Engaging Luther

Engaging Luther
A (New) Theological Assessment

Edited by
OLLI-PEKKA VAINIO

CASCADE *Books* • Eugene, Oregon

ENGAGING LUTHER
A (New) Theological Assessment

Copyright © 2010 Wipf and Stock Publishers. All rights reserved. Except for brief quotations in critical publications or reviews, no part of this book may be reproduced in any manner without prior written permission from the publisher. Write: Permissions, Wipf and Stock Publishers, 199 W. 8th Ave., Suite 3, Eugene, OR 97401.

Cascade Books
An Imprint of Wipf and Stock Publishers
199 W. 8th Ave., Suite 3
Eugene, OR 97401

www.wipfandstock.com

ISBN 13: 978-1-60608-818-0

Cataloging-in-Publication data:

Engaging Luther : a (new) theological assessment / edited by Olli-Pekka Vainio.

xvi + 256 p. ; cm. — Includes bibliographical references and indexes.

ISBN 13: 978-1-60608-818-0

1. Luther, Martin, 1483–1546. 2. Theology, Doctrinal — Finland. 3. Orthodox Eastern Church — Relations — Lutheran Church. 4. Deification — Christianity. I. Vainio, Olli-Pekka. II. Title.

BR333.5.J8 .E54 2010

Manufactured in the U.S.A.

Contents

Preface • *vii*
Acknowledgments • *xiii*
List of Contributors • *xiv*
Abbreviations • *xv*

1 Finnish Luther Studies: A Story and a Program
   —*Risto Saarinen* • 1
2 The Human Being—*Antti Raunio* • 27
3 Christ—*Sammeli Juntunen* • 59
4 Trinity—*Pekka Kärkkäinen* • 80
5 Baptism—*Eeva Martikainen* • 95
6 Eucharist—*Jari Jolkkonen* • 108
7 Faith—*Olli-Pekka Vainio* • 138
8 Theology of the Cross—*Kari Kopperi* • 155
9 The Virgin Mary—*Anja Ghiselli* • 173
10 Sex—*Sammeli Juntunen* • 186
11 Music—*Miikka E. Anttila* • 210
12 Luther as a Reader of the Holy Scripture
   —*Tuomo Mannermaa* • 223

Bibliography • 233
Subject Index • 249
Name Index • 253

Preface

THE PRESENT VOLUME COLLECTS the results of recent Luther studies carried out at the University of Helsinki. Our scholarly approach has for some time been known as "The New Finnish Interpretation of Luther." However, there is nothing exceptionally Finnish in this particular understanding of the Reformer (had that been the case, the approach probably would not have aroused any particular interest). Instead, it is Martin Luther's thought that has been found to be fascinating and engaging by us as well as by our adherents and critics around the world. Since the 1980s Finnish scholars have read Luther in a new manner.[1] We do not consider, however, that there is anything really innovative in our approach. If something appears to be new, it is essentially an old treasure, which was lost, but has now been found again.

Having refuted both the Finnishness and the newness of our approach, I might be expected to refute the third point and claim that we do not really "interpret" Luther; we just say what he really meant. In a sense, this is the case. The Finnish scholars often call their way of reading texts "systematic analysis." This is a method, which aims at unfolding the so-called "structuring principles," which constitute the ideological and theological horizon of the texts under scrutiny. These principles operate in the background of thinking systems and have an effect to how humans proceed in their reasoning. This way of reading has turned out to be very fruitful; we have been able to point out aspects of the Reformer's thought that have either been forgotten or neglected for some reason. However, we do not claim that everything people do always falls within

---

1. The discussion surrounding our project is extensive, and we have a regularly updated website and a blog, which contain the major publications, news, and current assignments of our scholars. See the Finnish Luther studies webpage: http://www.helsinki.fi/~risaarin/luther.html. This page contains a short history of the project and a comprehensive list of publications. The Finnish Luther Studies Blog is found at http://blogs.helsinki.fi/luther-studies/ This blog is the more regularly updated source for current events.

these principles since few of us are actually that systematic in our thinking. We readily acknowledge that our reading is fragmentary and open to complementary approaches.

In order to place our approach in context, we try to see Luther as a theologian who works within the western theological tradition of being loyal to a great many traditional themes while simultaneously creating something new. In a way, we tend to see Luther as a less radical thinker than he is sometimes considered to be. Clearly, this reading has some ecumenical implications, as Luther is seen working *within* Catholic tradition (after all, he was an Augustinian eremite), yet this in no way is meant to downplay Luther's criticisms of late medieval Catholic theology and practice. We are not trying to create "A Catholic Luther." Nevertheless, we believe that a great deal of the opposition between Lutheran and Catholic theologies has been based on anachronistic and one-sided readings of the Reformer with the culprits on the both sides of the borderline.

This volume is intended to introduce to the English-speaking world the recent work of both established and younger scholars who have been affiliated with the Finnish project. In a way, this book is a sequel to our previous collection *Union with Christ*,[2] although the present volume targets a more general readership. Nevertheless, the previous volume helpfully supplements this book. The articles presented here attempt to cover the key themes of Luther's thought so that the reader can obtain an overall picture of the Finnish perspective on Luther.

In the introductory article, Risto Saarinen provides a short history of Finnish scholarship. He also outlines a program, which employs the Lutheran theology of "gift." Although the Finns do not agree on everything, Saarinen's sketch exemplifies some essential tenets of the Finnish approach. If we examine faith from the perspective of God as the giver, then the human being ceases to appear as an agent and becomes the recipient of the word and of Christ. In this seemingly passive perspective the individual reappears, paradoxically, as a vivid and animated partner. Luther's argumentative move from "works" to "faith alone" is therefore not a move from presence to absence, from activity to pure passivity, or from objectivity to subjectivity. Rather it is a move that proceeds from passivity to a living faith. In light of this perspective, Christians are seen as animate beings in their union with Christ.

2. Edited by Carl Braaten and Robert Jenson.

Antti Raunio continues this theme by sketching out the anthropological assumptions of Luther's theology. One of the crucial questions in this regard is what changes when a person comes to believe in Christ? Should this change be understood in substantial or relational terms? Raunio argues that Luther follows a classical Aristotelian understanding of creatures as substances, according to which creatures also possess substantial forms. The Reformer uses the same terms in a theological sense as well. If the rational soul is the substantial form of a human being in a philosophical sense, then in theology the form of a Christian is the word of God, Christ, or faith, and sometimes even love. Critics of the Finnish position often understand this question in a way that suggests a return to classical substantial ontology in Lutheran theology. This, however, is a misunderstanding. The relational aspect is crucial for Luther's theological ontology, because God's being (*esse*) is relational. Thus, in God himself, substantial and relational beings do not exclude each other. Participation in the divine life through Christ means participation in God's Trinitarian being, which is relational.

Naturally, the next question is how this participation is to be understood from the standpoint of Trinitarian theology. This question is answered in the chapters by Sammeli Juntunen and Pekka Kärkkäinen. Juntunen examines Luther's Christology in the context of soteriology. According to Juntunen, Christ's coming to humankind in the external Word is essentially connected to Christ's person and work: Christ's incarnation, *kenosis*, cross, resurrection, and ascension together make it possible that Christ's kingdom can exist and that the proclaimed word truly joins the believer with the Triune God in saving union. The article has appeared in a longer form in the *Seminary Ridge Review* and is published here with the *Review's* kind permission.

Perhaps more than any other field of Lutheran thinking the theology of the Trinity reveals Luther's strong urge to return to the sources of true theology. Pekka Kärkkäinen argues that these sources consisted of the Scriptures, as well as the theology of the ancient Church, which formulated scriptural message into Trinitarian creeds and which were for the most part passed down through tradition up to Luther's own time. Guided by such a vision, Luther provided the later Reformation with treasure for a new kind of Trinitarian theology.

For Luther, the application of Christ's merit and gifts is a communal and sacramental event. Eeva Martikainen treats the doctrine of baptism from the standpoint of incorporation into Christ's righteousness with special attention to the faith of infants. Luther understood God's gift as real gifts to human beings. In keeping with this idea, the gift of baptism is also a treasure that God gives and human beings grasp and therefore possess in faith. That is exactly how Luther understands the gift of baptism when speaking of the faith of newborns. On the one hand, the child receives its own faith through baptism and, on the other, precisely through this faith the child comes to Christ himself. So the child does not depend on an instrument received through faith; rather, the child is united directly with Christ.

Jari Jolkkonen's article deals with the connection of doctrine and practice in Luther's theology of the Eucharist. According to Luther, the Triune God is self-giving Love (*agape*) who gives and applies all the gifts of creation, redemption, and sanctification to Christians through the word and the sacraments. The Eucharist is, in the first place, God's gift and reflects the nature of God as the giver. Therefore, in Luther's teaching the Eucharist also has a strong ecclesiological and ethical dimension: the sharing of the sacramental bread and wine unites Christians into one communion of love in which all joys and sufferings must be shared.

Olli-Pekka Vainio examines Luther's notions of faith and love. Vainio argues that when the sinner focuses on Christ in the Gospel, he or she "apprehends and owns" Christ. This means that Christ's presence in the believing person cannot be understood in terms of the redirection of the human faculties or as new psychological and anthropological entities alone. Instead, the life and bliss bestowed by Christ are not entities separate from his person, but are divine attributes. This makes it possible to understand how the union with Christ also means union with divine, active love.

When Luther argues for the reality of Christ's presence, the efficacy of sacraments, and communal understanding of the Christian faith, there are elements in his thought that underline the hiddenness of God and the mystical nature of Christian faith. Especially the theology of the cross is usually considered the very centre of Luther's thought. Interestingly, the theology of the cross has been seen as the heart of Luther's criticism of metaphysics as well. Kari Kopperi, however, argues that this reading betrays the original context of Luther's thought. The theology of the cross is essentially a criticism of human love, not metaphysics per se. This challenges traditional metaphysics to some degree but does not entail its total abandonment.

A practical example of the theology of the cross in Luther's thought is his treatment of the Virgin Mary. Usually, Luther's attitude towards Mary has been seen as negative. Anja Ghiselli, however, argues that Luther's criticism does not imply suspicion of Mary's essential place in the context of Christian faith and theological deliberation. In Luther's theology, Mariology is always connected to Christology and soteriology. Ghiselli especially concentrates on how the Virgin Mary appears to be a paradigm of the theology of the cross.

If the Virgin Mary appears as an exemplary Christian for Luther, it is interesting to see how Luther understands the role of sexuality in Christian life. This question is addressed in Juntunen's second contribution to our volume. Juntunen argues that Luther's treatment of sexuality is integrated into his overall theology, especially in the notions of sinfulness and goodness of creation. As a critical point, Juntunen argues that Luther's own thought contained elements that could have made Luther's attitude to sexuality even more positive than it actually did. Even if many of his statements treat sex as "medicine against whoring," his personal writings show affection and the affirmation of enjoyment.

Regarding music—another source of enjoyment—Luther states: "Indeed I plainly judge, and do not hesitate to affirm, that except for theology there is no art that could be put on the same level with music, since except for theology, music alone produces what otherwise only theology can do, namely, a calm and joyful soul." In his article, Miikka Anttila examines how and why Luther comes to consider music the "greatest gift of God." Anttila argues that the greatest blessing of music is its ability to touch human emotions. This is related to Luther's view of faith. When the word of God is sung, it moves both human intellect and affect, and thus faith encompasses all of personhood.

Lastly, Tuomo Mannermaa's article offers practical applications of how Luther's theology and how it can affect the way we read the Holy Scripture. In a spiritual reading of the Scripture, God personally reveals his face so that the reader truly encounters God. In this encounter God's word is joined together with the reader's heart, the centre of the personality and the real participation takes place where the reader is made one with God the Father, in the Holy Spirit, through Christ. The article was originally written for the ministers of the Evangelical Lutheran Church in Finland.

The articles thus cover a wide range of theoretical and practical questions. We do not claim that we are able to offer completely new perspectives on all of the old theological themes yet by placing our interpretation of Luther in a wider context, we hope to offer our readers something that may enable them to see the Reformer in a way that is both old and new, both Catholic and Evangelical.

Olli-Pekka Vainio
Editor

Acknowledgments

THIS BOOK HAS BEEN a joint project of a group of people who have been engaged with Luther and who have had the remarkable opportunity of sharing their interest with other like-minded people. As the editor, I would like to thank Professor Tuomo Mannermaa on behalf of all contributors for his cordial support, inspiration, and the evening gatherings we have been privileged to enjoy with him. I wish also personally to extend my gratitude to all those who have worked in Mannermaa's Luther project.

The Academy of Finland kindly supported this project financially. Our English was revised by Glenda Goss, Lisa Muszynski, and Riitta and Tom Toepfer. Of course, all remaining errors, limitations, and oversights are completely our own.

Contributors

MIIKKA E. ANTTILA, Lic. Theol., Pastor in Janakkala.

ANJA GHISELLI, Dr. Theol., Researcher.

JARI JOLKKONEN, Dr. Theol., Dr. habil., Secretary to the Bishops' Conference, Adjunct Professor of Ecumenical Theology at the University of Joensuu and Adjunct Professor of Practical Theology at the University of Helsinki.

SAMMELI JUNTUNEN, Dr. Theol., Dr. habil., Vicar of Savonlinna, Adjunct Professor of Ecumenical Theology at the University of Helsinki.

KARI KOPPERI, Dr. Theol., Director of the Church Institute for Advanced Training, Järvenpää.

PEKKA KÄRKKÄINEN, Dr. Theol., Dr. habil., University Researcher, Adjunct Professor of Philosophy of Religion at the University of Helsinki.

TUOMO MANNERMAA, Professor Emeritus of Ecumenical Theology at the University of Helsinki.

EEVA MARTIKAINEN (†), Professor of Systematic Theology at the University of Joensuu.

ANTTI RAUNIO, Dr. Theol., Dr. habil., University Lecturer of Ecumenical Theology at the University of Helsinki.

RISTO SAARINEN, Professor of Ecumenical Theology at the University of Helsinki.

OLLI-PEKKA VAINIO, Dr. Theol., Dr. habil., Post-Doctoral Researcher, Adjunct Professor of Ecumenical Theology at the University of Helsinki.

Abbreviations

AWA	Martin Luther. *Archiv zu Weimarer Ausgabe der Werke Martin Luthers*. Cologne: Bohlau, 1984–.
BC	*Book of Concord: The Confessions of the Evangelical Lutheran Church*. Edited by Robert Kolb and Timothy Wengert. Philadelphia: Augsburg Fortress, 2001.
BSLK	*Die Bekenntnisschriften der evangelisch-lutherischen Kirche*. Hrsg. im Gedenkjahr der Augsburgischen Konfession 1930. 8. Aufl. Göttingen, 1979.
CA	The Augsburg Confession.
Coll	Gabriel Biel. *Collectorium circa quattuor libros Sententiarum*.
DS	*Enchiridion symbolorum: definitionum et declarationum de rebus fidei et morum*. Denzinger Henricus. Freiburg im Breisgau: Herder, 1960.
FC	The Formula of Concord.
GK	The Large Catechism.
LuSt	Gerhard Ebeling. *Lutherstudien*.
LW	Martin Luther. *Luther's Works*. American Edition. Philadelphia: Fortress, 1955–1986.
KK	The Small Catechism.
MPL	Patrologia Latina. Migne.
MW	Melanchthon's *Werke*. Gütersloh: Mohn, 1961.
ST	Thomas Aquinas. *Summa Theologiae*.
StA	Martin Luther. *Studienausgabe*. Berlin: Evangelische Verlagsanstalt, 1979.
WA	Martin Luther. *Werke. Weimarer Ausgabe*. Weimar: Bohlau, 1883–.

WA Br		Martin Luther. *Werke. Weimarer Ausgabe. Briefe.* Weimar: Bohlau, 1883–.
WA DB		Martin Luther. *Werke. Weimarer Ausgabe. Deutsche Bibel.* Weimar: Bohlau, 1883–.
WA Tr		Martin Luther. *Werke. Weimarer Ausgabe. Tischrede.* Weimar: Bohlau, 1883–.

1

Finnish Luther Studies

A Story and a Program

Risto Saarinen

Martin Luther is a figure of world historical proportions, but today Luther and Lutheranism are often considered as parochial phenomena in world Christianity. Generally Luther's thought and impact are closely connected with the emergence of German language and cultural practices; this connection has not enhanced the global popularity of Lutheranism. Theological studies of Luther have remained predominantly German ventures, although prominent exceptions, like Roland Bainton and Heiko Oberman, can be named.

If we look at today's theological schools and fashionable discussion topics in the English-speaking world, Luther is either absent or his views are regarded as problematic. Communitarians, following Alasdair MacIntyre, tend to regard the Reformation as the beginning of problematic modernity.[1] The negative attitude towards Luther and the Reformation is even stronger in Radical Orthodoxy since, for John Milbank, Luther exemplifies the kind of nominalism which follows Duns Scotus and William Ockham and thus deviates from true Augustinianism.[2] Benedict XVI has recently stated that Luther preferred a subjective understanding of faith which differs from the Catholic concept thereof.[3]

1. MacIntyre, *After Virtue*, 165–67.
2. Milbank, *Being Reconciled*, 110, 223.
3. Benedict XVI, *Spe salvi*, 7.

Luther is rejected by the adherents of patristic nostalgia, but he fares no better among liberal postmoderns. Luther was a white male university professor who had anti-Semitic leanings, rejected Copernicus's astronomy, and showed complicity with the worldly rulers. Some Luther scholars have argued that the Wittenberg reformer at least had Kierkegaardian or existential-philosophical ideas, but Kierkegaard himself denied this and stated that Luther was not capable of existential dialectics.[4]

Although Luther's thought still can play a positive role in some prominent social philosophies, these have not inspired much theological reflection. Charles Taylor's political philosophy is a good example of the common dismissal of Luther in this regard. In his *Sources of the Self* Taylor argues that the Reformers initiated "the entire modern development of the affirmation of ordinary life."[5] This is in many ways true and valuable, but at the same time the statement seems to confirm a certain dullness of the Reformation: it legitimized the middle-class lifestyle with its orientation towards family and consumerism. In *A Secular Age* Taylor links the Reformation with the "disenchantment" that took place in early modernity; the Reformation led to the "new 'police state' which undertakes to organize the lives of its citizens in rational ways."[6] In this manner the Reformation was not so much an exciting theological project as a forerunner of modern secularization.

In view of all these dismissals of Luther and the Lutheran Reformation one needs certain boldness in claiming that Luther's theology is intellectually fascinating and contains exceptional resources. This is precisely what the present volume claims. The studies collected in this volume aim at showing in which sense Luther remains a fully Catholic and genuinely Augustinian theologian who is not so much a forerunner of problematic modernity as a representative of classical Christianity. At the same time, Luther's theology contains ideas that can be made fruitful in dialogue with currents like communitarianism or Radical Orthodoxy. Luther certainly has his faults and dark sides, but many of the accusations connected with his name are more due to the distorted picture given by biased research.

---

4. Helmer, *Global Luther*; Pelikan, *From Luther to Kierkegaard*; Bornkamm, *Luther im Spiegel*, 95–100 (Kierkegaard) and 114–17, 156 (Kierkegaardian Luther scholars).

5. Taylor, *Sources of the Self*, 218.

6. Taylor, *Secular Age*, 86.

In order to understand the claims that unite the contributors of this volume, one first needs to outline the "story" behind the new wave of Finnish Luther research. Obviously, the following narrative cannot legitimize the claims made in individual contributions, but it can make visible why and in what sense we want to liberate ourselves from much of the earlier research and why we want to connect Luther and the Reformation so closely with the patristic and medieval periods. The story also serves as a background to the theological "program" outlined in the second part of my essay. Although we have not developed our theological program in detail, our critics have repeatedly pointed out that a certain program is implied behind our historical studies. I believe that the critics are right on this point: we do have a program but we also have to work it out in more detail. The second part is my own attempt to outline such a theological program.

THE STORY

The study of the Reformation has seldom been a theologically neutral venture for the Protestant churches. Confessionally committed scholars of Luther have traditionally regarded that a merely historical understanding of the Reformation is not sufficient. In addition to this, one should provide a theological legitimation of the constitutive ideas of the period. In European theology, this has traditionally meant that the Lutheran or the broader Protestant identity needs to be normatively defined so that it remains sufficiently distinctive from the Roman Catholic Church. If Catholicism is perceived as "medieval," Protestantism is seen as "modern"; if Catholicism is defined by its "hierarchy," Protestantism defends "democracy."

The confessional writings of the Reformation period, as well as the decisions of the Council of Trent, paved this way of doing theology already in the sixteenth century. The Lutheran Confessions outline not only the valid doctrine, but also the wrong opinions and practices of the opponents. The doctrinal condemnations of the Council of Trent proceed in a similar manner. Over the centuries, these texts became the normative source of information regarding the other part of conflict. For this reason, it does not always help if group B states: "this is not how we teach," when the normative text of group A states that this is indeed the way B teaches. One hermeneutical problem of both the Protestant confessions and the decisions of the Council of Trent is, therefore, that they define the doctrines of both insiders and outsiders, irrespective of whether the outsiders approve of this definition.[7]

Some cracks in the confessional walls of the Reformation can be found in Anglicanism, which appreciates its Catholic heritage in ways that deviate from Continental European Protestantism. The Nordic Lutheranism of Sweden and Finland also exemplifies an ecclesiastical tradition which understands itself in terms of "Evangelical Catholicity."[8] In the Reformation, Sweden and Finland took over the Lutheran Confessions but preserved historical episcopacy and medieval dioceses. For centuries, they nurtured a Lutheran monoculture in the traditional dioceses.

While the Church of Sweden has, during the twentieth century, moved towards an ecumenical understanding of the ecclesial communion, the Finns have tended to focus on the theological resources of Lutheranism. A new and important period in this regard was initiated when ecumenically-minded Roman Catholic scholars started to study Luther in the 1960s. In the writings of Erwin Iserloh, Peter Manns, and Otto Hermann Pesch, Luther appears for the first time as a figure who in many respects continued the Catholic teachings of the Church and opposed a late medieval Catholicism which was no longer itself fully Catholic because it was tainted by questionable practices and such new currents as Ockhamism.[9]

When Tuomo Mannermaa, Professor at the Faculty of Theology in Helsinki, initiated his study project on Luther in the early 1980s, he created close contacts with the Institute for European History in Mainz, Germany, of which Peter Manns was director. A generation of young Finnish theologians, many of whom are contributors in the present book, were supervised in Luther's Augustinian and Catholic background by Manns, while Mannermaa worked with them on Luther as an ecumenical theologian. Mannermaa also participated in the ecumenical dialogue between the Evangelical Lutheran Church of Finland and the Russian Orthodox Church. In this dialogue already in 1977 he presented his thesis that the Lutheran view of "Christ present in faith" offers a theo-

---

7. For this phenomenon, see Lehmann and Pannenberg, *Condemnations*.

8. For the theological program of Evangelical Catholicity, see, e.g., Tjorhom, *Visible Church*, 21–37.

9. See Pesch, "Twenty Years" and Manns, *Vater im Glauben*.

logical counterpoint and parallel to the Orthodox doctrine of theosis or deification.[10]

This thesis has become the most often discussed and contested point of Finnish Luther research. We shall return to it below, but need to state already here that the thesis belongs to a broader framework of which the dialogue with Eastern Orthodoxy is only an aspect. Mannermaa's program, as it can be read from his other studies of contemporary theology[11] is critical of several features of modern Protestantism. In his view, the modern period has often replaced the content of doctrine, the sacramental presence of God and the personal encounter with the core (*res*) of theology with an existential experience regarding the phenomenal—or even epiphenomenal—traces of God. This is because the post-Kantian epistemological spectacles of modernity do not allow an encounter with the "ontology" of Christianity.[12]

In some respects Mannermaa follows Karl Barth's criticism of cultural and liberal Protestantism. He does not, however, share the Reformed and Barthian axiom according to which the finite cannot contain the infinite. He wants to affirm the Lutheran principle *finitum capax infiniti*, "the finite is capable of receiving the infinite," and thus claims that a genuine theological ontology, a study of divine being, is possible. The biggest obstacle for this ontology lies in the preconditions of modernity, which have pushed theology and religion into the realms of value and phenomenal experience, thus denying the possibility of theological real presence. Because Eastern Orthodox theology has not embraced modernity as strongly as Protestantism, it has preserved a healthier view of theological ontology.[13]

Although Mannermaa hardly ever quotes George Lindbeck, it may be proper to label his theological approach in terms of a Lutheran "postliberalism." Lindbeck[14] and Mannermaa are critical of the theological value of experience and consider language to relate to specified lifeforms. In ecumenical and systematic-theological contexts, Mannermaa's students have often adhered to postliberal views. In Finland, Mannermaa

10. See Saarinen, *Faith and Holiness*, 38–54; Braaten and Jenson, *Union with Christ*, vii–ix, 1–17.
11. Mannermaa, *Von Preussen*; *Kontrapunkteja*; *Paralleeleja*.
12. Mannermaa, "Why Is Luther," 4–9; see also his *Von Preussen*.
13. Cf. Mannermaa, "Justification and Theosis."
14. See Lindbeck, *Nature of Doctrine*.

is well-known for his moderately non-liberal stances in church politics: he opposed the Lutheran-Reformed *Leuenberg Agreement*, but supported the Anglican-Lutheran *Porvoo Agreement* and the Lutheran-Roman Catholic *Joint Declaration on the Doctrine of Justification*. He supported women's ordination in the 1980s, but opposed the new Finnish Bible translation, claiming that a more literal translation technique is needed to preserve the doctrinal core of the Bible.[15]

This broader context shows that Mannermaa's Luther studies have not been driven by patristic nostalgia or ecumenical opportunism, but by an original variant of Lutheran postliberalism. The influence of Roman Catholic Luther scholars, in particular Peter Manns, has been considerable. Mannermaa wrote his doctoral thesis on Karl Rahner[16] and was helped in this process by Karl Lehmann. Lehmann's subsequent activity as the Catholic bishop of Mainz and leading ecumenist has also left traces on Mannermaa's thinking. These reasons have contributed to the ecumenical interest of Mannermaa's younger colleagues and students, in particular Eero Huovinen and Simo Peura, who have focused on the Lutheran–Roman Catholic relationships.

As the present volume introduces Finnish Luther studies to readers beyond Scandinavia and Continental Europe, they should keep the historical context of Finnish Lutheranism in mind. Mannermaa's approach stems from a monoculture in which about 80 percent of all Finns belong to the Lutheran church. For this reason, a more relaxed attitude towards Roman Catholicism can be assumed than is the rule in German Protestantism. The Lutheran bishops can still look at their dioceses as carriers of the entire Christianity in that region. Theology is nowhere made in a historical or sociological vacuum, but in Finland the monocultural context of Lutheranism is particularly influential. In earlier times this monoculture promoted confessionalism, but today it expresses a mixture of ecumenical generosity and, for better or worse, remaining self-confidence.

The postliberal attitude of Finnish Luther studies is thus in its own peculiar way a product of late modernity. It aims at being historically reliable and academically solid research within the context of a state university. In this context, confessional claims cannot be based on unquestioned authority, but rather they need to follow certain argumenta-

15. See Mannermaa, *Von Preussen* and his *Paralleeleja*.
16. Mannermaa, *Lumen fidei*.

tive rules. The academic guise of the studies may sometimes confuse the theological expectations of a committed reader. At the same time it would be illusory to state that the historical claims would be theologically neutral because they appear in this academic environment. Mannermaa's realist approach is indebted to the German tradition of systematic theology, which, while being strictly academic, also seeks to influence the doctrinal reflection of the church through making informed arguments concerning the nature and content of ecclesial teaching. In this sense it continues the tradition of theological study, which does not remain in the refuge of historical neutrality.

In his seminal study, *Der im Glauben gegenwärtige Christus* (*Christ Present in Faith*) Mannermaa interprets Luther's doctrine of justification as holding that justification contains the effective holiness and makes it present in Christians. This effective side is not, however, a meritorius property of human beings but the presence of Christ in faith. For this reason, justification is not merely a new ethical or juridical relation between God and a human being. When a human being believes in Christ, Christ is present, in the very fullness of his divine and human nature, in that faith itself.[17]

While later Protestant theology tended to differentiate between justification and sanctification, Mannermaa claims that for Luther union with Christ contains both terms and that they are, as a result, not really different from one another: In faith, human beings are really united with Christ. Christ, in turn, is both the forgiveness of sins and the effective producer of everything that is good in them. Therefore "sanctification" — that is, the sanctity or holiness of the Christian—is, in fact, only another name for the same phenomenon of which Luther speaks when discussing the communication of attributes, the happy exchange, and the union between the person of Christ and that of the believer.[18]

Because salvation is in this way constituted by the real indwelling of Christ, human and divine, in the faith of the Christian, Mannermaa can state that Luther's doctrine of justification involves a way of thinking that can be described by using the technical term "divinization" or "deification." The idea of divinization is present in Luther's theology not only as a term but also in content. Luther's idea of divinization finds succinct

---

17. Mannermaa, *Christ Present in Faith*, 87.
18. Ibid., 49.

expression in his well-known sentence: *in ipsa fide Christus adest* (Christ is present in faith).[19]

In addition to this outline of justification, the German volume *Der im Glauben gegenwärtige Christus* contains a thematic study titled *Zwei Arten der Liebe* ("two kinds of love"). This study reinterprets, in the light of Luther's theology, Anders Nygren's classic book *Agape and Eros*. While Nygren argued that the mystical union between Christ and Christian exemplifies a peculiar aspect of eros, Mannermaa claims that union with Christ exemplifies the divine love of agape. He is not, however, happy with Nygren's basic distinction but prefers to speak, in Luther's terms, of the distinction between human love and divine love. While human love is directed to pleasant and lovable objects, divine love creates the lovability of its object.[20]

Although the initial difference between human and divine love is radical, the union of divine love with the Christian in faith can have a united concept of love as its final result. Given this, the Christian cannot only love his or her neighbor but also God:

> When the person—in faith and through the word—unites with God who is love, then he or she unites in faith with divine love. Where Christ dwells within the Christian, this love is alive in him or her ... the love received in faith is not merely directed towards other people, but it also has God as its object.[21]

In this union of human and divine love, human love is transformed so that it receives the properties of divine love:

> When the Christian participates in faith in God's love which prompts her to love both God and neighbor, this love which is active in her also displays features of divine love. It is an altruistic love which does not seek its own good. The Christian loves both God and other people with an altruistic, pure love ... For Luther, this love of God is pure when the person loves and praises God only for the sake of divine goodness, without any regard for the benefits which she receives from God.[22]

---

19. Ibid., 49.
20. *Der im Glauben*, 108–15.
21. Ibid., 174 (my translation).
22. Ibid., 175 (my translation).

Zwei Arten der Liebe shows, first, that Luther is not only a theologian of faith but also a theologian of love who can formulate his insights in terms of a reorientation of love. Although this reorientation is critical towards some medieval understandings of the so-called order of love (*ordo caritatis*),[23] it also remains deeply Augustinian in its emphasis on the transforming power of divine love. Second, Mannermaa shows in this study that the dichotomies between human and divine love are not unbridgeable, pure "motifs," as Nygren claimed, but aspects which belong to the broader transformative process. Third, this study connects the theology of justification with the dynamics of love, showing how the divine presence transforms human attitudes and conduct.

One particularly strong background reason for Mannermaa is the conviction that both modern German Protestantism and the confessional traditionalism have remained defective in their understandings of justification.[24] This key doctrine of Lutheranism has either been understood in purely forensic and externalist terms, or it was seen in the context of existential experience. Both of these alternatives fail to pay sufficient attitude to the realistic, or, in Mannermaa's terms, "real-ontic" character of salvation. In his characterization of salvation as real-ontic presence of Christ in faith Mannermaa wants to affirm the continuation of classical sacramental soteriology in the Lutheran Reformation. At the same time he adopts Barth's criticism of modernity insofar as the concept of experience was concerned. The categories of "ontic" and "ontological" may echo his early study of Rahner, although Mannermaa remains critical of all modernist-existential interpretations of reality.

The further development of this approach was undertaken by Mannermaa's numerous students. My own book *Gottes Wirken auf uns* aims at consolidating the view that the earlier Protestant studies on "Christ present in faith" are highly problematic in their interpretation of this presence as a *Wirkung* (*a posteriori* consequence) of God's self-revelation. This interpretation does not allow for sacramental or ontological view of effective justification but, staying faithful to the anti-Catholic leanings of Protestant theology, regards Luther as a forerunner of the post-Kantian rejection of metaphysics.

---

23. This has been worked out in Raunio, *Summe des christlichen Lebens*.

24. Cf. Stjerna, "Editor's Introduction," xiv–xv; Braaten and Jenson, *Union with Christ*, viii.

My own research history in *Gottes Wirken auf uns* is limited to the period between 1880 and 1950, but the subsequent books of my colleagues apply, in their chapters of research history, my views to cover more recent relevant studies. More importantly, they investigate a great variety of significant topics to consolidate Mannermaa's approach. In his *Mehr als ein Mensch?* Simo Peura tackles the difficult issue of deification in Luther. Although the Wittenberg professor employs the term only rarely, his theology of participation, transformation, conformity with Christ, and Christian progress employs the idea of deification. Peura also argues that Luther's views in this respect did not undergo sharp changes after the beginning of the Reformation.[25]

Antti Raunio's *Summe des christlichen Lebens* analyses Luther's interpretation of the Golden Rule (Matt 7:12, Luke 6:31) by using Mannermaa's insights concerning the twofold character of love. Raunio argues that the Golden Rule primarily expresses the dynamics of divine love in which God is seen as the giver of everything good. Although one can, to an extent, set oneself in the place of the other by means of natural reason, the loving application of the Golden Rule is only possible for Christians because Christ has first fulfilled its demand and does so continually as present in the heart of the believer through faith. Thus the Golden Rule is, fundamentally, a theological principle of ethics. Earlier studies that have either made the rule autonomous or denied its significance have failed to pay attention to the complex interaction of theological principles and natural dynamics.[26]

The Finnish approach was further consolidated in three German collections, *Thesaurus Lutheri, Luther und Theosis* and *Luther und Ontologie*, in which also European scholars comment on Mannermaa's views. The Mannermaa Festschrift, *Caritas Dei*, as well the first American collection, *Union with Christ*, broadened the discussion to the English-speaking world. The dissertations of Sammeli Juntunen and Pekka Kärkkäinen apply the Finnish theses to new theological realms. Olli-Pekka Vainio's study, our first monograph written in English, shows that the paradigm of "participation in Christ" is relevant not only for Luther but also for the broader development of the doctrine of justification in the sixteenth century.[27]

---

25. In addition to *Mehr als ein Mensch?*, see also Peura, "What God gives."

26. In addition to *Summe des christlichen Lebens*, see also Raunio, "Natural Law."

27. Juntunen, *Der Begriff des Nichts*; Kärkkäinen, *Luthers trinitarische Theologie*; Vainio, *Justification and Participation in Christ*.

The further continuation of the story can be told by referring to the European and American reception of Finnish studies. For some German Luther scholars, the Finnish approach is not Protestant enough and can therefore be dismissed; other voices demand a more historical grounding of the theses.[28] The most thorough German criticism has been presented by Reinhard Flogaus; he echoes many other German voices in saying that the concept of substance is employed by the Finns in a sense which brings a problematical "ontological added value" to the concept of divine gift in justification.[29] At the same time Flogaus affirms the need for ontology in theology. He thinks that Protestant theology can basically relate positively to theosis, provided that it is understood in terms of "participation in the love revealed in Jesus Christ."[30] Although Flogaus in this way reduces the ontological concept of Mannermaa, he also remains in constructive discussion regarding the possibility of theological ontology and theosis.

Among other constructive European Protestant voices, Karsten Lehmkühler has investigated the history of the doctrine of divine inhabitation in great detail. He shows that inhabitation is not merely a Roman Catholic and Orthodox doctrine, but also plays a role in the Lutheran Orthodoxy as well as in Schleiermacher, Ritschl, and Bonhoeffer.[31] Bo Holm has developed many Finnish views in a highly original manner, claiming that Luther's theology can be understood as a theology of giving in which a relationship between the divine and human agent can be conceived in terms of reciprocity.[32]

Several European Catholic theologians have commented on Finnish research. Reinhard Messner states that Mannermaa's approach is ecumenically fruitful. In his textbook on the Reformation, Angelo Maffeis regards the Finnish studies as helpful corrective to the prevailing Protestant views, although he also warns of making Luther a completely systematic thinker. Pedro Urbano connects the Finnish research with

---

28. On the early German reception, see Saarinen, "Die Teilhabe an Gott." Among later German criticisms, Wenz, "Unio" and Mahlmann, "Unio cum Christo" are particularly valuable.

29. Flogaus, *Theosis bei Palamas und Luther*, 328–35.

30. Ibid., 439.

31. Lehmkühler, *Inhabitatio*.

32. Holm, *Gabe und Geben bei Luther*. Holm, "Nordic Luther Research" is a concise and insightful overview of recent Northern European scholarship.

the late medieval context of Augustinian mysticism. At the same time he states that Luther's strong dualism of flesh and spirit remains difficult for many Catholics. In this manner the Catholic reception has been constructive while also presenting critical theological issues.[33]

A rich diversity of positions can be found in the American reception of Finnish studies. Some strictly Protestant authors, like Mark C. Mattes, have taken over the critical doubts of German scholars. Conservative Lutherans, like Kurt E. Marquart, have been positive to Mannermaa since his approach contains a criticism of liberal modernity and emphasizes the salvific realism in ways which come close to the Lutheran Orthodoxy. In a thematic issue of *Westminster Theological Journal*, four American scholars present the Finnish studies to the Reformed readers. While they appreciate the connections made with the Pauline theology of participation, they also demand a more historical picture of the different shades of the Reformation.[34]

Among other Reformed theologians, Carl Mosser states that not only Luther but also Calvin presents a theology of deification. This observation leads J. Todd Billings to a certain criticism of John Milbank's view of the Reformation. While Milbank claims that Luther was a typical nominalist and the Finnish Luther scholars cannot therefore make their point convincingly, Billings remarks that the doctrine of deification in Calvin provides possibilities for a genuinely Western language of participation. Allen Jorgenson likewise defends Luther against Milbank's criticism. Veli-Matti Kärkkäinen, a Pentecostal scholar and pupil of Mannermaa, argues extensively that the doctrine of deification is also present in Pentecostal and Methodist soteriology and can thus provide opportunities for an inner-Western ecumenism.[35]

The most positive reception process of Finnish studies has occurred in the Evangelical Catholic wing of American theology. This reception was initiated by Robert Jenson and Carl Braaten who edited the volume *Union with Christ*. Among their colleagues, Bruce Marshall develops the

---

33. Messner, "Rechtfertigung und Vergöttlichung"; Maffeis, *Teologia della Riforma*, 29–60; Urbano, "Christus in fide adest."

34. Mattes, *Role of Justification*; Mattes, "A Future"; Marquart, "Luther and Theosis"; Metzger, "Mystical Union"; Seifried, "Paul, Luther"; Trueman, "Is the Finnish Line"; Jenson, "Response."

35. Mosser, "Greatest"; Milbank, *Being Reconciled*, 110, 223; Billings, "John Milbank's Theology"; Billings, "John Calvin"; Jorgenson, "Luther on Ubiquity"; Kärkkäinen, *One with God*.

theology of transformation in Luther, using Finnish studies. David Yeago outlines a sacramental and ontological reading of Luther's theology. Jonathan Linman considers that the Finnish scholars have adequately met the contemporary need for Lutheran mysticism. Reinhard Hütter follows the Finnish criticism of German Protestant research and attempts to see Luther in the light of Patristic and Catholic theology.[36]

One clear but also in many ways ambivalent background reason for the increased interest in Mannermaa's approach has been the ongoing debate on the nature of deification in Christian theology.[37] For many Protestants who follow the line from Ludwig Feuerbach to Karl Barth, this doctrine is fundamentally problematic since it may lead to a non-Christian apotheosis in which the fundamental distinction between human and divine is blurred.[38] This has of course never been the intention of the Finnish scholars, but it remains to be debated whether the problematic side of theosis can be successfully avoided.

On the other hand, some defenders of theosis see the Finnish claims as threatening. Some Orthodox theologians want to show that the Lutheran approach cannot adequately grasp the depth of the Orthodox doctrine.[39] John Milbank likewise considers theosis to be an important doctrine. At the same time Milbank thinks that theosis cannot be adequately expressed in an early modern context.[40] Among Catholic theologians, Gösta Hallonsten argues that the Western theology cannot contain the Orthodox view of theosis in its totality but only some fragments of it.[41] In spite of all this vivid discussion on deification, it should be emphasized that the story of new Finnish Luther studies should not be reduced to the debate on this one topic.[42] Theosis is but the tip of the iceberg which moves in a new direction under the Northern waters.

---

36. Marshall, "Justification as Declaration and Deification"; Yeago, "Luther on Grace"; Yeago, "Ecclesia sancta"; Hütter, *Suffering Divine Things*; Linman, "Little Christs"; Hütter, *Bound to Be Free*.

37. See Finlan and Kharimov, *Theosis*; Christensen and Wittung, *Partakers of the Divine Nature*.

38. See the discussion in my *Gottes Wirken auf uns*.

39. Tselengides, *He Soteriologia* (German summary in Flogaus, *Theosis bei Palamas und Luther*, 416–20); Briskina, "Orthodox View."

40. Milbank, *Being Reconciled*, 64–74.

41. Hallonsten, "Theosis in Recent Research."

42. For my own account, see Saarinen, "Theosis."

THE PROGRAM

Given this story, how can the actual theological program of Finnish Luther studies be outlined in more detail? Let us start from Pope Benedict XVI whom we mentioned above as one of Luther's contemporary critics. In his encyclical letter *Spe salvi*[43] Benedict lays out the correct understanding of Heb 11:1: "Faith is the substance [*hypostasis*] of things hoped for; the proof [*elenchos, argumentum*] of things not seen." It is important for Benedict that faith already brings the proof of things hoped for. Thus these things are not merely in the future:

> Precisely because the thing itself is already present, this presence of what is to come also creates certainty: this "thing" which must come is not yet visible in the external world (it does not "appear"), but because of the fact that, as an initial and dynamic reality, we carry it within us, a certain perception of it has even now come into existence.

Benedict comes close to Mannermaa's understanding of Christ present in faith: salvation is not merely subjective or eschatological, but rather carries an ontological significance here and now. Benedict further underlines the importance of *hypostasis* or substance as an initial and dynamic reality. Faith is, therefore, not subjective conviction but an objective "proof." Benedict, however, regards Luther's view as diametrically opposed to the Catholic reading of Heb 11:1:

> To Luther, who was not particularly fond of the Letter to the Hebrews, the concept of "substance," in the context of his view of faith, meant nothing. For this reason he understood the term *hypostasis*/substance not in the objective sense (of a reality present within us), but in the subjective sense, as an expression of an interior attitude, and so, naturally, he also had to understand the term *argumentum* as a disposition of the subject.

This is the standard Protestant interpretation put forward by Gerhard Ebeling. He interprets Luther's early Augustinian dialectics between "in hope" (*in spe*) and "in reality" (*in re*) so that there is no present holiness but everything lies in the future. Erwin Iserloh expresses a Catholic view, pointing out that Luther's Augustinian phrase does not deny the initial reality of salvation.[44] Benedict reads Heb 11:1 in this

---

43. The following quotations are all from *Spe salvi*, 7.
44. Ebeling, *LuSt I*, 24–25, 33–35. Iserloh, "Existentiale Interpretation." They discuss

manner. Unlike Iserloh, however, the pope believes that the subjective reading of Heb 11:1 stems from Luther. Benedict emphatically refutes Luther's alleged view:

> Faith is not merely a personal reaching out towards things to come that are still totally absent: it gives us something. It gives us even now something of the reality we are waiting for, and this present reality constitutes for us a "proof" of the things that are still unseen. Faith draws the future into the present, so that it is no longer simply a "not yet." The fact that this future exists changes the present; the present is touched by the future reality, and thus the things of the future spill over into those of the present and those of the present into those of the future.

The Pope's reading of Luther is backed not only by Protestant scholars like Ebeling, but also by those conservative Catholics who think that Luther adheres to problematic subjectivism.[45]

The Finnish scholarship, however, sets out to prove that, first, Luther's theology is ontologically richer and contains an effective view of justification as the presence of things hoped for, and, second, that the subjectivist picture of Luther to a great extent stems from the anti-Catholic prejudices of modern Protestantism. In his *Mehr als ein Mensch?* Simo Peura investigates in detail the theological background of *in spe/in re* dialectics. On the basis of Luther's *First Lectures on the Psalms*—the very text discussed by Ebeling and Iserloh—Peura concludes that

> For Luther, the person who is *pars Christi* or *sors Christi* is already in this life partially "divine." This partial, ontological understanding of deification takes place in a real fashion, because God himself . . . becomes "a part" of the person, when the person participates in Christ. But this participation is not yet fulfilment. . . . The definition that the Christian is now healed *in spe* and in the future life *in re* does not deny the reality of that effective becoming righteous which has already been initiated.[46]

In Luther's own words, the dialectics of presence and hiddenness can be expressed as follows:

---

in particular Luther's interpretation of Heb 11:1 in WA 3, 279, 30–32 (*First Lectures on the Psalms*).

45. Especially Hacker, *Das Ich im Glauben*, plays here a role. For the relevance of this study in papal thought, see Nichols, *The Thought of Benedict XVI*, 277.

46. Peura, *Mehr als ein Mensch*, 81 (my translation).

> That in the holy of holies there was no light, signifies God to be present in the Church via the faith of Christ in their hearts, that does not comprehend and is not comprehended, does not see and is not seen, but still sees all things. It is a powerful "proof" [*argumentum*] of present, but "not visible things" [Heb 11:1]. Likewise the Ark of Covenant was present in the holy of holies, but was not visible, because the Tabernacle was around—in the middle of which at the holy of holies the very seat of God was—as is said in Ps. 46 "God is present in the middle of the congregation," so that they cannot be shaken, as this and similar prophesies state.[47]

This ontological understanding of hidden presence comes very close to the Pope's own teaching in *Spe salvi*. While Benedict thinks that Luther is opposed to this understanding, the Finns rely on the Catholic nature of Luther's theology and maintain that only the modern Protestant interpretations need to be refuted. In this sense, the program of Finnish Luther research advocates a Reformer who is "Evangelical and Catholic."

The burden of proof in this program is for a great part historical; therefore many studies in this volume proceed historically. Given the enormous quantity and pluriform character of Luther's texts the historical issue is complex: one can find prooftexts for different positions, and one needs to interpret a great amount of sources. This is precisely what Peura, Raunio, Juntunen, Kärkkäinen and Vainio have done in their monographic treatises. Our short introduction must, however, limit the discussion of the "program" to a brief and condensed outline.

We have already seen that the Finnish program revolves around the issues of justification, faith and love. Sacramental theology and fundamental ecclesiology are also considered as important.[48] The questions of ordained ministry, church order, canon law, and liturgy do not, however, play much role. In this sense the Finnish approach is not distinctively "high church," although it advocates a return to many patristic topics and sees Luther as a continuation of the ancient and medieval Church. The core of the program concerns salvation and life in Christ. Ontological and other philosophical issues are sometimes discussed in detail, but they are not treated for their own sake; rather, they are treated as related to this core. For this reason, the program is predominantly theological.

---

47. WA 5, 506, 12–20. (*Second Lectures on the Psalms*)

48. See Huovinen, *Fides infantium*, Forsberg, "Die finnische Lutherforschung" and the contributions regarding the sacraments in the present volume.

Is there an inner development or unfolding of the Finnish program? My conviction is that a fruitful paradigm cannot afford to remain stagnated, but rather that it undergoes a certain development. As far as I can see, no ruptures are found in Mannermaa's own texts. They are short and even laconic treatises which are impressive but remain in need of more elaboration. The monographic studies mentioned above perform much of this elaboration, explaining, for instance, in which sense the concept of substance is a theological concept, or how the Christian figure of the Golden Rule transcends a merely rationalist view of natural law.

At the same time we can perceive not only further elucidation but new developments. Recent collective volumes connect Luther's thinking with much broader currents of theology, philosophy, and the law.[49] Olli-Pekka Vainio's work modifies the view put forward in Mannermaa's early writings. He argues that while Mannermaa thinks that Luther remains in many ways distinct from Melanchthon and later doctrinal developments, one actually finds a stronger continuity between Luther and the theologians behind the *Book of Concord*.[50]

My own recent work likewise aims at moving in new directions. In *God and the Gift* I construct a systematic theology around the concept of the gift. This theology is employed in discussion with other contemporary approaches, for instance those of John Milbank. *God and the Gift* also aims at seeing some traditional issues of Reformation theology, for instance, freedom, reciprocity and forgiveness, in a new light. My own work on the concepts of forgiveness and gift has probably provided a basis for some differentiation between my own thinking and some earlier Finnish achievements. While Simo Peura strongly pleads for the unity of forensic and effective justification,[51] I am more inclined to grant God's merciful favor a conceptual primacy over the *donum*, the effective fruit. I believe that a gift can only be identified as gift if we know the intention of the giver. Thus divine mercy and benevolence in a way precedes

---

49. See Mäkinen, *Lutheran Reformation and the Law* and Kärkkäinen, *Trinitarian Theology in the Medieval West*.

50. Vainio, *Justification and Participation in Christ*. For the same phenomenon, see also Mahlmann, "Unio cum Christo."

51. Peura, "Christ as Favor and Gift," 56–60.

divine gifts.[52] At the same time, however, I interpret forgiveness in more effective terms than has been customary in Finnish research.[53]

In the following I will present a current vision of the Finnish program as I see it. Although this version is based on Mannermaa's insights, it also represents a certain stage of systematic development. Five successive points are needed to characterize my version.[54] These points do not cover the ethical and political implications of Luther's theology. There are certainly such implications, and they deserve to be worked out in detail in other contexts. The five points only lay out the theological constitution of the gift which needs to be circulated.

Theology of the Gift: Basic Relations

The theological and sociological concepts of "gift" (*donum*) and "favor" (as act, *beneficium*, as benevolent attitude, *favor*) characterize divine action and interpersonal human activities in various ways. Although these concepts are frequently used in theological texts, they are seldom understood as *loci communes*, that is, as doctrinal points which would have their own entries in theological dictionaries or chapters in dogmatics. Gift and benevolence are normally understood as interpretative concepts, which mediate between human experience and theological truth. As such they are often understood to be pedagogical concepts.

It would nevertheless be misleading to conceive "the gift" as a merely pedagogical or otherwise auxiliary notion. "The gift" belongs to a group of concepts and corresponding phenomena that constitute elementary theological concepts with the help of the idea of giving. Forgiveness and redemption, thanksgiving and some other forms of prayer, offerings and sacrifice, the processes of handing over and tradition, to name but a few, are among the phenomena which are conceptualized by means of giving. Caritative aid, hospitality, and generosity are also phenomena that relate to the concept of giving. The verbs denoting such action are called ditransitive verbs, because they take two objects, expressed through the relational places of gift and recipient.

---

52. Saarinen, "Gunst und Gabe." See also below.
53. Saarinen, "Forgiveness, the Gift, and Ecclesiology."
54. Some, though not all, of the following topics are discussed in more detail in my *God and the Gift* as well as in "Gunst und Gabe" and "Forgiveness, the Gift, and Ecclesiology."

Christian tradition has elaborated theological language which can adequately express the ditransitive and sometimes even tritransitive nature of giving. Ditransitive action presupposes the giver (A), the gift (B), and the recipient (C). At least since Augustine Christian theology has very consciously identified a fourth place in such relations, that of beneficiary (D). In the theological figures of sacrifice and redemption, for instance, A gives B to C in order that D may benefit from this act. A beneficiary is thus sometimes clearly distinct from the recipient, and we can say that the action, for instance sacrifice, is expressed by a tritransitive verb.[55]

Augustine formalizes the logic of the gift[56] by employing the phenomenon of sacrifice. In sacrifice, A offers the gift (B) to the recipient (C) in order that the beneficiary (D) can profit from this act. The Christian theology of atonement and redemption is, obviously, highly dependant on the proper understanding of the distinction between the four relational places. The same protagonist can occupy two or even more relational places simultaneously. Augustine says in this context that Jesus Christ occupied all four relational places in the event of crucifixion: as God he was the giver and recipient of this sacrifice, as human being he belonged among the beneficiaries, as crucified he was the gift. Luther often employs the figure of Christ's self-giving: in the salvific act of self-giving, Jesus was both the giver and the gift.

The understanding of the gift in terms of four-place relation is connected with another classical principle, formulated by Seneca, saying that an act of favor (*beneficium*) is identified through the intention of the giver and the awareness of the recipient rather than through any material circumstances of the act.[57] If you find my book laying on your table, you cannot know whether I have 1) given it as a gift, or 2) simply forgotten it there, or 3) paid back an old debt. Only your knowledge of my intention can reveal the true meaning of this act. This principle is also needed when the theological meaning of four-place relation is investigated. Normally, both the giver and the recipient should be favorable in order that the intended act of gift-giving can take place.

---

55. While "ditransitive" is commonly used in linguistics, "tritransitive" is a more tentative concept. Like Augustine, contemporary linguistics calls the third transitive position that of a beneficiary. See Kittilä, "A typology of tritransitives."

56. Augustine *De trinitate* 4, 3, 19.

57. Seneca, "De beneficiis," 1, 5, 1–2 and 1, 5, 5 as well as 1, 6, 1.

Giver-Oriented Perspective

This rudimentary understanding can be helpful in understanding various theological acts of giving. Because gift-giving presupposes an intention, both givers and recipients are normally portrayed as living persons. I give this book to you, but I put it on the bookshelf. The semantics of "giving" and "the gift" normally requires a living recipient, a feature which may be puzzling in some theological contexts. Lutheran theology in particular has been accustomed to think of the gift in terms of unilateral and non-meritorious act. Baptism, for instance, is understood as God's unilateral gift to the infant.

At the same time, however, all Christian theology teaches that baptism can only be administered to living persons. This is logical, since an act of gift-giving requires a living recipient. But it also means that some reciprocity is embedded in the very concept of the gift. A purely unilateral transfer cannot, for semantical reasons, qualify as giving. This paradox of gift and giving has received an extensive treatment in philosophical and sociological literature,[58] but its theological implications have remained poorly understood. We may call the awareness of this paradox and related phenomena a "giver-oriented perspective."

In its discussion on freedom, Western theology has often preferred a recipient-oriented perspective in which the free will or some other capacity of the recipient is under scrutiny. Because of its focus on the recipient, this perspective has often favored a minimalist view of human freedom. Given this focus, Catholics prefer Augustine to Pelagius, while Protestants side with Luther and Calvin rather than Erasmus and Arminius. Examined from a recipient-oriented perspective, God's monergy and sovereignty tends to minimize human freedom.

We see the constraints of this framework in a comparison with Eastern Orthodoxy. The Orthodox churches affirm free will and synergy in salvation. But this Orthodox belief is not Pelagian. Basically, Orthodox anthropology claims that human beings have "self-determination" (*autexousion*), that is, humans are not machines and they are something more than animals.[59] The freedom implied by this view is one of responsiveness and responsibility, that is, an ability to react and initiate something as a response to the external world. At the same time, Orthodox

---

58. See my *God and the Gift* and Kass, *Giving Well*.

59. For this Greek concept, see Sorabji, *Emotion*, 320–25. Note the connection with the biblical concept of *exousia*.

theology is essentially God-centered and regards the human being from a theo-logical perspective. This is an essentially giver-oriented perspective, since it aims at understanding freedom not from an anthropocentric focus but from the theo-centric perspective of giving. In looking at human freedom in this sense indirectly, Orthodox theology manages to conceptualize freedom in ways which remain beyond the recipient-oriented scope of Western theology.

When the Finnish Luther studies focus on salvation as gift (*donum*), they have the possibility to focus on the gift-character of theological reality. This gift-character needs a proper perspective in order to be grasped adequately. The semantics of giving and the gift can lead towards this proper perspective. Freedom is but one example of a theological reinterpretation which can take place with the help of a giver-oriented perspective.

Recipients and Beneficiaries

Another many-sided feature in this regard concerns the distinction between recipients and beneficiaries. As we have seen, some tritransitive theological acts, most notably those of sacrifice and redemption, require this distinction. Its neglect can lead to a soteriology which does not understand the work of Christ properly. When the Finnish studies underline the importance of Christ present in faith, the most important issue to be discussed may not be mysticism or ontology, but the proper understanding of the work of Christ.

Some of the most vehement critics of Finnish studies are proponents of a strictly forensic theology of justification. By "strictly forensic" I mean a theology which basically denies the effective or ontological side of salvation, claiming that the justification of the sinner is a merely declarative act in God's mind, *in foro caeli*. In terms of Christology, Christ "for us" stands for this imputative declaration, whereas Christ "in us" approaches effective justification. If a theologian claims that Christ "for us" is the primary content of justification and that Christ "in us" can be reduced to that primary aspect, then he or she defends a strictly forensic theology of justification.

Among the critics of the Finns, Mark C. Mattes is a good example of this kind. He claims that

> Christ is so for us that he becomes one with us in this marriage of the conscience to Christ. Christ and the conscience are then "one body." The reason that Christ lives in me is not to accentuate a mystical teleology of ascent into the triune life but to "abolish the law"... Luther emphasizes Christ in us because it is the strongest scriptural affirmation to support the truth that Christ is for us. The efficacy of Christ in us is logically subordinate to the forensic declaration that Christ is for us.[60]

Mattes in this manner states that "Christ for us" is the primary truth, while "Christ in us" is an affirmation which is designated to support that primary truth. The union with Christ takes place in the conscience, but the essence of this union is to highlight how intimately Christ is for us.

In terms of our four-place relation, we are beneficiaries of the work of Christ since "for us" signifies this relational place. But we do not receive Christ in any such sense which would put us into the position of the recipient: because the work of Christ in justification is, in Mattes's view, reduced to Christ "for us," our union with Christ only highlights our role as beneficiaries. Such a strictly forensic understanding of justification clearly deviates from Mannermaa's concept and cannot be reconciled with it. It belongs to the central claims of the Finnish program that humans are both beneficiaries of Christ's work and recipients of salvation. The union with Christ has obvious connections with eucharistic and sacramental theology in which the faithful receive the body and blood of Christ.

Luther's theology of the Lord's Supper and the Mass exemplifies particularly well the fact that the salvific self-giving of Christ comprises humans as both beneficiaries and recipients. The fundamental problem of Catholic Masses was that the laypeople could be interpreted as mere beneficiaries: they did not need to attend the Mass but could benefit by the performance without participation. Luther, however, emphasized that the eucharist needed to be personally received. Likewise, the theology of justification needs both Christ for us and Christ in us—one aspect cannot be reduced to another. Paradoxically, the strictly forensic concept of Mattes thus approaches the theology of eucharistic sacrifice that Luther rejected.

The Augustinian distinction between recipients and beneficiaries is used abundantly in Luther's theology of the eucharist and Christian life.

---

60. Mattes, "A Future," 446.

Luther emphasizes that the believers perform a response to Christ's act of self-giving. In their response to the eucharist, the faithful give themselves to their neighbors in loving service; the neighbors thus benefit from the response. In this sense the common priesthood of all believers also contains a sense of becoming a living sacrifice. In order to grasp this secondary sacrifice, a response to Christ's primary self-giving, the interaction of different relational places has to be clearly defined.[61]

Favor and Gift

It was shown above that my development of the Finnish program is critical of a purely forensic understanding of justification. Such an understanding reduces the work of Christ so that humans remain mere beneficiaries without personal participation in the salvific reality. Salvation and Christ need to be received in Christian theology. The giver-oriented perspective contains, however, another angle from which the relationship between forensic and effective justification ascribes some primacy to the forensic aspect.

Since the gift can only be a gift when the giver's intention is recognized, the intention has a certain non-temporal, conceptual primacy over the effective gift. When Melanchthon stresses that God's merciful attitude, *gratia* or *favor*, must in some way precede the gift given,[62] he affirms Seneca's classical principle. Luther scholars have often debated whether Luther also teaches the primacy of *gratia* over *donum*; the Finns have defended the view that Luther advocates a unity of these two concepts such that neither of them has primacy over the other in the doctrine of justification.[63]

My own development of the Finnish paradigm in terms of "giver-oriented perspective" modifies this view slightly. While it is true that God's benevolence and God's gift appear together, one also needs to say that God's gift needs to be preconditioned by benevolence in order that it can be a gift. As Luther himself remarks, God can generously give the very same material things to the pious and the impious, but this thing

---

61. This has been worked out in detail by Simon, *Luthers Messopfertheologie*. See also Simon, "Worship and the Eucharist."
62. See Melanchthon, *Loci communes 1521*, 5, 4–7.
63. See Peura, "Christ as Favor and Gift."

is a healing gift only for the pious, because God's merciful intention is limited to the pious.[64]

As this example shows, the logic of favor and gift is complex. I do not say to my children at Christmas time: "I only give you my good intention, but not the present." Similarly, there is little point in saying "cheers" when the glass is empty. In this sense the benevolence often needs the subsequent gift. But this observation concerns a factual, not conceptual unity of favor and gift. It is entirely possible to say that I only give my good will—and one often does, for instance, in saying "farewell." The other way round, however, a conceptual link is required: my transaction to you can only be a gift if my intention is favorably gratuitous. In this very specific and limited sense, there is a conceptual priority of favor over the gift. I think that both Luther and Melanchthon defend this specific view and that their conceptualizations of justification are, therefore, basically similar in this regard.[65]

Let it be finally reiterated that the issue at stake in my third and fourth point is fairly complex. Various debates related to the Lutheran doctrine of justification fail because they do not differentiate the matter adequately. Adherents to forensic justification readily affirm the primacy of merciful favor, but they fail to see the dynamics of one's being both recipient and beneficiary. Adherents of effective justification grasp this dynamics, but they do not see the fine differences between the concepts of favor and gift. But when over-simplifications are adequately avoided, the third and fourth points are both historically valid and systematically clear.

Three Powers of Faith

We saw above that Benedict refutes Luther's alleged concept of faith by saying that "faith is not merely a personal reaching out towards things to come that are still totally absent: it gives us something."[66] Our reading of Luther has yielded a view in which the faithful is not merely reaching out towards absent things; divine benevolence accompanies the gift such that Christ is really present in faith. Luther's concept of faith can be aptly summarized with his view of the three powers of faith laid out in his

---

64. For God's "gifts" to the impious, see Luther, *StA* 2, 491, 1–5 (*Against Latomus*).
65. See Saarinen, "Gunst und Gabe."
66. Benedict XVI, *Spe salvi*, 7.

*On the Freedom of the Christian.*⁶⁷ The three powers show how the faith comprises both the subjective element of *fides sola* and the more objective elements of forensic justification and the presence of Christ.

The first power of faith emerges from Luther's discussion of "faith alone." It portrays the situation in which word and faith rule united in the soul. This union of faithful soul with the word is compared with the unity of fire and iron. This unity is predominantly an ascetic union of promise and trust. Luther does describe it in terms of participation, union, and sanctification, but because of the centrality of "faith alone" this first power of faith is a personal reaching out. Its objective counterpart is word and promise.⁶⁸

The second power of faith is closely connected with forensic justification. When God sees that the faithful give God honor, righteousness, and truthfulness in their act of faith, then God also regards the faithful as righteous and truthful. Their faith is the basis of this divine consideration of righteousness. The second power thus exemplifies a coexistence of subjective and objective elements: while, on the one hand, "faith makes truth and righteousness," the justifying act of God is, on the other hand, a monergic and objective divine decision.⁶⁹

The third power of faith is

> that it unites the soul with Christ as a bride is united with her bridegroom. By this mystery, as the Apostle teaches, Christ and the soul become one flesh. And if they are one flesh and there is between them a true marriage—indeed the most perfect of all marriages, since human marriages are but poor examples of this one true marriage—it follows that everything they have they hold in common, the good as well as the evil. Accordingly the believing soul can boast of and glory in whatever Christ has as though it were its own.⁷⁰

While the second power expresses God's benevolence or favor, the third power expresses God's gift. This gift is Christ himself present in faith. While the first power expresses an ascetic and subjective union between word and faith, promise and trust, the third power enriches this union so that it becomes, in Mannermaa's terms, "real-ontic," and in that

---

67. The following is an analysis of *StA* 2, 270–78.
68. *StA* 2, 270–72.
69. *StA* 2, 272–74.
70. *StA* 2, 274, 37–276, 1. Translation from *LW* 31, 351.

sense ontological and sacramental. The third power thus expresses the power of the gift which enriches the promise through becoming foretaste; the benevolence is transformed into an effective power and gift. Thus Luther's concept of faith alone does not lead to a subjective reduction of sacramental presence: through its third power, faith continues to meditate the hidden but present nature of the gift.

The third power is described with the language of donation: Christ gives (*donat*) the faithful his body and very self and takes the sins of the faithful, thus transforming the being of the Christians. The role of "faith alone" in this exchange and "blessed struggle" is not limited to its subjective nature; on the contrary, the presence of the promised good is abundantly given in the third power.[71] "Faith alone" is not contrasted to real presence but to "works" (*opera*): since works are "inanimate things,"[72] they cannot achieve what faith can. Through its three powers (*virtus*), faith emerges as an animated, living principle to which word and Christ can adhere. Peace and freedom are qualities of the Christian soul who lives in faith.[73]

This description of faith reveals a final connection with our "giver-oriented perspective." If human beings are investigated from the viewpoint of their own activity, their works come into focus so that they, paradoxically, become inanimate and thus incapable of bringing about the union with God. If, however, the perspective is shifted to God as giver, the human person ceases to appear as agent and becomes the recipient of the word and Christ. In this new, seemingly passive perspective he or she reappears, again paradoxically, as vivid and animated partner. The argumentative move from "works" to "faith alone" is, therefore, not a move from presence to absence, from activity to passivity, or from objectivity to subjectivity. It is a move which proceeds from assumed passivity to a living faith. In the light of this perspectival move, Christians are seen as animated beings in their union with Christ. In this manner Luther's faith draws the future into the present.

---

71. StA 2, 276, 6–10.
72. StA 2, 278, 9: "res insensatae."
73. StA 2, 272, 17–20.

2

The Human Being

ANTTI RAUNIO

THE CENTRAL THEMES OF Finnish Luther research, namely, the believer's participation in the divine life, union with Christ through faith, and theological ontology, all stand in close relation to the notion of the human being. Thus far, there has been no Finnish monograph on this topic. However, different aspects of Luther's concept of the human being have been dealt with in several studies.[1]

Luther's anthropology is a complicated issue. The reformer did not leave any systematic presentation, but commented on anthropological themes in many writings and from different points of view. Only with a thorough historical reconstruction can we therefore arrive at a general view of Luther's anthropology. This reconstruction is challenged by Luther's terminology, which changes from text to text, and by the concep-

---

1. The most important so far have been Eero Huovinen's *Kuolemattomuudesta osallinen. Martti Lutherin kuoleman teologinen perusongelma* [*A Participant in Immortality: The Fundamental Ecumenical Problem of Martin Luther's Theology of Death*] and Simo Peura's article on the Christian's participation in Christ, "Die Teilhabe in Christus bei Luther," in S. Peura and A. Raunio, *Luther und Theosis*, 121–61. In his study, which exists complete only in Finnish (short German summary will be published in Eero Huovinen, *Baptism, Church and Ecumenism*), Huovinen analyzes specifically Luther's understanding of the human being in the initial state and the influence of the fall on the human being as *imago Dei*. Huovinen's main topic is Luther's view of death and immortality, and therefore, he does not deal with all the questions which are important for anthropology. His study nevertheless contains anthropologically relevant insights. In this article I also draw on my earlier study "Die Gegenwart des Geistes im Christen bei Luther," in J. Heubach, *Der Heilige Geist: Ökumenische und reformatorische Untersuchungen*, 89–104.

tual distinctions that he often assumes without explanation. However, he has made fundamental distinctions in some texts, and these distinctions can be applied in analyzing passages in which such distinctions are not explicitly mentioned.

There has been widespread scholarly discussion of Luther's concept of the human being. Recently, Robert Kolb has described the central theses of Finnish Luther research as they apply to the understanding of the human being. According to Kolb, the Finnish view veers in Osiander's direction by interpreting some of Luther's statements in a way that brings him into accord with an Eastern Orthodox view of salvation by "divinization." Osiander believed in the ontological transformation of a person, by contending that the believer is united with the divine nature of Christ. Osiander maintained that the essential righteousness of Christ's divine nature becomes the believer's righteousness before God. By being united with Christ, sinners are transformed by his eternal divine righteousness, which swallows up our righteousness, thereby transforming us into pure brides. As a critique of such view, Kolb states that Luther opposed the view of salvation by psychological transformation and the view of salvation by ontological transformation, both of which make sense only in a Platonic, spiritualizing frame of reference. For Kolb, Luther held that the verdict of justification does not come at the beginning or at the end of a movement; instead, it establishes an entirely new situation. The joyous exchange is thus not a substantial exchange, but a relational exchange. It puts one in a different set of relationships, whether it means substantial change or not.[2]

---

2. Kolb, *Genius of Luther's Theology*, 48–49. Kolb's interpretation of the Finnish view of Luther's idea of deification is clearly a misunderstanding. Tuomo Mannermaa and Simo Peura, who have studied the theme of deification, have never maintained that Luther's view is "in accord" with the Orthodox view. For Mannermaa, the Lutheran understanding of the indwelling of Christ is analogous to the Orthodox doctrine of participation in God. This means that the concepts are not similar but have some common features, especially the real participation in Christ. See Mannermaa, "Justification and Theosis," 25. Peura has also explicitly addressed the crucial difference between Luther and Osiander. Luther never believed that in the union with the believer, Christ's human nature has nothing but an intermediary function and that the believer only participates in Christ's divine nature; see Peura, "Gott und Mensch in der Unio," 33–61. Furthermore, the Finnish researchers have emphasized that the term "ontology" is used in a general and "technical" sense without reference to any philosophical (Platonic, Aristotelian, Kantian, existential) ontology. Cf. Mannermaa, "Why is Luther So Fascinating?" 12.

The main line of German Luther research also represents a relational and extrinsic view of the human being. This means that the "being" of human creatures is not substantial, but exists in relationships, which set the human beings outside themselves. Human being cannot be substantial simply because humans do not exist in themselves as do substances, but only in relations to God and to other creatures. According to Peters, the extrinsic humanity of the Christian "theological man" has its center not in the human being but in the word addressed to humans. In the word the human conceals self-confidence and a relationship to the world.[3]

On the other hand, some scholars have pointed out that the contradiction between substantial and relational ontology and the view of the human being is too simple and perhaps not at all fruitful.[4] The question is not which of the two we should choose in order to understand Luther correctly, but rather how we should understand these categories in relation to each other. In the philosophical sense Luther, of course, understood the terms "substance" and "relation" as Aristotelian categories. He was also well aware of the late medieval discussions concerning the substantial forms of creatures. However, a relational philosophy and a view of reality in the proper sense is a modern phenomenon, one that has developed slowly. A relational ontology as an alternative to substantial ontology is in fact a more or less a Kantian idea, which was developed further by Hegel.[5]

As for theology, it had always been relational, because it examines the Trinitarian God, his internal relationships and his relation to the created world. Thus, the main idea of Finnish Luther research can be presented such that, in philosophical terms, Luther follows a classical Aristotelian understanding of creatures as substances, in which creatures also possess substantial forms. The reformer uses the same terms in a theological sense as well. If the rational soul is the substantial form

---

3. Peters, *Mensch*, 55. Cf. Zur Mühlen, *Reformatorisches Profil*, 206–7. The paradigmatic presentation of the relational conception of human being in Luther is Wilfried Joest, *Ontologie der Person bei Luther*. It develops certain ideas of Gerhard Ebeling's early Luther studies. For Joest, in the Reformation a substantial concept of person is challenged by a dialogical one. See Joest, *Ontologie der Person*, 28.

4. See, for example, Mannermaa, "Hat Luther eine trinitarische Ontologie?"; Saarinen, "Gottes Sein—Gottes Wirken"; Beutel, "Antwort und Wort"; Dieter, "Du musst den Geist haben."

5. Shults, *Reforming Theological Anthropology*, 20–25.

of a human being in a philosophical sense, then in theology the form of a Christian is the word of God, Christ, or faith, and sometimes even love, but the form of a non-believer contradicts the form of a Christian. Critics of the Finnish position often understand the matter in a way that suggests a return to the classical substantial ontology in Lutheran theology. This return, however, is not the case. The relational aspect is crucial for Luther's theological ontology, because God's being (*esse*) is relational.[6] In God himself, thus, substantial and relational beings do not exclude each other. Participation in the divine being or in the divine life through Christ means participation in God's Trinitarian relational being.

In the created world the connection between substance and relation has to be treated in both the philosophical and the theological senses. Philosophy is the realm of human reason, but theology assumes faith. Both realms have their own language, and each signifies reality in different ways. Despite their differences, they are not totally exclusive. In Luther's view philosophical reason or language cannot comprehend the theological signification and view of reality, yet theological language does not exclude, but rather includes the philosophical signification of the terms.[7] This point is very important, because it means that philosophical and theological language, ontology, and anthropology are not alternatives. When understood correctly, they each have their own realms of knowing and understanding, but they also belong together and complement each other.

My purpose here is to present the main lines of Luther's concept of the human being,[8] who in the beginning was created in God's image,

---

6. Mannermaa, "Why is Luther so Fascinating?" 12: "…I have tried to outline some of the elements of Luther's ontology. God is in relation to himself in the movement of Word at the same time that he is this movement of the Word. The being of God is relational, and as such has the character of *esse*. This understanding of the being of God is the basis for understanding the being-present-of-Christ-in-faith. In Christ the inner-Trinitarian Word, which is the being of God, becomes incarnate. The presence of Christ's word and the word about Christ in faith are the presence of God himself."

7. White, "Luther as Nominalist," 318–19; 345–46 has come to the same conclusion in his detailed analysis of Luther's conception of philosophical and theological language. His result is that the so-called primary signification of a proposition remains the same in both languages, whereas the assertive signification changes. This means that the part of the signification which is necessary for picking out an object remains. In addition the signification contains a further part, which allows inferences from one proposition to another.

8. The most comprehensive presentation of Luther's anthropology is Gerhard Ebeling's *LuSt II*, in which the author explains the reformer's *Disputatio de homine*. In

then lost this image, but may regain it through the Gospel of Christ. This description also answers, at least to some degree, the question of what Luther means by the human being's participation in divine life. However, the problem of theological ontology is too complicated to be discussed comprehensively here.[9]

As with all his thinking, Luther's concept of human being is theologically informed. However, Luther's theological anthropology is difficult to understand without taking into account his concept of the relation between philosophy and theology. This is perhaps especially relevant to the reformer's anthropology, because often he relates his theological views of human beings by using philosophical insights. Even though Luther believes that theology is able to know the human being better than philosophy, he does not reject all philosophy. Gerhard Ebeling has described Luther's criticism of philosophy as mainly directed to the role of philosophy in theology. It should not be understood as a rejection of philosophy as such. According to Ebeling, theology deals with things *coram Deo*, and philosophy's proper task is to understand the things *coram mundi*. When understood correctly, philosophy and theology do not exclude each other but coexist peacefully.[10] This is without doubt an important aspect of Luther's view. One may still ask whether it covers the whole relation between philosophy and theology. If we apply this distinction to the concept of the human being, then the result would be that theology provides knowledge about the human's relation to God, and philosophy tells about the relationships between human beings and other creatures. Luther's understanding of the difference between theological and philosophical knowledge contains this distinction, but also something else.

Luther's main point is that philosophical or rational knowledge is "objective," but theological knowledge is "practical." The principal difference is that objective knowledge is based on rational reasoning whereas practical knowledge assumes certain kind of personal experience. We have to ask how objective and practical knowledge relate to each other. Do they refer to different areas of reality or do they have some com-

---

a Nordic context most influential has been Hägglund *De homine*. See also Hägglund, "Luthers Anthropologie."

9. See especially Mannermaa, "Hat Luther eine trinitarische Ontologie?"; Dieter, "Du musst den Geist haben!"; Juntunen, "Luther and Metaphysics."

10. Ebeling, *LuSt II, Disputatio de homine 3. Teil*, 6–15.

mon realm? In searching for answer to this question, it is important to consider Luther's philosophical background. He had learned the tools of semantic analysis of language in the school of *via moderna*.[11] It is well known that, for Luther, the concepts of philosophical language have to be "baptized" when they are used in theology. He also says that they become "new words." The idea is that in theology the words refer to their objects in a different way than in ordinary language. However, the signification of ordinary terms does not disappear, but is included in the new, theological significations. Consequently, when we speak about a "human being" in the philosophical sense, we speak about the person in this world and in relation to other beings. Theologically, we speak about human beings in relation to God, but this does not exclude the *coram mundi* aspect.

THE HUMAN BEING AS GOD'S IMAGE AND LIKENESS

Luther adheres to the general theological view that the human being is a creature of God. God creates the human being—like all creatures—by speaking. The creation has taken place through the Son of God, that is, the Word, who is God's invisible image.[12] The existence of the human being is continuously dependent on God's creative speech. Luther points out that in a theological sense, the term "to create" does not signify some singular act at a given moment, but rather the Holy Spirit's continuous guidance, conservation, and increasing of spiritual actions in the hearts believers.[13] The theological concept of creating also naturally includes the "first moment" or the beginning of creation when God called up the creatures out of nothing into existence.

In the beginning the human creature, which consists of a body and a breathing soul, was made in God's own image and without sin. The purposes of man's creation in the image of God are generation, dominion over other created things, and immortal life. But since the fall of Adam the human being has been under the power of the Devil, sin, and

---

11. See White, *Luther as Nominalist*, 299–348. Pekka Kärkkäinen has recently published studies on Luther's teachers' philosophical psychology. See Kärkkäinen, "On the Semantics of 'Human Being' and 'Animal'; Theology, Philosophy, and Immortality of the Soul"; "Nominalist Psychology and the Limits of Canon Law"; "Objects of Sense Perception."

12. *WA* 42, 167, 15–16.

13. *WA* 40 II, 422, 34–423, 17.

death. Humans are also unable to overcome these powers with their own capacities alone. Only through the Son of God, Jesus Christ, can humans be liberated and eternal life be given. All this assumes a human belief in Christ. In his Disputation on the Human Being (*Disputatio De homine*) Luther calls this set of ideas the definition of the whole and perfect human being, which is based on the "plenitude of theological wisdom."[14]

Philosophy, which is human wisdom, defines the human being as a rational, sensitive, and corporeal animal. For Luther, this definition holds true as far as the human being is seen as a mortal and living this life.[15] Luther also accepts the philosophical view that reason is the essential difference between human beings and animals as well as other creatures.[16] Reason is the head of all things and better than everything else. Luther even says that, in a way, reason is divine.[17] Reason invents and governs all the arts, medicines, and laws as well as all wisdom, virtue and honor that concern this life.[18] In short, from the philosophical point of view, reason is the essential specific difference that makes a creature a human being.

Even though Luther criticizes the philosophical understanding of the human being, it is worth noting that the theological definition is not contrary to the philosophical view. In fact, the theological concept of a human being contains a philosophical aspect. Luther's point seems to be that the philosophical definition of man is not wrong as such, but it would be wrong to believe that this definition alone is sufficient without the theological point of view.

---

14. *WA* 39/I, 176, 5–13: "20. Theologia vero de plenitudine sapientiae suae Hominem totum et perfectum definit. 21. Scilicet, quod homo est creatura Dei, carne et anima spirante constans, ab initio ad imaginem Dei facta, sine peccato, ut generaret et rebus dominaretur, nec unquam moreretur. 22. Post lapsum vero Adae subiecta potestati diaboli, peccato et morti, utroque malo suis viribus insuperabili et aeterno. 23. Nec nisi per filium Dei Iesum Christum liberanda (si credat in eum) et vitae aeternitate donanda."

15. *WA* 39/I, 175, 3–4, 7–8: "1. Philosophia, sapientia humana, definit, hominem, esse animal rationale, sensitivum, corporeum."; "3. Sed hoc sciendum est, quod haec definitio tum mortalem et huius vitae hominem definit."

16. *WA* 39/I, 175, 14–15: "6. Ut hinc merito ipsa vocari debeat differentia essentialis, qua constituatur homo, differe ab animalibus et rebus aliis."

17. *WA* 39/I, 175, 9–10: "Et sane verum est, quod ratio omnium rerum res et caput et prae caeteris rebus huius vitae optimum et divinum quiddam sit."

18. *WA* 39/I, 175, 11–13: "5. Quae est inventrix et gubernatrix omnium Artium, Medicinarum, Iurium, et quidquid in hac vita sapientiae, potentiae, virtutis et gloriae ab hominibus possidetur."

We will return to the question of what Luther means by "reason." First, however, we need to ask how Luther's philosophical understanding of the human being as a rational creature relates to his conception of *imago Dei*. Luther scholars have often emphasized that, for Luther *imago Dei* is not any inherent quality that a human being possesses. As an alternative to such an "ontological" view, they suggest that Luther understands the *imago* as a relational term, as a value, for example, which God gives to the human being by making humans capable of answering God's speaking.[19] However, these alternatives do not exactly correspond to Luther's explicit dicta about *imago Dei*.

The human being has much in common with animals. The whole of corporeal life is in fact very similar to other creatures. Simultaneously, the human being differs from animals because human existence is based on God's particular thought (*consilio*) and providence (*providentia*). God's thought was to create man in his own image, and this image refers to something much higher that the corporeal life shared by all creatures.[20] The human being has been created for a double life: the corporeal or animal life and the spiritual, immortal life. In a theological sense then, the spiritual or immortal life is the difference between human beings and other creatures. However, the immortal life is not yet revealed perfectly but "in hope."[21] The phrase "in hope" does not suggest that immortal life was awaited first human beings only in the future. Huovinen has shown clearly that for Luther, the first human beings lived immortal lives from the beginning. But the immortal and spiritual life was not perfect, because human beings still lived a corporeal and animal life, and for the human senses, the immortal life was hidden. Immortality was not yet confirmed. So the human being could still lose immortality and become mortal.[22]

Luther says that the human being is created in the animal life and is also made in God's image and likeness, thus signifying another and bet-

---

19. See, for example, Bayer, *Martin Luthers Theologie*, 142.

20. WA 42, 41, 38–42, 20.

21. WA 42, 43, 7–11: "Habuit igitur Adam duplicem vitam: animalem et immortalem, sed nondum revelatam plane sed in spe. Interim edisset, bibisset, laborasset, generasset etc. Haec paucis admonere volui de differentia ista, quam Deus facit per suum consilium, quo discernit nos ab aliis animalibus, cum quibus nos sinit vivere."

22. Huovinen, *Kuolemattomuudesta osallinen*, 58–72.

ter life than the animal life.²³ These words raise the question of whether "the other and better life" refers to the *imago Dei* in an exclusive sense or does the image of God also include the animal life, that is, the human being as body and soul.

Luther criticizes the Augustinian idea that to be created in God's image means to have memory, mind or intellect, and will, but to be created in God's likeness is to possess those capacities perfected by the theological virtues, faith, hope, and love.²⁴ For Luther, these and other speculations contribute very little to the correct understanding of *imago Dei*. He rejects the concept of the three capacities of the soul as image of God. If that were true, the Devil too would have been created in the image of God. The Devil's natural capacities are even much more developed than human beings' memory, intellect and will.²⁵ However, in spite of these well-developed natural capacities, the Devil is not God's image.²⁶ Consequently, the phrase that "human beings have been made in the likeness of God" does not mean that human beings resemble God only by possessing reason and will. God's likeness, which for Luther is the same as the image of God, means that the human being's intellect comprehends God and wills what God wills.²⁷

Anyone who still wants to maintain that the image of God consists of the capacities of the soul has to take into account that the human capacities are perverted and weakened by sin. Luther concludes that the image of God does not refer to natural capacities, but is a quite special work of God.

For Luther, the sinful weakness of the natural capacities seems to prove that they cannot be the image of God. Luther's point here is that the traditional differentiation between image and likeness is not correct, but image means about the same or even more than likeness in the ear-

---

23. *WA* 42, 42, 40–43, 6: "Sed quod additur: conditum esse hominem ita in animalem vitam, ut esset tamen factus ad imaginem Dei et similitudinem, haec est significatio alterius et melioris vitae, quam animalis."

24. *WA* 42, 45, 1–17.

25. *WA* 42, 46, 5–10.

26. See Luthers Entwurf, *WA* 42, xx.

27. *WA* 42, 248, 9–3: "Quod igitur Moses dicit Hominem etiam ad similitudinem Dei factum esse, ostendit, quod homo non solum referat Deum in eo, quod rationem seu intellectum et voluntatem habet, sed etiam, quod habet similitudinem Dei, hoc est, voluntatem et intellectum talem, quo Deum intelligit, quo vult, quae Deus vult etc."

lier tradition, namely, pure and perfect human nature. Luther believes that all capacities of Adam's soul and body were totally pure.

In Luther's view *imago Dei* means that the human being lives a divine life. And this image, that is, the divine life, the first human beings Adam and Eve too had in their own substance.[28] Luther explicitly emphasizes that being created in God's image means not only knowing God and believing in his goodness, but also living an immortal life like God. For this reason Adam and Eve did not fear death or dangers. Instead of fearing, they were satisfied with God's grace.[29]

Luther describes the human being as imago Dei in several places in his *Lectures on Genesis*. As was already indicated above, *imago Dei* means to live without fear or danger. In addition, *imago Dei* makes human beings wise, just, good, and free from all spiritual and corporeal adversities. But what is even more important, the human being as *imago Dei* is capable (*capax*) of eternal life.[30] The phrase *eternae vitae capax* has to be understood in the context of Luther's concept that the image of God, that is, the divine eternal life, belongs to the substance of human being. The image of God includes eternal life and security as well as everything that is good.[31] Luther's statements indicate that he believed human beings were created to participate in divine life and goodness.

Luther also says this explicitly: God himself forms the human being according to his reasoning in his own image and as though in participation in God.[32] One might oppose the thought of real participation in God

---

28. Most descriptions of Luther's concept of *imago Dei* ignore the reformer's view that the image refers to the divine life that belonged to the human substance. Cf. Bayer, *Martin Luthers Theologie*, 141–43; Lohse, *Luthers Theologie*, 259–61; Albrecht Peters, *Mensch*, 43–49. Hägglund, however, in *De homine*, 77–90 takes note of this aspect, which is analyzed by Huovinen in *Kuolemattomuudesta osallinen*.

29. WA 42, 47, 8–17: "Ergo imaginem Dei sic intelligo: Quod Adam eam in sua substantia habuerit, quod non solum Deum cognovit et credidit eum esse bonum, sed quod etiam vitam vixerit plane divinam, hoc est, quod fuerit sine pavore mortis et omnium periculorum, contentus gratia Dei. Sicut in Heua apparet, quae cum serpente sine omni metu loquitur sicut nos cum agno aut cane. Ideo etiam istam poenam proponit Deus, si transgrediantur praeceptum: 'Quacunque die comederis es ligno hoc, morte morieris', quasi dicat: Adam et Heua, vos nunc vivitis securi, mortem non sentitis nec videtis. Haec est imago mea, qua vivitis, sicut Deus vivit. Si autem peccaveritis, amittetis hanc imaginem et moriemini."

30. WA 42, 49, 1–4.

31. WA 42, 48, 38–39: "Ergo fuit praestantissimum quiddam illa imago Dei, in quam inclusa fuit vita aeterna et securitas aeterna et omnia bona."

32. WA 42, 63, 30–31: "Sed ipse eum format ad imaginem sui, tanquam participem Dei et qui fruiturus sit requie Dei."

by pointing out that Luther uses the expression *tamquam participem Dei*. However, Luther is referring to participation elsewhere without any reservations. In the same context Luther says that when creating Adam God used a lifeless piece of clay and shaped it into a noble creature who would participate in immortality.[33] Later, Luther states that the human being is a unique creature, whose uniqueness is based on participation in divinity and immortality.[34] Consequently, Luther's conception of human beings as God's image includes the idea of participation in God, the divine life, goodness, and all divine qualities such righteousness, wisdom, friendliness, and helpfulness.

For Luther, Adam and Eve were totally absorbed in God's goodness and righteousness.[35] Thus, in the human being who is in God's image shines the likeness of the divine nature through illuminated reason, justice, and wisdom.[36] As Huovinen has shown, Luther believes that the human being before the fall was equal in form with God and alike with God.[37] Of course, Luther does not indicate that human beings could be gods in an absolute sense or in themselves. The *imago Dei* is not an inherent quality in the sense that one could possess it without God's real presence. Nevertheless, it is inherent in the sense that it belongs to the original and pure human substance. The original human being created in God's image participated in the divine life and its qualities.

Original righteousness was also one of the divine qualities in which the human being participated. Like *imago Dei*, it belonged to the humans' original nature. Adam's nature was to love God, to believe in him and to know him. For this reason, Luther rejects the view that righteousness is an additional gift that adorns the human nature, but does not belong to it. Because original justice was initially part of human nature, the loss of it means that the fallen human is depraved in nature.[38]

---

33. WA 42, 63, 31–33: "Itaque Adam, antequam a Domino formatur, est mortua et iacens gleba eam apprehendit Deus et format inde pulcherrimam creaturam participem immortalitatis."

34. WA 42, 87, 14–19.

35. WA 42, 50, 17–19.

36. WA 42, 49, 18–20: "Hic pulcherrimae creaturae, quae cognoscit Deum et est imago Dei, in qua lucet similitudo divinae naturae per rationem illuminatam, per iusticiam et sapientiam..."

37. Huovinen, *Kuolemattomuudesta osallinen*, 33–34.

38. WA 42, 123, 38–124, 6.

As a consequence, Luther's understanding of the *imago Dei* differs from the previous teachings, which saw in it the capacities of the human soul. Whereas Augustine counted reason, will, and memory among these capacities, Thomas Aquinas saw the reason or the mind as the feature that most resembles the divine nature.[39] By contrast, for Luther the image is not based on the created natural capacities, but on the divine immortal life which at the beginning belonged to the human substance or nature. The image of God, which belonged to human substance, affected the natural human capacities and made them perfect. Human persons who lived a divine life loved and knew God and all the creatures perfectly. If humans had not sinned against God's will and word, they would have kept the image of God, and their eternal life would have been confirmed. But when humans fell in sin, they also lost their godly image.

Thus, according to Luther we can say that the human being was created in God's image, but about fallen humans we cannot speak of *imago Dei* without qualifications. Luther believes that fallen human beings lost the image of God. This image has been so thoroughly lost that to speak about *imago Dei* is to speak about something unknown.[40] However, this loss is not quite total; we still have some weak remnants of it.[41] Therefore, when Luther describes his view exactly, he says that the image has been almost totally lost.[42]

Thus, the human being is no longer in the image of God. Adam was created in God's image and likeness, but he did not remain such. Therefore, his son Seth was not born in God's image, but in the image of his father. Seth was like Adam both in body and spirit and reflected the likeness of his father in his outlook, manner of speech, habits, and will. This likeness was not created by God, but inherited from Adam. This likeness also includes the initial sin and the punishment of eternal death.[43] As result, the "real" human being after the fall consists of Adam's inherited image and weak remnants of the created *imago Dei*. But the *imago Dei* in proper sense, the participation in divine immortal life, is gone.

39. *ST* 93.6.
40. *WA* 42, 47, 31–33.
41. *WA* 42, 50, 6–12.
42. *WA* 42, 50, 16–17.
43. *WA* 42, 249, 29–250, 3.

RESTORING AND REFORMING GOD'S IMAGE

Still, Luther does not think that human beings have to remain without God's image and likeness. The Gospel repairs human beings in God's image and renews humans in an even better way. For example, God impressed his likeness on Seth, who was no longer in God's image, through the word. Luther combines this effect of the word with the Apostle Paul's idea of "Christ being formed in the believers."[44] The word renews believers because they are reborn through faith in eternal life or rather in the hope of eternal life. They hope for life in and with God and unity with Him.[45]

"Christ's form" does not refer to a natural or a metaphysical meaning. In the spiritual sense his form or beauty means his real divinity and humanity. Christ has been conceived by the Holy Spirit and born of the Virgin Mary without sin. By contrast, all human beings are born in original sin, and they live and die without righteousness or wisdom without Christ's help. So in the spiritual sense, human beings have to receive their form from Christ's spiritual substance, because he is pure and holy both in spirit and in body.[46] Luther refers to the reforming of God's image in his *Lectures on the First Letter of John*, even though he does not explicitly speak about the *imago Dei*. Luther begins the lectures by emphasizing the union between divinity and humanity in Christ. Christ is the eternal word of God and the word of life, who has become a man. Where Christ is, there is salvation, joy, and life, but where he is absent, only death is present.[47] Luther indicates that Christ is the divine, eternal, and immortal life, although without using these terms.

This immortal life has been manifested, because Christ has risen from the dead, and the apostles witnessed this resurrection. Luther explains that the apostles first saw this life when Christ became man, but

---

44. WA 42, 250, 5–7.

45. WA 42, 48, 11–16: "Hoc autem nunc per Euangelium agitur, ut imago illa reparetur. Manserunt quidem intellectus et voluntas, sed valde viciata utraque. Euangelium igitur hoc agit, ut ad illam et quidem meliorem imaginem reformemur, quia in vitam aeternam vel potius in spem vitae aeternae renascimur per fidem, ut vivamus in Deo et cum Deo, et unum cum ipso sumus, sicut Christus dicit."

46. WA 40/II, 484, 25–485, 14.

47. WA 20, 607, 11–14: "Ipsa vita, scilicet quae est Christus, est manifestata: Christus est verbum vitae et vita. Ubi ille est, ibi salus, gaudium, ubi plus per cognitionem adest, plus vitae, ubi abest, mera mors. Potentior est ista vita quam universae mortes &c."

after the resurrection they saw the immortal life manifested when Christ was declared the victor over death. This victory has been revealed to everyone and is told through the word. The Apostles also endeavored to convince others to participate in salvation.[48] Through proclamation of the word, people partake salvation and eternal life.

Luther also quotes 2 Pet 1:4, where the writer speaks about the believers' participation in divine nature. For Luther this means that in Christ, the believers have everything good that God is and has. Hence, this "word of salvation and life"[49] contains and gives everything that God is and has, and above all, the eternal life and salvation.

Father and Son have eternal life, justice, and truth in themselves. But human beings have death, sin, and desperation. In order to help them, Father and Son unite with human beings. Luther here changes the plural form to singular by saying, "He comes with the Word." This assumes that the Son actually comes and communicates with human beings, but according to the maxim *opera trinitatis ad extra semper sunt indivisa* the Father is always present in the Son's actions. By coming with the word, the Father acts as if he himself were in death and sin. The Father also takes the death and sin of humans upon himself. And those human beings, who believe in the word of life see how their sins will be absorbed in the righteousness of Christ which is now theirs.[50] In other words, God unites himself with human beings through Christ, who is the word, and gives them his righteousness, which conquers and annihilates their sins.

Consequently, Christ's coming and communicating himself to believers makes them participants in God's substance and qualities, that is, of what God is and what he has. As shown above, this does not come about without the real humanity of Christ. This is precisely what happens when the image of God is restored in human beings by the Gospel.

Through faith, believers are reborn not only in eternal life but also in righteousness. Faith grasps Christ's merit and concludes that through Christ's death, people are free. Receiving Christ's merit by faith is then followed by the beginning of believers' "second righteousness": a new

---

48. WA 20, 607, 17—608, 2.

49. WA 20, 611, 1-2: Petrus: "Ut participes essetis divinae naturae i. e. in Christo habemus omnia bona, quae est deus et habet deus, das ist verbum salutis, nostrae vitae."

50. WA 20, 611, 8-17.

life in which they strive to be obedient to God, instructed by the word and helped by the Holy Spirit.[51] Luther thus refers here to two kinds of righteousness, a distinction that he made as early as in the late 1510s. The first kind of righteousness is the "alien" righteousness of Christ, which is given to the believer through faith and which the believer has completely. The second righteousness is the believer's "own" righteousness. It indicates the effect of the first righteousness upon the believer's soul and body. For Luther, the image of God clearly includes both aspects of righteousness.

Retrieving the image of God also assumes that the believer hears the Gospel and is reborn through faith. However, the *imago Dei*, that is, eternal life and unity with God, is not complete.

In this life the *imago* of the new creature only begins to be reformed, and the righteousness described above is only a beginning; neither can be perfect. Nevertheless, through the Gospel, people receive righteousness of heart and trust in God's mercifulness in Christ. They also receive the Holy Spirit, who fights unbelief, envy, and other vices so that the believers hope to live for the glory of God and his word.[52]

The new creature will become the perfect image of God in the Father's kingdom. The human being will have really free will, an illuminated mind or intellect, and constant memory. And all creatures will be even more subject to the human being than they were Adam's subjects in Paradise.[53] Luther describes the will as free as well as joyous and obedient to God. To life in the likeness of God belongs the fullness of joy. During this life believers receive the initial gifts of everything that is in God's image: through faith, people begin to know God, and the Holy Spirit helps them to want to follow God's precepts. The will is raised in praise and thankfulness to God, and it becomes willing to confess sin and to have faith as well as to be patient in all kinds of difficulties. At the

---

51. *WA* 42, 48, 17–20.

52. *WA* 42, 48, 20–28: "Sed haec iusticia in hac vita incipitur tantum, neque potest in hac carne esse perfecta. Placet autem Deo non tanquam perfecta iustitia aut tanquam precium pro peccatis, Sed quia proficiscitur ex corde, quod nititur fiducia misericordiae Dei per Christum. Deinde hoc quoque fit per Euangelium, ut conferatur nobis Spiritus sanctus, qui resistit in nobis incredulitati, invidiae et aliis vitiis, ut serio optemus ornare nomen Domini et verbum eius etc. Ad hunc modum incipit imago ista novae creaturae reparari per Euangelium in hac vita, sed non perficitur in hac vita."

53. *WA* 42, 48, 28–31.

same time the flesh still seeks of "its own" and struggles against what is God's will and property.[54]

Luther may thus say on the one hand that believers receive everything that God is and has, yet on the other hand believers are given the first gifts of everything that belongs to *imago Dei*. These statements only seem to be contradictory. They are to be understood in the context of distinguishing between two kinds of righteousness. With the first, Christ's righteousness, the believer does get everything: both God himself and his qualities. But from the point of view of the second, one's own righteousness, the believer has only inchoate righteousness.

Luther is referring to the second kind of righteousness when he says that the believers live in a situation in which they is slowly become more and more in the image of Christ. The reality of the second righteousness implies that living in faith is a kind of progress in which the Christ-likeness of the believer constantly increases.

PHILOSOPHICAL AND THEOLOGICAL ANTHROPOLOGY

As stated above, God created human beings, who consist of body and soul. Humans' animal life with its needs has much in common with other living creatures, but unlike them, humans have a rational soul, with capacities such as reason or intellect, will, memory, and conscience. The human substance as a composition of body and soul and with all its created natural capacities can be regarded from both the philosophical and the theological perspectives.

Luther does this as early as in the beginning of 1520s in his famous booklet *On Christian Freedom* and his interpretation of the *Magnificat*. In the texts from the 1530s he often deals with the relationship between philosophy and theology by differentiating among four "causes" and applying the differences also to the concept of the human being.

In his interpretation of the *Magnificat* Luther explains his view of Christian anthropology. He makes distinctions that he also assumes elsewhere, even though he does not always explicitly state them. As is repeatedly the case with Luther, his terminology changes in different contexts. Luther often uses the terms of the Bible translation. In the interpretation of *Magnificat*, his starting point is 1 Thess 5:23, where the Apostle Paul presents the anthropological trichotomy of the spirit, the soul, and the

---

54. WA 42, 248, 14–27.

body. According to Paul, the whole human being, including these three "parts," may become holy. Luther points out that the whole human being as well as all these three parts, is also differentiated into two aspects called spirit and flesh. The first division refers to human nature, and the second, to its qualities. Accordingly, human nature has three parts, all of which may be holy or unholy, good or evil. To be the spirit in the qualitative sense means to be good, and to be the flesh in this sense refers to wickedness.[55]

In this same text Luther is interested in human nature in a philosophical sense. The spirit is the highest, deepest, and noblest part of the human being. The spirit is able to grasp incomprehensible, invisible, and eternal things. It is the house where faith and God's word dwell. Although the spirit belongs to the nature of the human being, it does not imply that human beings are able to grasp incomprehensible and eternal things without the word or without faith.[56]

The second part is the soul. The soul is actually by nature the same spirit as the first part, but in another "work" or function. The task of the spirit as the soul is to make the body alive and to act through it. Moreover, its aim is to understand what the reason is able to know and measure. Reason is thus the light in this house of human nature. Reason, however, is too weak to deal with divine things. Consequently, without faith, reason will always err about divine matters.[57]

For Luther, the two functions of the spirit thus include two different kinds of understanding. The spirit as spirit is able to attain wisdom, but the spirit as soul seeks knowledge of the sensible world. Anthropologically, it is important to note that Luther also places the affects, like hatred, love, enjoyment, horror, and the like, in the soul.[58] About the third part, the

---

55. WA 7, 550, 19-28: "Wollen ein wort nach dem andernn bewiegen: das erst 'Meyn seele'. Die schrifft teilet den menschen ynn drey teil, da S. Paulus 1. Thessal. ult. [1. Thess. 5, 23.] sagt: 'Got der ein got des frids ist, der mache euch heilig durch und durch, alszo das ewer gantzer geist und seele und leip unstreflich erhalten auff die zukunfft unszers herrnn Ihesu Christi'. Und ein iglichs dieszer dreier sampt dem gantzen menschen wirt auch geteylet auff ein ander weisz ynn zwey stuck, die da heissen geist und fleisch, wilch teilung nit der natur, szondernn der eygenschafft ist, das ist, die natur hat drey stuck: geist, seel, leip, und mugen alle sampt gut oder bosz sein, das heist denn geist und fleysch sein, davon itzt nit zu reden ist."

56. WA 7, 550, 28-34.

57. WA 7, 550, 35—551, 9.

58. WA 7, 551, 9-11: "Dieszen zweien stucken eygent die schrifft viel dings, als sapientiam und scientiam: die weiszheit dem geist, die erkenntnisz der seelen, darnach auch hasz, liebe, lust, grewel und des gleichenn."

body, Luther states briefly that its task is practice and use things following the in accordance with of the soul and the faith of the spirit.[59]

The Reformer describes the Christian human being with a comparison to the temple, which is also divided into three parts: The Holy of Holies, the Holy, and the Atrium. The spirit of a Christian is the Holy of Holies. God himself dwells there in dark faith without light. Luther thus combines God's dwelling in the spirit with the faith, which does not see or experience or understand. Accordingly, the human being or human nature is not able to see, to experience, or to comprehend God. The Christian's soul is the Holy. There is the light of reason, knowledge, and the virtue of perception. The body can be compared with the Atrium, which is open to all. Everyone can see what the Christian is doing and how she lives.[60]

The dual division between spirit and flesh is treated thematically, for example, in *De libertate Christiana*. There the Biblical basis (2 Cor 4:16) and the terminology differ from the *Magnificat*. Luther states that a human being has a dual nature, spiritual and corporeal. The first problem is thus how Luther understands this "dual nature." In my view his text is possible to read as coherent with his presentation in the *Magnificat*. Luther continues by saying that, concerning the spiritual nature, which is also called the soul, the human being is described as spiritual, interior and a new man. So his use of the term "spiritual nature" assumes the concept of human nature as a soul. Consequently, "spirit" has two meanings as in the *Magnificat*: it refers both to human nature and to the human being as a "new man." Correspondingly, Luther speaks about "flesh" in two meanings in presenting the corporeal aspect of human nature. Even though Luther's presentation is not terminologically quite univocal, it very likely contains the same basic idea as the interpretation of the *Magnificat*. Only now the focus is on the spiritual and carnal "qualities"[61] that are fighting each other in one and the same human being, that is, in a Christian.[62] In *De libertate Christiana* Luther stresses that the spiritual

59. WA 7, 551, 12–13.

60. WA 7, 551, 15–24.

61. "Qualities" are not to be understood here in philosophical or psychological sense as "habits" or "accidents" of the human substance.

62. WA 7, 50, 5–12: "Altiore et crassiore petamus ista principio. Homo enim duplici constat natura, spirituali et corporali: iuxta spiritualem, quam dicunt, animam, vocatur spiritualis, interior, novus homo, iuxta corporalem, quam carnem dicunt, [2. Cor. 4, 16.] vocatur carnalis, exterior, vetus homo, de quo Apostolus 2. Cor. 4. 'Licet is qui foris

new man is the interior man in contrast to the outer man. This is not meant in an absolute sense but it depends on the point of view. Luther is speaking about becoming a Christian and arguing for the idea that real Christian freedom and righteousness do not consist of external things. He especially rejects all external deeds in the process of becoming a free and righteous Christian.

Only one work (*opus*) is needed for the Christian life. This work is God's Holy word, the Gospel of Christ: "I am the resurrection and the life; whoever believes in me shall never die." God's word is the word of life, light, peace, righteousness, salvation, joy, freedom, wisdom, strength, grace, glory, and everything good. For this reason the human soul (or spirit) may lack everything but the word. With the word it has everything it needs.[63]

In *De libertate Christiana* Luther thus uses the term "soul" primarily to refer to the new man. This is clear when he says that preaching about Christ—that is, his incarnation, suffering, resurrection, and glorification—builds, justifies, frees, and saves the soul if the soul believes the sermon.[64] Both the word of God and faith are necessary assumptions for the existence of the inner or the new man.[65] So in a theological sense, "soul" refers to the same reality as *imago Dei*.

Luther also explains more precisely the relationship between word and faith. The divine word consists of the law and promises. The law orders and demands, but it does not have the ability to fulfill the commandments. In fact, the inner man cannot be saved by any outward deeds. Luther assumes here that without faith, the human being or reason understands salvation as the result of certain outward deeds required by the law. This is an unavoidable misunderstanding of human reason.

But the promises or the Gospel fulfill the law. The promises are holy, true, righteous, free, and peaceful words, and full of goodness. And because they are such words, the human soul that embraces them firmly in faith becomes united with them. The soul not only participates in them,

---

est noster homo corrumpatur, tamen is qui intus est renovatur de die in diem". Haec diversitas facit, ut in scripturis pugnantia de eodem homine dicantur, cum et ipsi duo homines in eodem homine sibi pugnent, [Gal. 5, 17.] dum caro concupiscit adversus spiritum et spiritus adversus carnem, Gal. 5."

63. *WA* 7, 50, 33—51, 3.
64. *WA* 7, 51, 13–19.
65. *WA* 28, 180, 1–3.

but also is saturated and filled by all the virtues of these words. With this healing touch of Christ in the soul, the receiving of the word communicates all the properties of the word to the soul. The word therefore makes the soul alike with the word. Moreover, it makes the believers children of God.[66] Luther uses similar expressions when describing the *imago Dei* in his *Lectures on Genesis*.

Luther's description of the relationship between word and faith also confirms that in *De libertate Christiana* the term "soul" is used in the same sense as "spirit" in the interpretation of the *Magnificat*. For Luther, faith is needed in order to receive the word, because there is no human work that could adhere to the word. In the soul there cannot be any works; only faith and the word are governing the soul. The word thus defines the quality of the soul. The latter becomes like the word. Luther compares the relationship between the word and the soul to a hot iron. The iron glows like fire because of their union.[67]

In the disputation *De homine* Luther states that in comparison to theology, philosophy and reason impart almost nothing about the human being. He explains this by differentiating among four "causes." Philosophical reason does not recognize the *causa originalis* or the *causa finalis* of the human being. Nevertheless, philosophy offers some knowledge of material and formal causes. At its best, reason is used to research the material cause, that is, the body of the human being. Reason also offers some knowledge of the soul, which is the formal cause of a human being. But this knowledge is vague, and philosophers cannot reach any consensus concerning the soul.

Aristotle gave speculative or philosophical definition for the soul by calling the soul the first act of the body. However, this definition gives only the "objective" meaning of the soul, without reaching its proper essence. The reason can only conclude from the affects and their consequences that the soul is the noblest and most amazing being, which

---

66. WA 7, 53, 15–23: "Cum autem haec promissa dei sint verba sancta, vera, iusta, libera, pacata et universa bonitate plena, fit, ut anima, quae firma fide illis adheret, sic eis uniatur, immo penitus absorbeatur, ut non modo participet sed saturetur et inebrietur omni virtute eorum. Si enim tactus Christi sanabat, quanto magis hic tenerrimus in spiritu, immo absorptio verbi omnia quae verbi sunt animae communicat. Hoc igitur modo anima per fidem solam, sine operibus, e verbo dei iustificatur, sanctificatur, verificatur, pacificatur, [Joh. 1, 12.] liberatur et omni bono repletur vereque filia dei efficitur, sicut Iohan. 1. dicit 'Dedit eis potestatem filios dei fieri, iis qui credunt in nomine eius.'"

67. WA 7, 53, 24–28.

is so present and powerful that the body cannot resist its influence.⁶⁸ A more accurate understanding of the soul is achievable through "practical" knowledge.

Theologically speaking, the human soul is either flesh or spirit. In the theological sense the human being is actually a sinner, so deeply that being a sinner is the substance of being human. Theology's first task is to get people to realize that their human nature is corrupted by sin.⁶⁹ After realizing one's of own sinfulness, the human being can understand the second part of practical theological knowledge: grace and justification, that is, how God restores the human being through Christ. In fact, a Christian's soul is both flesh and spirit, because Christians are both sinners and righteous beings at the same time. Luther surely thinks of the simultaneity in its two aspects. Christians are sinners in themselves, but in Christ they are totally righteous, because Christ has been made into righteousness for human beings.⁷⁰ This aspect refers to the "first and alien righteousness," which is given to the Christian by Christ's presence in faith. But for Luther there is also the "second, one's own righteousness": the Christian begins to become righteous because Christ is cleaning sin away.⁷¹ This partial sinfulness and righteousness corresponds to the return of the *imago Dei* through the Gospel.

THE CORRUPTED HUMAN CAPACITIES AND THE REFORMATION OF THE *IMAGO DEI*

To be renewed, the human being must be turned into God's material for a future life.⁷² The human being has to be reduced to "nothing".⁷³ This applies first of all to the whole human person or substance. In his *Large Lectures on the Letter to Galatians*, Luther assumes both the traditional philosophical definition of a "person" and his own theological understanding.⁷⁴ He emphasizes that a Christian does not live in himself or

---

68. WA 44, 589, 31–38.

69. WA 40/II, 327, 20–22.

70. WA 40/II, 327, 26–35.

71. WA 40/I, 537, 21–34; 538, 14–25.

72. WA 39/I, 177, 3–4: "35. Quare homo huius vitae est pura materia Dei ad futurae formaesuae vitam."

73. For Luther's conception of nothingness of the creatures and annihilation of the human being see Juntunen, *Der Begriff des Nichts bei Luther*.

74. See also Dieter, *Der junge Luther und Aristoteles*, 228–34.

in his substance.⁷⁵ Here the decisive term is "self." If a human being gets stuck in the self, then the person inevitably becomes an actor under the law. The idea here is the human being or the self separated from Christ. A person without Christ thinks that the works of law are the way to Christ and eternal life.⁷⁶ The person who is obliged to do the works demanded by the law belongs to the outward, animal life. In the theological sense this person is the "old man," which has to be neglected in the spiritual life or in the issue of Christian righteousness.⁷⁷ If the person of Christ and a human being's own person are separated in the issue of justification, then the human being remains under the law and lives in the self. But then the person is dead to God and is judged by the law.⁷⁸

By contrast, the Christian person is living, but not in or for the self.⁷⁹ Accordingly, Christian righteousness is not in the human being's own person, that is, in the person who acts as enacts the works of law. Christian righteousness is Christ's living in us. Christ is the form of the believer and adorns the believer's faith. This means that Christ is inherent in humans and united with them. So he remains within them and lives their lives, or, to put it more exactly, Christ himself is the life that the believer lives. Thus, as for the justification, Christ and the believer have to be united so that Christ lives in the believer and the believer in Christ. Then all grace, righteousness, life, peace, and salvation in the believer are Christ's, but through union and adherence to faith, which make Christ and the believer one spiritual body, all these qualities also the believer's. Luther concludes that through faith, Christ and the believer are united as one and cannot be separated.

At the end of the examination of this concept of the person Luther differentiates between the natural or animal and the alien or spiritual life. The latter is alien because it is not innate but given through Christ in faith. For Luther, the Apostle Paul's statement, "I live, although not I but Christ lives in me," means that a believer is dead to the animal life and lives already the alien life. Paul no longer lives, but the Christian lives. In other words, Paul who is living in himself is dead, but in Christ he is

---

75. WA 40/I, 282, 16.
76. WA 40/I, 282, 19–26.
77. WA 40/I, 282, 18–19; 284, 20.
78. WA 40/I, 283, 23–25; 285, 15–17.
79. WA 40/I, 283, 21–22.

living the alien life, or more exactly, Christ is living the alien life in him and doing actions and deeds in him.[80]

Luther thus refers here to the "person" in the sense of the natural life and also in the sense of the alien life. From the point of view of the alien life, which is life in Christ, the natural life has to die. For the alien life the natural life is the life of the old man, who understand himself as obedient to the law and an actor of good deeds. As stated above, for Luther, the person or the self is still living in another sense. Then he is not living in or for himself. In my view this idea assumes the natural life, but now united with Christ so that Christ is the human's life and the actor of all inward and outward deeds.

Luther emphasizes that the form of the old man or the flesh has to be annihilated so that the form of a new man can be born. Annihilation and the nothingness of the human being take place in the theological sense. The human being is material for future form as long as she will be transformed in the perfect image of God. Prior to that she is still in sin, but will daily become either more righteous or more corrupted.[81] In light of Luther's writings, it is therefore clear that the renewal of God's image is a process in human beings.

How does the return of God's image and the beginning of the "second" righteousness influence the capacities of the soul? Because Luther often treats the reason and the will together, I will follow this practice. These two capacities have reciprocal effect on each other, but also have functions of their own. Furthermore, the power to decide (*arbitrium*), which may be either free (*liberum*) or bound (*servum*), belongs to both reason and will. In reason, free decision is the capacity to discern between right and wrong; in will, it is the power to decide between the two.[82]

The reformer describes reason, will, and decision in both the philosophical and theological meanings. He makes this distinction concerning reason and will, for example, when he explains the theological sense of "doing" (*facere*). As for decision, Luther deals with this question especially in *De servo arbitrio*. The question is what does a good work mean and what does it assume in theological language? Both in moral

---

80. WA 40/I, 287, 28–288, 16.

81. WA 39/I, 177, 9–12: "38. Talis est homo in hac vita ad futuram formam suam, cum reformata et perfecta fuerit imago Dei. 39. Interea in peccatis est homo, et in dies vel iustificatur vel polluitur magis."

82. WA 18, 664, 17–24; 665, 6–10.

philosophy and in theology, a good work assumes right reason and good will.[83] In the philosophical sense the aim of right reason and good will is the common good, morality, and peace in the political community. But moral philosophy does not have God as its object and final cause. As a consequence, the moral good will and the good deeds of a human being do not constitute good actions in the theological sense.[84] Luther's conclusion regarding the free decision making is that in the philosophical sense, the human being has this capacity. Humans are thus able to discern and decide what is good or right in things that are within their power.[85] In the theological sense, however, "free decision" is only an empty phrase. In other words, it should not be used about human beings because there is no any real object for the term in humans. The only being who can freely make decisions in a theological sense is God himself. Therefore, Luther stresses that free decision-making is a divine quality. Luther's view of free decision-making is also an example of rejecting an erroneous assimilation of divinity and humanity. The reformer stresses that freely making decisions is an attribute of divine majesty. If this attribute is ascribed to a human being, then divinity itself will also be ascribed to humans.[86] This would mean a substantial change in the human being, which Luther clearly denies.

By denying any substantial change, Luther refers to the factual state of a believer. If the change were substantial, then the person would become a sinless new man in an instant. In fact, the human being is changed and renewed only very slowly and through battle against flesh or sin. It is important to note that when denying any substantial human change Luther is speaking in the theological sense. He thus assumes a theo-

83. WA 40/I, 410, 15–17; 26–27; 411, 24–28.

84. WA 40/I, 410, 27—411, 23: "Hinc in Theologia dicimus moralem Philosophiam sophiam non habere in obiecto et causa finali Deum, Quia Aristoteles, Sadducaeus vel homo civiliter bonus vocat hoc rectam rationem et bonam voluntatem, si quaerat communem utilitatem Reipublicae, tranquillitatem et honestatem. altius non assurgit Philosophus vel Legislator, non cogitat per rectam rationem etc. consequi remissionem peccatorum et vitam aeternam, ut Sophista aut Monachus. Ideo Gentilis Philosophus longe melior est tali Iusticiario; manet enim intra limites suos, habens tantum rationem honestatis et tranquillitatis publicae, non miscens humanis divina. Hoc Sophista non facit; imaginatur enim Deum spectare suam bonam intentionem et opera. Ideo miscet divinis humana polluitque nomen Dei et has cogitationes plane haurit ex Philosophia morali, nisi quod ea peius abutitur quam homo Gentilis etc."

85. WA 18, 638, 4–11.

86. WA 18, 636, 27–637, 2.

logical substance in the fallen being, that is, sin. The renewal of believers does not make them sinless, which implies that the human theological substance still exists, even though believers have began to be righteous. Consequently, when humans are said to be righteous, this can be said only in relation to Christ. The relational understanding of the believer's righteousness does not exclude the real, substantial, or "formal" presence of Christ and the Holy Spirit or the union of the believer with them.[87]

Human reason as a "natural" ability is capable of theoretical and moral reasoning. This means that it contains some information about reality and can attain additional knowledge through syllogistic inference.[88] Reason is also able to acknowledge the principles of morality. About God, human reason has some "natural" knowledge. It connects to the term God such qualities as "good, graceful, merciful, and lenient," but recognizes these only in an objective sense without being able to apply the knowledge to the human situation. And natural reason is also unable to understand to whom these qualities actually belong. So human

---

87. *WA* 40/I, 283, 25–32: "Ideo inquit: 'Iam non Ego, sed Christus in me vivit'; Is est mea forma ornans fidem meam... Christus ergo, inquit, sic inhaerens et conglutinatus mihi et manens in me hanc vitam quam ago, vivit in me, imo vita qua sic vivo, est Christus ipse. Itaque Christus et ego iam unum in hac parte sumus." *WA* 40/I, 285, 24–286, 15: " Verum recte docenda est fides, quod per eam sic conglutineris Christo, ut ex te et ipso fiat quasi una persona quae non possit segregari sed perpetuo adhaerescat ei et dicat: Ego sum ut Christus, et vicissim Christus dicat: Ego sum ut ille peccator, quia adhaeret mihi, et ego illi; Coniuncti [Eph. 5, 30] enim sumus per fidem in unam carnem et os..." *WA* 40/II, 421, 36–422, 19: "Habitat ergo verus Spiritus in credentibus non tantum per dona, sed quoad substantiam suam. Neque enim sic dat dona sua, ut ipse alibi sit aut dormiat, sed adest donis et creaturae suae conservando, gubernando, addendo robur etc. Petit igitur Propheta, ut, postquam iustificatus est et remissionem peccatorum accepit, ut iste sensus misericordiae Dei altissime per Spiritum sanctum infigatur animo. Ideo his verbis utitur: 'Cor mundum crea in me, Deus.' Non enim loquitur de momentanea aliqua operatione, sed de continuatione coepti operis." *WA* 40/II, 353, 36–354, 19: "Ergo Christianus non est formaliter iustus, non est iustus secundum substantiam aut qualitatem (docendi causa hisce vocabulis utor), sed est iustus secundum praedicamentum ad aliquid, nempe respectu divinae gratiae tantum et remissionis peccatorum gratuitae, quae contingit agnoscentibus peccatum et credentibus, quod Deus faveat et ignoscat propter Christum pro peccatis nostris traditum et a nobis creditum." *WA* 40/II, 354, 33–355, 18: "prodest orationem Davidis bene considerare, in qua, postquam remissionem peccatorum quoad culpam rogavit et in misericordia Dei laetatur, etiam hoc petit, quod restat, ut lavetur ab iniquitatibus, ut donetur sibi Spiritus sanctus, virtus et Domini illud, quod intus in corde vivat et expurget reliquum peccati, quod per baptismum coepit sepeliri, sed nondum plane sepultum est. Atque haec est vita Christiana,..."

88. See Työrinoja, "Proprietas verbi," 141–78.

natural reason recognizes that there is a God, but only the Holy Spirit teaches who the real living God is.[89]

Luther says repeatedly that the Commandment of Love was written in the human mind or heart already before the promulgation of the Ten Commandments. He often presents the first principle of natural moral law in the form of the "golden rule."[90] When he speaks most exactly, Luther says that "being in mind" refers to knowing, but "being in heart" refers to emotion. Thus the law should not be written only objectively (*obiective*) in the soul but it needs to be formally (*formaliter*) in the heart. The objective writing of the law refers to the law's "letter," which presents the commandment, but does not give the power or the motivation to fulfill it. The formal writing of the law takes place when the Holy Spirit is present as love of the law and thus fulfills the law.[91] *Formaliter* here signifies the healing presence of the Holy Spirit, which reforms mere moral understanding into theological understanding. From the context it is clear that the "formal writing" of the law includes both the Spirit as the subject of inward and outward fulfilling of the law and the correct understanding of the theologically-good action. The content or matter of reason remains, but it receives a new form in a theological sense. As a consequence, the believer understands the nature of good deeds and their subject in a new way.

With rational theoretical knowledge one cannot comprehend the whole of reality, because such knowledge does not recognize the origin or the end of creatures. In order to know these things, that is, to know God, one needs theological, experiential knowledge. Rational moral knowledge contains the divine law in the sense of objective knowledge. Luther believes that people are principally able to follow the law in the outward sense.[92] When they do, they are acting appropriately in a moral or philosophical sense. However, in theology "a good work" is also a new term, and it assumes faith.

---

89. WA 19, 205, 27–207, 13.

90. WA 42, 205, 22–25: "Nimirum, ut ultro [3. Mose 19:16] fateatur se legem hanc nihil curare: 'Dilige proximum sicut teipsum.' Item: 'Quod tibi non vis fieri, alteri ne feceris.' Haec enim lex non in Decalogi primum promulgata sed omnium hominum inscripta est."

91. WA 57/III, 195, 20–196, 19.

92. WA DB 7, 34.

Luther recognizes natural reason in Aristotelian sense: such reason follows syllogistic form, which consists of a major premise, a minor premise, and a conclusion. This way of reasoning applies both to theological and to practical knowledge. In practical inference the major premise identifies some good to be achieved, and the minor premise locates the good in some situation at hand. Luther never presents his understanding of practical reasoning as a whole. Nevertheless, he discusses the role of the major and minor premises. For him the major premise consists of the natural knowledge of God and divine law. This premise presents the good to be achieved both in the theological and in the moral sense. Yet the content of the major premise does not guarantee that human beings will obey the law. The obstacle to that occurs mostly on the level of the second premise. In practical philosophy, which Luther had learned in Erfurt, the term "right reason" referred to the ability to establish the minor premise of a syllogism. Luther stresses that a good work in the philosophical sense precedes a good work, but in the theological sense, there is no right human reason because faith is the only theologically right reason. The theological right reason, that is, faith, reveals a God who is willing and able to help. The theologically right reason turns human knowledge the other way round: it does not show what a person should do in a given situation, but rather how God is ready to help and do good for the person. Luther's view of the natural knowledge of God follows exactly the idea that the error takes place on the level of right reason.[93] From this error it follows that the human being is not able to understand the theological sense of good works in human relations. For the believer, it is God, not the human being, who is the only one who enacts good works and the only source of knowing what is right or wrong.

In theology the term "do" receives new significance. As in moral philosophy, it assumes right reason and good will, but now understood in the theological sense and not in the moral meaning. Theological right reason and good will mean that through the Gospel, one knows and believes that God has sent his Son into the world to save human beings from sin and death. This kind of action is new and unknown to human reason.[94] In theology, "doing" thus presupposes faith. Correspondingly, the theological understanding of right reason and good will is incomprehensible to human reason. So human reason is blind at this point,

---

93. For a more detailed analysis, see Raunio, "Luthers politische Ethik," 163–67.
94. WA 40/I, 411, 24—412, 13.

and a new reason, namely, faith is generated. Faith includes theological right reason, and theological good will.[95] In other contexts theological good will is presented as the love of God and of one's neighbour or as the presence of the Holy Spirit.

Luther concludes that the human being in the theological sense is a believing or faithful (*fidelis*) human being whose right reason and good will are correspondingly formed by faith. This means that faith is the divinity in the works, the person, and all parts of the human being. Faith is moreover the form of theological works. This implies that faith is also the form of the whole human being, who now has right reason and good will. Faith is thus the only cause of justification. When faith is present as the believer's form, also the matter of the believer is justified. Theologically righteous works assume a theologically righteous human being.[96]

When the Gospel reforms the human being, it annihilates the natural light and transforms it into a new light. The annihilation should again be understood in the theological sense. Consequently, the natural light is not annihilated totally, but only as far as such light is intertwined with sinfulness and carnal understanding. For Luther, the transformation of sinful light into a new light results in other human abilities being reformed as well. The human being is transformed into a totally new person who sees everything different from before. The transformed human being thinks and evaluates in new ways, and also wills, loves, and acts in new ways. Luther says nevertheless that the natural light is a part and the beginning of the proper light. In this statement he is referring to natural light in the philosophical sense. From this point of view the

---

95. *WA* 40/I, 412, 14–24: "Ergo facere in Theologia necessario praerequirit ipsam fidem. Quare sic respondebis ad omnes sententias Scripturae de operibus, in quibus adversarii urgent vocabula operandi et faciendi: Ea esse vocabula Theologica, non naturalia aut moralia; Quae si naturalia vel moralia sint, accipi in suo usu; Si vero Theologica, includere rectam rationem et bonam voluntatem, incomprehensibilem rationi humanae quae ibi excaecatur, et alia ratio generatur quae est fidei. Ergo facere in Theologia intelligitur semper de fideli facere, Ut facere fidele sit alius circulus ac novum quasi regnum a facere morali. Itaque cum nos Theologi loquimur de facere, necesse est nos loqui de fideli facere, quia in Theologia nullam rectam rationem et bonam voluntatem habemus nisi fidem."

96. *WA* 40/I, 417, 25–29: "Sic homo Theologicus est fidelis, item ratio recta, voluntas bona est fidelis ratio et voluntas, Ut fides in universum sit divinitas in opere, persona et membris, ut unica causa iustificationis quae postea etiam tribuitur materiae propter formam, hoc est, operi propter fidem."

light of grace or faith does not turn out the natural reason, but rejects its understanding of serving God and becoming righteous. Natural reason teaches that the human being becomes righteous by doing good works. By contrast, Christ teaches that good works will be done only after the human being has become righteous through faith.[97]

God's law provides the understanding and experience of the natural light's "nothingness" and the will's inability to do good works. When God begins to act in the human being and to fulfill his law in humans, he empties human beings from all own inward and outward deeds. So the human can no longer trust in the self's good works or the dicta of the natural reason, not to mention good intentions. Then the dictum of the natural reason is for God like matter without form. The premises of reasoning, its conclusions, and prudence as well as the good intentions of the will have to lose their forms and become reformed. In Luther's view the reason's natural light relates to the light of grace like darkness to light or like a formless being to the perfect form. The heart, that is, the whole human being in theological sense, becomes a new form through God's work in faith. In faith God is united with the human person through the word and acts in the human being, who opens up through faith to the word. Only when God acts in humans through faith, can human beings cooperate with God. In this state humans can also do truly good works.[98] It thus becomes clear that faith is the new form of the human being, but Luther also says that the new form, which renews the whole human being and human natural capacities, is divine love.[99] Faith and love are thus closely intertwined and should not be separated. Luther clearly speaks about faith and love here as divine affects and inner deeds, but does not refer to love as outward good deed. At the same time, he stresses faith as the new form when he speaks about becoming righteous, but he speaks of love when the issue is the Christian life and Christian actions.

The renewal of the will is realized when the Holy Spirit enters the living will of the heart. This renewal includes two aspects: the union of the divine will with human will and the reducing of the human will to God's will. Again, the human being has to abandon something that has been considered its own. Because human will and God's will are adversarial,

---

97. *WA* 10/I 1, 203, 5–9.; 205, 4–21.

98. *WA* 57/III, 13–17; 142, 18–143, 22.

99. *WA* 57/III, 195, 20–196, 19; *WA* 17/II, 97, 9–21. *WA* 18, 681, 12–34. This view should not be confused with Luther's criticism of the *fides caritate formata*–doctrine.

the human will has to be annihilated so that God's will may happen.[100] Here Luther also speaks about annihilation in the theological sense. With one's "own" being and "self," which should be returned to God, Luther refers to the depravity of human being. The created human self and will are not destroyed or abandoned, but the human is still the same human being, even though transformed in the theological sense when all sins are forgiven and wickedness is defeated through faith. Because of such faith, the human being is righteous, truthful, and free. Faith also fulfills all commandments of the law.[101] Through faith the believer participates in divine love and divine qualities and also gives the self and the will back to God. And when the human will has been returned to God, the whole human being has been given to God.[102] So God gives himself to the believer as love and becomes the believer's new will, and the believer gives everything that was ever desired of God, back to God.

The term "conscience" is used with several meanings. Luther applies it principally in theological sense as a divine evaluation of the whole human being and human action. But Luther also recognizes the evaluating conscience in the philosophical sense. Then it estimates the moral goodness of human deeds. However, sometimes with the word conscience Luther is referring to the conclusion of a practical inference. Then conscience is a suggestion of what to do in a given situation. Theologically, Luther often has this meaning in mind when he speaks about conscience which is bound to the word of God. In this sense the conscience does not evaluate the human person afterwards but recommends what one should do in a given situation. This was the case in Luther's famous statement at the Diet of Worms when he denied retracting his teachings.[103]

Luther differentiates between the inward and the outward activities of the conscience. Firstly, according to the moral and philosophical meanings the conscience evaluates how the outward works obey the law.[104] Secondly, the conscience evaluates the inner "good works," such as humility, leniency, patience, faithfulness, and love. Such works can be done in two different ways: either because of fear of punishment and desire for reward or simply because such works are good and please God.

---

100. WA 2, 102, 13–19.
101. WA 7, 22, 31–23, 5.
102. WA 2, 105, 20–25.
103. Brecht, *Martin Luther. Sein Weg*, 438–39.
104. WA 7, 795, 25–799, 10.

Luther believes that the conscience may accept such works erroneously when they are done before one understands clearly that no one by nature has such reason and will as God demands. For Luther, this is a case of false security, which, however, leaves the inner conscience insecure.[105]

The proper theological task of the conscience is to evaluate whether the deeds of a human being are acceptable in the eyes of God. The acceptance of the conscience in the theological sense has two aspects. First, for the justification and righteousness of the Christian, Christ and the human conscience have to become "one body" so that the human being sees only the crucified and the risen Christ.[106] Second, the conscience is good in the theological sense only when Christ and the Holy Spirit influence all good works in the human being and so fulfill the divine law. The theological conscience accepts only those works done out of love in order to "carry the others' weaknesses."[107] Such works cannot be done with the human being's natural abilities.

The theological conscience thus makes a distinction between the human being's own works and Christ's works. It rejects the first and accepts the second. The believing conscience (*fidelis conscientia*) holds to Christ's works simply because it knows that it can be secure and peaceful only in Christ. In Christ's works, all of which are done for the benefit of human beings, the conscience includes the reconciliation, forgiveness of sins, righteousness, and peace. The conscience seizes Christ's good works and leads the human being to the works that Christ has done for the individual and in turn teaches the human to do similar works for the benefit of neighbors and in order to exercise the body. The works are commanded in the Decalogue, but they should be done—as Luther says—according to the substance. This means that they should be done just as Christ's works in our behalf, freely and without charge. They are not works of law, but deeds of Christ who acts in his believers through faith.[108]

---

105. WA 5, 556, 26–36.
106. WA 40/1, 282, 16–22.
107. WA 2, 607, 15–19.
108. WA 8, 606, 34—607, 17; 808, 22–35.

CONCLUSION

The purpose of this article was to present some of the main features of Luther's concept of the human being. In the beginning humans were created in the image of God and of Christ. For Luther, this means that participation in the divine life and in righteousness belonged to humans' original substance. The human being thus possessed the substance both in the philosophical and the theological sense and these substances were united in the original state. With the fall into sin human beings lost the image of God and their theological substance almost completely. The human still has substance or personhood in the philosophical sense, but from the theological point of view, this substance is the "old," sinful man, because it is no longer united with God.

The only way to retrieve the lost image of God and righteousness is to receive these gifts in faith through the Gospel of Christ. The word brings Christ and all the divine qualities, and through faith the believer becomes united with these qualities. Through this union the believer acquires a new form, and is reformed in the likeness of Christ and God. Yet even though the believer's old form is annihilated, this renewal is not to be understood substantially, but relationally. This means that the Christian is not righteous in the self or in substance, but in relation to Christ. Luther sees at least two errors in the substantial concept of Christian righteousness. First, without the union with Christ, this kind of self-righteousness would exist as an inherent quality of the human being. Second, the human being could become perfectly righteous during this life, and the persons factual sinfulness be ignored. However, the Christian's relational righteousness assumes the substantial presence of Christ as well as the real union with him and participation in him as divine grace, life, righteousness, and peace.

3

Christ

Sammeli Juntunen

In examining Luther's understanding of Christ, we should not be surprised to find a connection to Luther's understanding of the Trinity. To begin with, it is extremely important for Luther that Christ is both truly God and truly human. The Savior has to be God in his essence (*Wesen*) in order to have to power to save people from sin. On the other hand, the Savior also has to be human in order to share his merit with us. Christ has obtained a human nature, by being born of the Virgin Mary at a given moment in time. He has had the divine nature he had throughout eternity, owing to his birth from the Father.[1] The Trinitarian dogma is an integral part of Luther's thinking about which I will make a few comments.

First, Luther uses traditional Trinitarian concepts. God is one *essentia/Wesen/natura* in three persons. The Son is not created (*creo*), but is born (*nasci/anboren*) of the Father, not in time, but in eternity.[2] The Spirit proceeds (*procedo*) from the Father and from the Son.[3] In this sense Luther is clearly a follower of the Western "filioque" tradition.[4] On the other hand, Luther seems to think, that the Father is the "first/

---

1. *WA* 15, 798, 803; *WA* 27, 529.
2. *WA* 27, 524–25.
3. *WA* 17/I, 278–79.
4. E.g., *WA* 10/III, 150.

original person in the divinity" and "the whole essence and spring of the divinity."[5] This introduces a certain "Eastern" tinge into his thinking.[6]

Second, in the Trinity there is a unity of the essence (*Wesen*), but not of the persons. Therefore, it may be said, "Whatever (*quidquid*) is God, that is the Father, and whatever is God that is the Son". But it may not be said, "Whoever is God, he is the Father or the Son".[7] For Luther an "economic" Trinity would not be enough;[8] he requires that parishioners hold fast to the view that we would call the "immanent Trinity." Simple people must simply believe in this Trinity on the basis of the Credo, but the literate should read biblical passages that prove Christ's divinity, and memorize and believe them.[9] The most important such passage according to Luther is the prologue to the Gospel of John.[10]

Third, Luther is skeptical of "speculation" about the Trinitarian dogma and wants to replace it with biblical teaching. On the other hand, even in his parish sermons Luther himself uses some traditional "explanations" of the Trinity, such as the analogy between a human thought or word (*verbum internum*) and God's Logos, the Son.[11] The difference be-

---

5. See *WA* 1, 600; *WA* 10/III, 150; *WA* 17/I, 278.

6. The idea about the Father as the "primary person" can also be seen in Luther's view that it is the Father whose Word and will the Son is. It is the Father who sends the Son into the World. It is the Father, whom the Son obeys. See also Lienhardt, *Luther*, 323. This does not mean, however, "subordinationism" or "monarchism." See Saarinen, *Gottes Wirken*, 93–94.

7. *WA* 1, 21–2. All translations from *WA* are my own.

8. In a few sermons Luther refers to what in scholasticism is called the "appropriations." See, e.g., *WA* 29, 385; *WA* 15, 468–69. On the other hand, Luther seems to follow the Augustinian principle *opera trinitatis ad extra indivisa sunt*. Even though the work of creation is attributed to the Father, still the Son and the Spirit also partake of that creation. Similarly, Luther can attribute the "sanctification" (i.e., making salvation effective) to Christ (e.g., *WA* 11, 109), even though usually it is the work of the Spirit (e.g., in *WA* 29, 364; *WA* 28, 82–83; *WA* 1, 269) Despite the fact that the economic appropriations "overlap" in this way, it is clear that Luther does not intermingle the persons.

9. See *WA* 27, 523. In one sermon Luther describes such reading of important passages of the Bible "picking flowers for a garland." *WA* 15, 801–20.

10. Luther preaches on the prologue of John in *WA* 1, 20–23, *WA* 12, 585–91, *WA* 15, 798–803 and *WA* 11, 226. The use of the prologue stays essentially the same over the years. When John writes that the Word "was (*erat*) in the beginning" of the creation, according to Luther, he denies that the Word himself has began in time. Therefore, the Word is the eternal Creator, i.e., God. On the other hand, the words "*apud Deum*" make the Word personally distinct from God the Father, because nothing can be by (or with) itself. See *WA* 1, 21; *WA* 17/I, 278–79.

11. *WA* 1, 26–27, 527.

tween Luther and scholastic Trinitarian speculation is easily overemphasized. Even in his later years Luther said that the scholastics had treated the theme of the Trinity rather well. But it is understandable that, especially for uneducated people, a speculative treatment of the Trinitarian dogma could easily go against Luther's "*pro me*"-principle of faith.[12]

Fourth, for Luther the Trinitarian doctrine is not an absolute value. It is needed for a certain purpose, to secure the full divinity of salvation, as this can be seen from Luther's description of the words *Dreyfaltigkeit* as well as *trinitas* and *persona* as unbiblical and linguistically unfitting. Still, they have to be used, in the same way as the Church Fathers did, in order to avoid heresies.[13] Luther mentions Arianism and the modalistic heresy in his sermons. They must be fought against, because they make the saving faith in Christ impossible. The Savior must be a "natural God" (*naturalis deus/wesentlich Gott*), distinct from the person of the Father.[14]

CHRIST'S PERSON AND THE DOCTRINE OF *ENHYPOSTASIS*

In his Christological teaching Luther is a follower of the Chalcedonian two natures-doctrine. He also follows the traditional doctrine of *enhypostasis*.[15] According to this doctrine, Christ is the same person as the Logos, God's eternal Son. In his incarnation the Son accepted a human *nature*, not a human *person*. The purpose of the doctrine was to prevent the idea that Christ could be two persons: He is only one person, the divine Son, who is also a true human being, because he has assumed a human nature. Luther emphasizes that the Son did not "desert himself," i.e., does not change into other than what he is in his divine person.[16]

12. See, e.g., *WA* 20, 432; *WA* 29, 385; *WA* 20, 393; *WA* 15, 802; *WA* 15, 468; *WA* 17/I, 169.

13. *WA* 27, 187; *WA* 29, 385. Luther would have perhaps agreed with George Lindbeck's point in his book *Nature of Doctrine*: The Trinitarian dogma is not a set of propositions that grasps its referent, but rather a set of rules that has to be followed in order to speak the saving Gospel correctly. See, e.g., *WA* 1, 21–22.

14. *WA* 1, 21, *WA* 11, 226; *WA* 27, 189, 521; *WA* 27, 522–27; *WA* 15, 799, 803; *WA* 12, 588; *WA* 17/I, 279. Luther does not explicitly state, how a modalistic doctrine would distort the saving faith. However, in texts where he "proves" Christ's divinity by means of the Scripture, Luther also says, that the same biblical passages clearly show, that Christ is distinct from the Father (e.g., *WA* 28, 88–89). This seems to indicate that it was important for Luther to oppose modalism for soteriological reasons.

15. Nilsson, *Simul*, 179–80; Lienhardt, *Luther*, 234–35; Peters, *Luthers Christuszeugnis*, 3–5.

16. *WA* 1, 20, 28; *WA* 20, 428.

In his sermons Luther usually concentrates on what Christ is like and how he acts in the narrative of the Gospel. This means that his point of looking at Christ is different from the traditional *enhypostasis* doctrine, which deals with the event of incarnation from God's point of view. Seen from the viewpoint of *enhypostasis*, Christ's person is for Luther clearly the divine Son, who assumes a human nature, and not a human person. But from the "lower" viewpoint of the concrete Gospel narratives the concept "Christ's person" does not mean for Luther the divine Son only. It refers to Christ, who is a concrete, living person (*viva persona*). In such a context Luther says that Christ is a "person constituted of God and man" (*persona constituta ex deo et homine*).[17] Humanity is a constitutive element of Christ as well as of divinity. This does not mean that Luther would deny the *enhypostasis*. He wants to emphasize that the Son has assumed humanity in a deep way, not just as an external "garment." After the incarnation the Son not only "has flesh" (*habet carnem*) but also he "is flesh" (*est caro*).[18]

THE UNITY OF CHRIST'S PERSON

A central aspect of Luther's Christology is the unity and undividedness of Christ's person. When Christ is dealt with "from the outside" (*ab extra*), according to Luther, we see only one concrete person, not two natures, which could be separable from each other. The viewpoint "from the outside" means for Luther, that Christ is "an object, which is given to me," with "whom I deal," for example, when one reads a story about Christ in the Gospels. Even though Christ's two natures are distinct (*distincta*) "in themselves," (*in se*) that is, when considered "from the inside" (*ad intra*), they still are so deeply united that one can never "meet" just one of the natures, but only one person, the *totus Christus*, God and man.[19]

On the other hand, the unity of Christ's two natures in one person is not just a point of view. The unity is real and the natures mutually affect each other. This so-called *communicatio idiomatum* is central to Luther's entire theology.[20] He illuminates the concept with the following

17. WA 20, 605.

18. WA 1, 28. See also Lienhardt, *Luther*, 231; Siggins, *Martin Luther's Doctrine of Christ*, 224.

19. WA 20, 604.

20. Nilsson, *Simul*, 228. Later the Lutheran orthodoxy made differentiated between the various *genera* of *communicatio idiomatum* on the basis of whether the divine prop-

example: when a dog bites Peter on the leg, the injury has to do with Peter's whole person, not just with his leg. In a similar way, whatever concerns one of Christ's two natures, concerns the whole of his person. Christ's human properties, such as being visible, tangible, able to suffer and die, are also properties of his person, which is divine. Therefore, God is seen in Christ, even though God in himself is not visible.[21] For the same reason, not did only the human Jesus suffer and die on the cross, but so did God's Son.

For Luther, to maintain the unity of Christ's person was a matter of life and death. The Christology of Zwingli and the *Schwärmer*, which separated Christ's natures at the cost of the unity of the person, is something diabolical for Luther. According to Luther, the devil tempts people to make exactly such a separation between Christ's humanity and God. When the devil has been able to accomplish this in the consciousness of a poor sinner, the sinner can no longer find relief in Christ and his sacrificial love. He sees in his mind how Christ dies on the cross, but does not understand that Christ is God, dying for him. He is left searching for God in heaven and in the thoughts of his own mind.[22]

THE DISTINCTION BETWEEN NATURES

According to Luther the unity of Christ's natures does not mean that these natures would change so that Christ would neither be a true God nor a true man. In his sermons on the Gospel of John, Luther describes Christ's humanity first of all as corporality. Christ ate, drank, and was in all other respects a bodily human being.[23]

---

erty affects human nature, human property affects the divine nature or the properties collectively affect the person. Luther does not make these distinctions, when he speaks of *communicatio idiomatum*. See Nilsson, *Simul*, 241, and Lienhardt, *Luther*, 344. If we apply the later division to Luther's sermons, it seems that Luther most often uses the so-called *genus idiomaticum*, which means that both natures affect the one person. However, Luther also recognizes other kinds of *communicatio*: e.g., the properties of the divine nature affect the human nature. Such a communication is behind the idea that Christ's flesh is *divina caro*, which can bring salvation (WA 4, 702) and also behind the idea that Christ's humanity is everywhere (*ubique*) after the ascension (WA 20, 377). See also WA 1, 296.

21. WA 20, 603, 605; WA 28, 224–26.

22. WA 28, 117–19, 487; WA 20, 602–5.

23. WA 29, 640; WA 28, 65; WA 33, 65: "leibliche Mensch." WA 17/I, 271: "infirma creatura."

Second, Christ's humanity means for Luther that Christ had to live under the requirements of God's law, just like any other human being. Christ fulfilled the law of un-egoistic love, even to the point that he took the sins of others upon himself in order to save them. This subordination under the law reached its climax on the cross, where Christ suffered the punishment required of sinners.[24]

Third, Christ's humanity means for Luther his humane, friendly, and gentle behavior toward others.[25] When Christ was with his disciples, none of them could see his divine majesty. This is a topic Luther discusses often in his sermons. Christ was so humane that he "played with John like a child" and "even forgot himself that he was God."[26]

When Luther preaches about Christ's true divinity, he emphasizes the creation. Christ is the Father's Word (*verbum*) through whom everything is created and continually preserved in being. As God's *verbum* Christ is also the principle of rationality, which enables people to understand the world, even logical and mathematical truths.[27] This means that the same God who created people is also their Savior.

The ability to save mankind from sin and death is another central property that Luther uses to describe Christ's divinity in his sermons.[28]

CHRIST'S *KENOSIS*

The idea of *kenosis* is central to Luther's Christology. *Kenosis* means "emptying" and refers to Philippians 2, according to which Christ "did not count equality with God to be something to be grasped, but he emptied himself, taking the form of a slave." For Luther this means first of all that the earthly Jesus did not make use of his divine properties, but put them aside. Nevertheless, he still had a divine nature, but one as if without supernatural properties.[29]

---

24. WA 10/III, 9, 1, 95; WA 28, 407. See also Nilsson, *Simul*, 197, and Lienhardt, *Luther*, 140, 168.

25. WA 20, 602.

26. WA 20, 312.

27. WA 15, 802; WA 11, 224; WA 20, 294; WA 17/I, 155; WA 20, 427, 602; WA 27, 530.

28. WA 28, 226; WA 15, 803. Other ways to describe Christ's divinity in the sermons are the divine power (WA 20, 376), honor (WA 1, 269; WA 27, 84), and *ubiquitas* (WA 20, 377; WA 28, 141–42).

29. WA 1, 269. Later, in Lutheran Orthodoxy, it became a matter of great dispute whether Christ had *hidden* his divine properties (*krypsis*) or emptied himself of them

Luther is especially interested in the divine properties that have to do with external behavior. Because Christ was God, divine glory and majesty belonged to him. However, Christ did not associate with people as a glorious Lord, but was friendly and served others.[30]

Second, for Luther *kenosis* means, that Christ became an especially wretched and sinful human being when he assumed the sin, guilt, and anxiety of humankind in himself.[31] It seems that, for Luther, Christ's whole life was a continuous *kenosis*, beginning with his birth.[32] However, it is important to note that for Luther, *kenosis* has to be separated from incarnation. Luther often emphasizes that in his incarnation Christ assumed a sinless human nature, which was not perverted by the egoistic self-love or concupiscence (*concupiscentia carnis*). Christ was born "of the flesh" but not "according to the flesh." He was a human being without guilt, because he fulfilled the Father's will through obedience and love.[33]

Despite his innocence, Christ was "in the flesh of the sinners," because he assumed the sin of others in order to serve them.[34] This means that the guilt concerned him *coram deo* as strongly as in the case of other sinners, or even in a stronger way: According to Luther, Christ had "loaded"[35] the sins of the world on himself and become the "greatest sinner."[36]

(*kenosis*). This dispute is quite interesting, because the actual topic behind it had to do with the understanding of justification. See Nüssel, *Allein aus Glauben*, 178–79, 207, 220–23, 237, 345–46. Luther does not deal with this question, but it seems to me that his theological position is closer to followers of the later *krypsis* theory (the theologians in Tübingen) than to the followers of the *kenosis* theory (the position of the University of Giessen).

30. WA 17/I, 27.

31. In the end he was less than a human being. He was even "less than worms" (WA 28, 80).

32. See e.g., WA 15, 509; WA 17/I, 284; WA 1, 269; WA 4, 628; WA 9, 435; WA 29, 344; WA 10/III, 129, 154; WA 12, 582; WA 20, 431; WA 20, 430; WA 28, 97; WA 15, 511. See also Nilsson, *Simul*, 221.

33. Here Mannermaa (*Der im Glauben Gegenwärtige Christus*, 23; "Justification and Theosis," 29) is clearly mistaken. See WA 20, 430; WA 28, 257, 343; WA 15, 464; WA 20, 427; WA 15, 803; WA 46, 231–32; WA 45, 48; WA 46, 136.

34. WA 1, 268.

35. WA 20, 431: "Das heisst, das er ein sunder ist worden, hat sie auffgeladen, die doch nicht sein war, und eben mit der sunde, die er so auff sich lud, und lies sich richten und verdammen als ein übelthetter hat er die sunde vertilget." WA 12, 582: "auf sich genomen"; WA 15, 509: "in se accipit"; WA 20, 431: "auf sich lud"; WA 20, 430: "ein sunder ist worden"; WA 10/III, 154: "gesteckt in meinem sünd."

36. WA 28, 390–91: "Er hat müssen der grossest sünder werden für uns und unser

CHRIST'S PERSON AND THE RESURRECTION AND ASCENSION

Christ's resurrection and ascension to heaven (*der Gang zu Vater*) is an event that stands in contrast to *kenosis*; through this event the servant becomes the king. Christ's divinity becomes the dominant character of his person. His human properties are left behind, just as his divine properties were hidden behind the human one's during his earthly life. It is difficult to believe in the true humanity of the resurrected Christ, just as it was difficult to believe in the true divinity of the earthly Christ.[37]

On the other hand, Luther seldom preaches about Christ in his heavenly glory. More often his theme is the earthly Christ, whose central feature is his kenotic humanity. Luther urges his listeners to meet Christ through his humanity, to believe that he is God and Savior, even though he looks so wretched.

In Christ's ascension the decisive element for Luther is that Christ again receives the property of *ubiquitas*, which belonged to him as God, but which he had laid aside in his *kenosis*. In his earthly existence Christ could meet people only in one local place at a time. In ascension this human property of locality is replaced by the divine property of *ubiquitas*. Because of the *communicatio idiomatum* Christ's human nature partakes in the divine *ubiquitas*. This idea becomes central for Luther in his doctrine of the Eucharist.

As is well known, the Swiss reformer Ulrich Zwingli taught that Christ's body couldn't be present in the bread of the Eucharist. Zwingli contented that Christ's body existed after the ascension in heaven, "at the right hand of the Father" and can therefore not exist on earth. Luther mocks Zwingli's reasoning: Zwingli understands the words of the Credo, "he ascended into heaven and is seated at the right hand of the Father," to refer to a specific heavenly place, where Christ's body "sits on a velvet pillow."[38] According to Luther, Zwingli does not acknowledge that Christ has ascended "to God the Father." The Father is present everywhere in the world, in water, in fire, in prison and in the sword, even "above the fish of the sea." When Christ went to this Father, it means that he also

---

sünder tragen, Auff das wir durch in erloset und selig würden wie auch S.P. sagt 2.Cor.5. er hat den der von keinen sünde wuste, fur uns zur sünde gemacht, auff das wir würden in Im die gerechtigkeit gottes." See also WA 20, 430. WA 17/I, 284.

37. WA 20, 315.
38. Leinhardt, *Luther*, 216–13.

became present everywhere. Therefore, his body and blood can truly be present in the material things of the sacrament, in different locations at the same time.[39]

CHRIST'S WORK AS RECONCILIATION

So far I have dealt with Luther's thinking about Christ's person. These concepts are closely related to Luther's understanding of Christ's work. There has been considerable discussion in Luther research concerning the question of whether the reformer understands Christ's reconciling work as *redemption* (that is, as a victory over the destructive powers) or as *satisfaction* (that is, as a juridical event, in which Christ suffers for the guilt of others).[40] It is clear that in Luther's sermons and lectures on the Gospel of John, both theories are represented. This duality of the soteriological theories results from the fact that Luther understands sin in a two-fold fashion. On one hand, sin is *guilt* before God; on the other hand, sin is a *destructive power* that holds the humankind captive (as can be seen when people suffer God's wrath, fear the devil or death, and have a troubled conscience).[41] From the duality in understanding sin there results a duality in understanding Christ's work: on the one hand, Christ conquers evil powers and rescues people from captivity. On the other hand, he took on himself the guilt of humankind and suffered on behalf of others the death, required by God's law for sinners.[42] Luther

---

39. WA 20, 366; WA 28, 143.

40 See, e.g., Aulen, *Den kristna försöningstanken*, 189; Lindroth, *Försöningen*, 187, 210; Peters, *Luthers Christuszeugnis*, 26, Tiililä, *Das Strafleiden Christi*, 212; Vainio, *Justification*, 25–26.

41. WA 15, 511, 534. See also WA 17/I, 247; WA 20, 301; WA 33, 32–34,45; WA 15, 466, 475, 534; WA 33, 45; WA 10/III, 159; WA 29, 82; WA 12, 455.

42. Olsson (*Schöpfung*, 106) gives a similar reason for the duality of Luther's understanding of reconciliation. There is a connection between sin as guilt and sin as diabolic destructive power: because of the guilt of the humankind God's law and his wrath give the devil the right to rule over people. See Bring, *Dualismen*, 155–56; Olsson, *Schöpfung*, 102, 105; Nilsson, *Simul*, 193, n. 8; WA 28, 348; WA 20, 399, 609. Concerning the frequency of the two theories, it is evident that the idea of Christ conquering the destructive powers appears more often in the sources of this article than does the theory of satisfaction. Satisfaction is fully developed only in the lectures on the history of the passion in John (WA 28, 201–478). On the other hand, one could claim that satisfaction is primary for Luther, because the destructive powers are, according to him, results of God's wrath, which has to do with guilt. (See, e.g., WA 20, 399; WA 28, 97, 231, 348–49, 406). See Seeberg, *Grundzüge der Theologie Luthers*, 96. This argument is weakened by the fact that Luther also deals with God's wrath as a power overcome by redemption.

does not explicitly distinguish these two aspects from each other. They are so intertwined, that he can use both in two successive sentences. For the sake of clarity I will deal with the two lines of thought separately: first, the victory over the destructive powers and then, satisfaction.

As already noted, according to Luther, Christ took the sin of humankind on himself in his *kenosis*. In his suffering and death Christ's sinfulness reaches its climax.[43] He becomes the greatest sinner.[44] The destructive powers and their leader, Satan, attack him with all their might.

Christ conquers sin and the destructive powers "in his own person."[45] The sin of the world is absorbed in Christ's person and conquered there. Luther can say for example, that Christ's flesh, his righteousness, his goodness, or his person conquers over the sin. Or he can say that Christ takes away or carries the sins or that they vanish, are annulled (*verschwinden, zu nicht gemacht*), or "drowned" because of Christ's victory.[46]

Behind all these expressions is the idea of the *communicatio idiomatum* and the immense contrast present in Christ's person.[47] Because of the unity of his person, the sin and destructive powers absorbed in Christ's human nature must do battle with the divine nature and its properties. Sin and destructive powers cannot destroy Christ, even though they drag him down to a hell "lower than worms." In the end righteousness, life, and other "goods" (*bona*) in Christ's person are victorious. Hell and its powers cannot keep him captive. He tramples death under his feet and is resurrected.[48]

See, e.g., WA 10/III, 127; WA 15, 466; WA 12, 581.

43. WA 27, 171; WA 15, 569; WA 10/III, 92.

44. WA 20, 430. WA 28, 390-91. See also WA 40, I, 434-35. The last passages are from the lecture on the Galatians, according to which Christ became the biggest sinner (*maximus peccator*) if the world. The sins are so totally absorbed in Christ's person, that in one sense sin can be found nowhere in the world, except in the person of the Crucified.

45. WA 28, 97: "E coelo missus in terram, ut expediret opus ei commissum, ut sequitur. Credendum quod Christus missus in terras, ut peccata in se sumeret et in sua persona vinceret peccatum." WA 17/I, 284; WA 29, 344.

46. WA 10/III, 157: "... sund und unglatt den grossen meer seinen grosen gutigkeit versenkt und erdrenkt." WA 11, 105: "peccatum abstulit" WA 4, 702; WA 10/III, 125; WA 20, 430-33; WA 22, 171.

47. WA 15, 569; WA 10/III, 130.

48. WA 22, 171.

Christ is victorious over sin, because he has the "Father's righteousness."[49] As the Son he is God's creative Word, i.e., life itself, which death, the devil, God's wrath, sin, or anxiety cannot vanquish. Therefore, for Luther, redemption is an intertrinitarian event, wherein God reconciles sinners with himself through his Son. However, this does not mean, that Christ's divine nature alone is active in the victory. Also Christ's human nature and its properties (such as his obedience to the Father, his innocence, or the fulfilling of God's law) have their part in victory over sin.[50]

Next I will deal with Luther's understanding of reconciliation as a vicarious death, that is, as satisfaction. Luther understands sin as guilt *coram deo*.[51] It's basis is that a human being has made himself a god for himself. He does not want to be a creature of the real God, but raises himself to his Creator and Savior by trusting his own wisdom, money, or other "goods" with the trust that should be given only to the Creator. In this way all people make gods for themselves (i.e., idols) and at the same time hope that the real God would not be God. Whoever does this, has deserved death. This is why Christ died. He had "dressed in our person" (*induit nostram personam*), suffered our punishment, and thereby taken away God's wrath, which without Christ is visited upon human beings because of their sinful self-divinisation.[52] Luther preaches about this, for example, by saying that "Christ's passion is given to me," "Christ died for me" (*pro me mortuus*) or "Christ's blood has flowed for me."[53] Also the idea that Christ has earned (*meruit*) salvation for us through his crucifixion, punishment, and death, appears in Luther's sermons.[54]

---

49. WA 20, 401, 403; WA 15, 467, 569; WA 10/III, 130; WA 28, 226; WA 15, 803.

50. E.g., WA 10/III, 91; WA 11, 116; WA 17/I, 493; WA 15, 464; WA 20, 431; WA 20, 430–31; WA 29, 369; WA 15, 534.

51. WA 28, 350–51; WA 28, 343; WA 4, 699. For passages about the demands of God's law, see, e.g., WA 4, 684; WA 10/III, 88–87; WA 12, 534.

52. WA 28, 348; WA 28, 343.

53. WA 12, 581; WA 15, 509, 566; WA 17/I, 262, 277; WA 20, 604, 639; WA 4, 596; WA 12, 544; WA 15, 511–12; WA 28, 273, 410, 411; WA 28, 97–98, 406.

54. WA 15, 568; WA 15, 512; WA 28, 45; WA 11, 120. According to Haikola (*Studien*, 109–10) and Althaus (*Die Theologie*, 179), Luther's idea of the satisfying *meritum* is different from Anselm's. According to Luther, Christ's obedience in passion does not deserve any "positive merits." His death is a merit only "negatively," because he dies in a way that sinners should die.

It is extremely important to note that for Luther, reconciliation (the victory over sin and its satisfaction) is *present in Christ's person and is given to people in his person.*[55] Luther does not recognize the result of Christ's reconciling work, the justification of the world, as a state of affairs that would somehow be separable from Christ's person. This is the reason why Christ's ascension to heaven is for Luther a part of his victory over sin; there Christ acquires the ubiquity that makes it possible for him and his victory to be given to those who believe. In Christ they become lords over sin and Satan.

CHRIST'S WORK AS CONDESCENDENCE

Christ's reconciling death and resurrection is a necessary but not sufficient reason for human salvation. It is not sufficient, because it does not explain, how people can *believe* in Christ and his salvific work, how to apprehend Christ and his righteousness in justifying faith, how forgiveness and Christ's victory over sin become a reality for me and in me.

Therefore, we have to consider other aspects of Christ's work, other christological assumptions for the justifying *unio cum Christo* in Luther's thinking. I have chosen to use the expression "Christ's work as condescendence" to discuss this aspect of Luther's thinking, even though Luther does not use the word "condescendence". It is derived from the traditional theological term *con-descendere*, which means that someone comes down to be with someone else. What I mean by speaking of Christ's work as condescendence, is that God in Christ has become such a human being, that through him mankind can be united with God. The "coming-to-our-level" which God accomplished in Christ, is for Luther a

---

55. *WA* 15, 543: "Ubi ergo fides Christi non est, ibi peccatum est, quia alia via in nobis non habitat Christus nisi per fidem." *WA* 15, 803. *WA* 27, 174. *WA* 28, 46; *WA* 20, 366; *WA* 11, 116, 126; *WA* 33, 37. *WA* 17/I, 245. Thus also Haikola, *Studien*, 108. The term "happy exchange" does not appear in sermons on John. However, the idea is expressed, e.g., in the following passages: *WA* 4, 703: "Ita hic quoque in spiritu qui manducat Christi carnem et bibit eius sanguinem, non id ore facit, sed spiritu et fide, quia fide hanc carnem sibi natam esse habet firmum, filium hunc suum esse tam sit persuasus, ut nulla morte, nulla periculo, nullo tormento cogi possit, ut aliter dicat, quam ut Christi iustitia et innocentia sua sit, et suum peccatum, suam noxam, suam miseriam esse Christi victoris. Atque it evanescit omne malum, et hoc ex gratuita Dei misericordia, ita Christi spiritus est cum spiritu hominis coniunctus, ut impossibile sit avellare hunc hominem a Christo, quem nemo potest corrumpere, ut corpus corrumpimus mortale. Atque ita hic, qui sic manducat carnem Christi, manet in Christo et Christus in eo." See also *WA* 15, 467. *WA* 11, 126; *WA* 20, 403.

necessary condition for our justification. Why? Luther's sermons on the Gospel of John suggest three reasons:

First, if God were "naked" (*Deus nudus*) and not "dressed" in Christ, he would be too great and too majestic for human beings. Luther often warns his listeners away from speculations, which are directed to God outside Christ. Before God's exposed majesty a human being "becomes dizzy" (*zu drummern gehen*), is horrified, "falls on his back," or at worst, commits suicide, because he cannot abide God's holiness.[56]

Second, God is present all over his universe, but not in a way that he could be known. According to Luther, to know God is to know his "heart" (*Herz*) and his "decision" (*consilium*), i.e., to know, that Christ has been born and has died for us, so that we would be saved through "alien righteousness" (*iustitia aliena*).[57]

Third, because of his sinful corruption, a human being cannot believe in God or love him in an unselfish way. A person considers himself as god, and the real God as a "tax collector," from whom human being tries to buy favor with merits. In such a situation a justifying faith is impossible.[58]

For Luther, God, in Christ, has drawn close to people to such a degree that all these obstacles have been overcome. Luther uses all the stages of Christ's life in order to describe how this closeness happens. According to some sermons the incarnation is the deciding point. Other sermons emphasize the humanity of Christ's kenotic life by saying that Christ has put aside or hid his divine properties so that people will not fear him. In many sermons Christ's ascension is the decisive point: there Christ's kingdom was established, a kingdom in which Christ comes to people by sending his Spirit to them through the Gospel and the sacraments. In his sermons Luther does not distinguish between these lines of thought. For the sake of clarity, I will analyze them separately.

Incarnation as Condescendence

For Luther Christ's incarnation is the basic soteriological event that enables the union between God and humans.[59] The incarnation is not

---

56. WA 28, 117; WA 4,704; WA 10/III, 161.
57. WA 28, 199; WA 15, 558; WA 27, 146.
58. WA 10/III, 155; WA 4, 704; WA 28, 350.
59. See, e.g., WA 15, 503: "Regnum Christi ita institutum, ut fieret homo." WA 15, 799: "Locus capitalis, quod verbum dei sit factam caro . . ." WA 10/III, 91; WA 15, 686,

a mere manifestation of God. The Son has assumed the human nature in his person. This means that God has given his Son to the world as a gift in order to be on the same ontological level with people, to be apprehended by people.[60]

In a sermon from 1524, Luther reproaches the pope for denying the doctrine of incarnation. In Luther's eyes the pope does not truly believe that Christ has become flesh. In other words the pope does not believe "with all his body" (*cum toto suo corpore*) that mere reality of the incarnation saves people, but rather that good works are also required. According to Luther, only the person who believes in Christ's incarnation, who confesses that Christ is born "in my favor" (*mir zu gut*) and "in my flesh and in your flesh" (*in meam et tuam carnem*), believes correctly.[61] In other sermons Luther emphasizes the idea that in the incarnation, the Son has come "to be mine," "has come for me, to be my righteousness."[62] After God gave his Son to the world, the whole world has been so full of the Son and God's mercy that there is nowhere people can run to God in order to receive the Son. The world is already full of the Son who is everywhere.[63]

From the unity of Christ's person it follows that whoever meets Christ through his human properties also meets God.[64] This is the background of the pastoral principle that Luther calls "starting from below" (*von unten Anfangen*). It means that one has to have dealings with God through Christ's human nature and its properties, which are told about in the Gospels. In a sermon from 1522, Luther preaches about the Trinity, saying, "it is not necessary to make Christ into a God." It is enough that Christ is preached as God's Son. It is the Holy Spirit's task to make it

---

799; WA 20, 403; WA 27, 171.

60. Luther himself does not use these expressions, but I think they express his thinking rather well. WA 28, 135; WA 10/III, 161–162; WA 28, 486–87.

61. WA 15, 685.

62. WA 20, 729; WA 10/III, 91; WA 4, 596; WA 27, 171; WA 15, 468. The idea that Christ is "given to me" in his incarnation is important for Luther when he preaches on the sixth chapter of John. Luther emphasizes that in John 6, Christ's flesh and blood does not refer to the Eucharist, but to Christ's natural humanity "in which he walked." This *divina caro* is given to humankind as "food for the soul" (*cibus animae*), to be eaten in faith. See, e.g., WA 4, 702: "Queso, quanta sit fames mortalium, quam talis cibus, nempe caro divina sit satiatura?" WA 4, 700; WA 11, 125; WA 15, 466–67; WA 20, 296; WA 4, 701; WA 15, 467.

63. WA 20, 403; WA 20, 741.

64. WA 28, 487; WA 28, 487; WA 33, 77–81; WA 20, 603–5; WA 33, 81.

clear, that Christ is God. When the Bible leads people to Christ, it first teaches them to know him as a human being, then to view him as Lord over all creatures, then as Lord over everything, and only after that as God. According to Luther, in this way we come to know God "in a fine way." Philosophers have not followed this way, but have "started from above" and become fools.[65]

In a sermon from 1528, Luther preaches about the temptation to speculate on predestination, whether one is consigned to heaven or to hell.

> The temptation of the eternal predestination is taken away as follows. Some people have tormented themselves with it so that they have become mad ... If you want to deal with the question in a more sensible way, then look at this text. Start from below, not from above. Look at whether these words taste good (*sapio*) in your heart. If the words that come from the mouth of this man [Christ], if they are precious to you and you can hear nothing sweeter than these words, then you start from below. Then he leads you inside and says to you: you are given to me; if you are given to me, then your name is written in heaven ... This is the right way to deal with the question, this way you start in Christ, in his flesh and blood (which the *Schwärmer* fight against). And let go the distress about what God thinks of you ... This is what I call "starting from below." Those who start from above let Christ preach, but they do not pay attention to his mouth or his words; they think instead: what does God think about me, where shall I be? ... It happens that they lose Christ from their heart. The oral word is not there, but their own thoughts make God terrifying, and they will be damned."[66]

In Luther's sermons on the Gospel of John the phrase *Von unten Anfangen* is explicitly used only two sermons. But the idea itself is found in other sermons as well. Luther starts from Christ's humanity, what Christ says and what he is like according to the text. In this context Luther uses the words "the bodily human" (*der leibliche Mensch*). One may not look for God anywhere but in the Incarnated "who is lying on his mother's lap."[67] Christ's humanity is like a bag, which is given to humankind. Inside is a treasure, namely God himself. In Christ God does a

---

65. *WA* 12, 386–87.
66. *WA* 28, 122.
67. *WA* 33, 15; *WA* 28, 487.

great service to humans and meets them in a form that humans can apprehend. The divinity is not given to us "naked" but "bagged" (*eingesackt*) in Christ's humanity.[68]

In his lectures on the gospel of John, Luther says: "Let no one be so stupid that he would have dealings with God without Christ, or with Christ without his humanity."[69] In his sermons Luther urges his listeners to pay attention to how the Gospels describe Christ: he is a servant, not a frightening king. His conduct toward sinners is not harsh; he even allows Judas to be in his company and does not reveal Judas's sins to the other disciples. On the contrary, Christ "takes the load of others' sins upon himself." By focusing on Christ's humanity in the Gospels, we learn just how good and loving Christ is. Christ's goodness attracts humans to Christ, and a "fine and lovely trust" is created. "If I know him as the Gospel depicts him, then I long for him as for my best friend."[70]

In another sermon Luther says that when a person pays attention to Christ's loving humanity, at the same time she will see the Father's will and heart, because Christ lived according to his Father's will. When a person realizes this, she "rises from the Son to the Father":

> In this way I know the Father's friendly will and his highest love, which one's heart can't oppose. I take hold of God, where he is at his sweetest, and I think: O, that is God, o that is God's will and pleasure, that Christ does such things for me![71]

The idea of "rising from the Son to the Father" does not mean that a person should actively try to go further than Christ the man: "The greatest thing is (*altissimum est*) if someone can abide this man. If Christ accepts you, then the Father also accepts you."[72]

Kenosis as Condescendence

So far I have dealt with incarnation as condescendence. In Luther's theology there are also other christological thoughts that have to do with

---

68. WA 28, 487. It should be noted that even though the bag metaphor is used in this context, it does not express Luther's thinking about the relationship of humanity to divinity in Christ's person.

69. WA 28, 487.

70. WA 10/III, 164.

71. WA 10/III, 154–55. See also WA 1, 273.

72. WA 28, 135.

God's condescendence, his coming near to us. One of them is *kenosis*.[73] I have found the following two aspects of *kenosis* to be key to Luther's understanding:

First, as already indicated, for Luther it is important that Christ not only became a human being, but also became humble and loving person who is not frightening. According to Luther, one of Christ's main goals was to instill into people a trust in himself. That is why the frightening divine properties were largely hidden beneath human properties. Christ lived such a humane life that he even "forgot himself that he was God"; the disciples thought that he was merely a man. Sometimes his divinity showed in miracles, but even then it served others. This unfrightening, kenotic Christ is obviously a very important theme in Luther's sermons.[74]

Second, however, the "kenotic Christ" is, according to Luther, not merely pleasant. In his role as a servant, Christ is sinful, despicable, the opposite to all that people normally consider good and lovable.[75] He reigns through the cross and suffering. According to Luther, this lowly and despicable way of existence was necessary in order for Christ to be the Savior of humankind. As the Savior, he came to heal the egotistical lust of humankind (*concupiscentia*).[76]

By *concupiscentia* Luther does not mean sexuality, but natural human love, which loves that which is exalted, good, and beautiful, but shuns that which is lowly. *Concupiscentia* separates one's neighbors into two groups, the lovable and the despicable. It wants to be in the first group, because there is something to be gained from them. Those in the other group are left alone; they have no wisdom, beauty, or other goodness that one could gain by associating with them.[77] In relation to God *concupiscentia* is manifested in such a way, that God is considered a judge or a "tax-collector" from whom a person can buy salvation with good works. A normal human being living under *concupiscentia* trusts with a trust that should be placed in God alone. Thereby the person divinizes himself and wishes that the true God would not exist.

---

73. See, e.g., WA 1, 274; WA 10/III, 154–59; WA 10/III, 164; WA 17, 17.
74. WA 20, 312; WA 1, 274; WA 10/III, 154, 158, 164; WA 17/I, 579.
75. WA 1, 270; WA 1, 269; WA 4, 628.
76. WA 9, 435.
77. WA 1, 270. WA 17/I, 247; WA 33, 26.

If Christ had had a glorious appearance, or in some other way had been such that the *concupiscentia* could love him, then Christ would not have been able to save people from the power of sin. People would consider Christ a reward, bought from God with their merits. In order to destroy *concupiscentia* Christ in his *kenosis* became the opposite of all that *concupiscentia* considers good. Christ carries the sins of the world. In this way he teaches people to serve others, with a pure divine love, which does not love in order to receive, but in order to give good things to those who lack. Also a relationship to God is made possible. In Christ the egotistical love cannot find anything lovable, or that could be used for self-divinization. Therefore, it has to recede and give place to faith and pure love.[78]

Christ's Ascension and Kingdom as Condescendence

For Luther, Christ's saving work cannot be reduced to his incarnation, death, and resurrection. It extends further, so that Christ brings about the reconciliation and the ontological union between God and humanity in his person, a reality among us and in us. Christ accomplishes these ends through his ascension (*hymelfart*),[79] after which he is established in his kingdom (*Reich*).[80] In this kingdom he reigns with the word and the sacraments, made effective by the Holy Spirit.[81] Two other aspects of the condescendence (*kenosis* and incarnation) continue after Christ's ascension, in his kingdom of the word and the sacraments. The kenotic aspect continues in the sense that the "external word," through which God comes to people is, according to Luther, "lowly" (*vilis*) and "simple" (*simplex*), in all respects something that human reason cannot help but despise.[82] The kenotic existence even becomes a property of the whole

78. WA 9, 435; WA 4, 628; WA 15, 570.

79. WA 17/I, 270; WA 12, 547; WA 29, 369; WA 32, 74; WA 17/I, 29.

80. In one sense, Christ's death and resurrection mean for Luther Christ's glorious victory over sin and death. On the other hand, they mean that Christ is transferred from a natural human existence into a new, immortal existence at the right hand of the Father. In this sense Christ's death, resurrection, and ascension together make for Luther—in accordance with John 16–17—Christ's "going to the Father" (*Gang zu Vater*). In this it is not only that reconciliation is accomplished, but also that Christ's kingdom is established. See WA 9, 469; WA 15, 542; WA 12, 546–47; WA 17/I, 270; WA 20, 397–98. WA 9, 469; WA 29, 368–69.

81. WA 12, 537; WA 20, 397–98; WA 11, 112: WA 20, 296, 754; WA 17/I, 29.

82. WA 20, 296: "Quando praedicatur Euangelium, est vilis vox, non habet speciem,

church. It lives under the cross. Christ has weak and sick sheep in his flock, and according to Luther, Christ wants it that way.[83]

The incarnational aspect continues, too. Luther emphasizes that in the word and the Eucharist, it is the *incarnated Christ* who meets us, not a spiritual Christ, "*contra schwermeros*," but the Incarnated, who has flesh and bones.[84] This raises the question of what sense does it have for Luther to hold on the idea that the ascended Christ has a human body, with "flesh and bones." Luther himself claims that the human body in question does not eat, drink, or suffer; neither is it bound by categories of time and space. Can such a body or such a nature still be human?

The answer is that Luther wants to hold on to the idea at any price whatsoever that the incarnation is the basic soteriological event. God became a human being in order for human beings to meet him on their own ontological level, on the material level, where they exist as bodily beings with flesh and bones. This basic soteriological event remains in force, even though Christ is taken to an unempirical existence in the divine *ubiquitas*.[85] Even at the right hand of the Father, Christ is still "Mary's son."[86] Therefore, he can still be met according to the principle of "starting from below." It is precisely Christ's human nature that enables Christ and his Spirit to be brought to mankind through the word and the sacraments.

The whole idea of Christ's kingdom is that because of Christ's person and his work the "external word" (*eusserliches Wort*)[87] can be spiritually effective. Words can hold Christ within them and convey him to

---

quod sit eterna salus."

83. *WA* 12, 539.

84. *WA* 20, 758-59; *WA* 28, 487. In this context Luther discusses what it means to be spiritual. Its opposite is not that one has "flesh and bones," but that one lives in a way that Luther calls "*animale*," which includes things like eating and procreation. This means that even though Christ really is a "spiritual" being—like the Zwinglians claim—this does not mean, that the spiritual Christ does not have "flesh and bones." See *WA* 20, 758-59.

85. *WA* 20, 366; *WA* 28, 143; *WA* 20, 377.

86. *WA* 11, 102.

87. I.e., the words coming from the mouth of the preacher, or words written with letters. See *WA* 12, 518; *WA* 20, 296-97, 302, 789; *WA* 15, 799-800; *WA* 29, 117; *WA* 12, 518.

people in a way that is more than the external knowledge of the brain.[88] How is this possible?

According to Luther, the preachers of the Gospel work as Christ's voice, as his "loudspeakers" (*Rufzeug*). When Christ went to his Father, he founded his kingdom and the instruments to reign in his kingdom: the sacraments and the ministry of preaching (*Predigamt*). God has decided that people receive their salvation "from the lips of the minister."[89] The external word is a word *about* Christ (*de/von Christo*), about his person and his deeds. A preacher "preaches Christ" (*Christum predigen*), not his own ideas. This is why in one sense the actual preacher is Christ himself, who speaks through his ministers.[90] Second, Christ is present in the external word. He "comes down to all people" in the preached or written words of the Gospel. One can analyze this thought a little further. The following ideas seem to be behind it:

1. The content of the external word is the revelation of God's deepest will, namely unconditional love. Christ as God's Logos, as his "internal Word" (*verbum internum*), is himself this divine thought (*consilium*), will, and love. Therefore, Christ is present in the external word (*verbum externum*); he himself is this word, expressed by human means.[91]

2. Because of Christ's incarnation, the human way of expressing God's deepest internal word does not annul its divinity. Luther almost identifies Christ's human nature and the human character of the proclamation of the Gospel. That the Son "was dressed" in human flesh is analogous to the fact that the spoken word of God dresses itself in a human voice and writing.[92] Preaching is therefore a continuation of Christ's incarnation in the world. This idea has to do with Luther's understanding of the semantics of the theological language. The language of the Gospel not only

---

88. *WA* 28, 155, 180; *WA* 20, 610, 727, 777; *WA* 12, 457; *WA* 29, 117; *WA* 27, 154.

89. *WA* 28, 478.

90. *WA* 12, 530; *WA* 20, 683, 748; *WA* 28, 478; *WA* 4, 99; *WA* 12, 531; *WA* 20, 667; *WA* 15, 800; *WA* 32, 140; *WA* 12, 523.

91. *WA* 1, 23–24; *WA* 20, 740. *WA* 11, 115. *WA* 27, 168–69

92. *WA* 1, 24–25; *WA* 20, 727, 748; *WA* 29, 373; *WA* 28, 119; *WA* 1, 274; *WA* 4, 704.

refers to their object (Christ), but it contains him ontologically and brings him to those who hear and understand.[93]

3. Christ's coming in the external word to humankind has to do with everything that was previously said about Christ's person and work as bringing reconciliation and condescendence. Christ's incarnation, *kenosis*, cross, his resurrection and ascension together make it possible that Christ's kingdom can exist. In this kingdom he comes to people, in saving union with them, through baptism, the Gospel, the Eucharist—in faith.[94]

---

93. WA 12, 518; WA 20, 296-97; WA 27, 154: "Hoc verbum est canalis, per quem venit spiritus sanctus ad nos." See also Työrinoja, "Proprietas Verbi," and "Nova vocabula"; Kirjavainen ,"Die Spezifizierung der Glaubensgegenstände bei Luther"; White, *Luther as Nominalist*, 328-31, 335, 342-46.

94. WA 4, 703: "Ita Christi spiritus est cum hominis spiritus coniunctus, ut impossibile sit avellare hunc hominem a Christus, quem nemo potest corrumpere, ut corpus corrumpimus mortale. Atque ita hic, qui sic manducat carnem Christi, manet in Christo et Christus in eo." WA 11, 126: "Haec fides heist mich essen, ut unum fio cum Christo." WA 20, 296: "Hic est cibus eternus vivens, qui ego sum. Hoc est, quando do Christo praedicatur. Non possemus Christum edere dentibus, ut Iudei dicebant, quomodo? Non tamen frustra secamus et dividimus eum, sed divisionem aliam facimus, quae venit in animam." WA 20, 754: "Si tantum manet fundamentum Christus, quod sit tota hereditas nostra, per sanguinem nos redemit, sed utitur babtismo, verbo, coena ad Christum distribuendum." See also WA 15, 467; WA 17/I, 29; WA 20, 401; WA 32, 140; WA 11, 109; WA 27, 174; WA 11, 112.

4

Trinity

Pekka Kärkkäinen

Throughout the late Middle Ages, students of theology were introduced to various problems of Trinitarian theology in lectures on Peter Lombard's *Sentences*. Luther's encounter with the theology of the Trinity did not take place *merely* on the basis of Lombard's *Sentences* and their scholastic commentaries. Already early in his studies he had revealed an enthusiasm towards the Bible itself, and, concurrently with his lecturing on the *Sentences*, he also read Augustine's works, particularly *De Trinitate*. By reading Augustine and the Bible, Luther became familiar with the very roots of the Trinitarian theology of Lombard and his commentators. With the help of this apparatus, it seems natural that Luther was gradually to form a theology of the Trinity, which was firmly grounded in the revelation of the Scriptures, but at the same time owed much to Augustine.[1]

During his early Wittenberg lectures, Luther discussed Trinitarian theology only incidentally. The situation changed after he began to preach regularly in 1519. For the rest of his life, he discussed the Trinity almost yearly in sermons on Pentecost and Trinity Sunday, and as a part of many series of catechetical sermons.[2] The latter resulted in Luther's

---

1. Wieneke, *Luther und Petrus Lombardus*, 86; Rosemann, *Story of a Great Medieval Book*, 178. On the relationship between exegesis and the Trinity in Luther's later works, see Mattox, "From Faith to the Text."

2. For an overview of Luther's catechetical sermons and sermons on Trinity Sunday, see Jansen, *Studien*, 9–12, 149–54; Helmer, *Trinity and Martin Luther*, 202–6. For the sermons on Pentecost, see also Kärkkäinen, *Luthers trinitarische Theologie*, 113–92.

most distinctive contribution to the theology of the Trinity, namely the explanations of the Creed included in his two catechisms. However, in his later years he commented on several themes of Trinitarian theology throughout his works; it seems that he never lost interest in these topics. During the 1540s he even showed a renewed concern for Trinitarian questions, partly in the context of the newly reintroduced practice of academic disputations and the challenge of the emerging anti-Trinitarian movements.[3]

STARTING POINT: EARLY MARGINAL NOTES

The marginal notes on Augustine's *De Trinitate* and Peter Lombard's *Sentences* present us with the earliest form of Luther's Trinitarian thinking. These glosses date from the time when Luther was a student of theology in Erfurt.[4] It is difficult to make a firm judgment on Luther's theological position, but there are reasons to believe that he was more or less consciously following the local tradition of the *via moderna*. His authorities included such theologians as William Ockham, Pierre d'Ailly and Gabriel Biel. It seems implausible that a writer who would have identified himself with the *via antiqua* would have referred to these thinkers in a favorable way.[5] On the other hand, scholars have noted that Luther also criticized the authorities of the *via moderna*.[6]

Luther's marginal notes are extremely brief, but they still reveal some distinctive traits in his early method of interpreting the theological tradition. The first of these is Luther's appeal to scriptural authority.[7] On the front cover of his copy of the *Sentences* he cites a passage from Hilary's *De Trinitate*, which states that God's own words express most adequately the truths about God.[8] A similar kind of attitude is reflected

---

3. Helmer, *Trinity and Martin Luther*, 43–44.

4. For a more detailed account of Luther's doctrine of Trinity in the early marginal notes, see Wieneke, *Luther und Petrus Lombardus*; Kärkkäinen, "Martin Luther." The current subchapter is partly based on the latter.

5. For the theological authorities of the Augustinians in Erfurt, see Zumkeller, *Erbsünde, Gnade, Rechtfertigung*, 461–504. According to Zumkeller (ibid., 460), Luther apparently had great freedom in choosing his sources for the lectures, which would explain why his sources were not directly connected with the theology of the Augustinian order. See also Kärkkäinen, "Martin Luther."

6. See Lohse, *Martin Luther's Theology*, 49.

7. On this, see Wieneke, *Luther und Petrus Lombardus*, 86.

8. WA 9, 29. Cf. Hilary of Poitiers, *De Trinitate* 7, 38.

in the discussion of individual questions. Thus, in his discussion of the emanations of the Son and the Spirit from the Father, Luther explicitly rejects the Scotist idea of the divine nature and will as two (formally distinct) principles of emanations.[9] He argues that such a view destroys the correspondence between the divine persons and the powers of the soul, that is to say, the psychological analogy of the Trinity. Luther does not stop here, but maintains that such a violation of the coherence of the psychological analogy is actually a sign of neglect of the scriptural authority, since according to the Bible, the "soul is an image of God." Although Luther strongly stresses here the idea of scriptural authority, which was hardly questioned by any Western theologian, his argument is focused on the alleged incoherence of the Scotist position.[10]

Another noteworthy feature in Luther's interpretation is his moderate criticism of Augustine and the Church councils. One might consider this a sign of his tendency to turn back to the scriptural roots of the theology. Moreover, Luther notes the inconsistencies among some statements in Peter Lombard's text, but at this time this does not lead him to disagreement, as in the case of his criticism of Scotus. In one such case Luther questions the internal coherence of Augustine's way of using the notion of relation in Trinitarian theology. Luther presents a view according to which the Father is Father only through the Son, whose sonship is constitutive of the Father's fatherhood. This corresponds to the notion that the Father is wise only through the Son, who is the wisdom of the Father. Luther is not willing to insist on this position or the one following from it, namely, that "being Father differs from being wise," since he considers the contrary view as being "consonant with the truth as defined by the blessed Augustine."[11]

---

9. Luther does not, contrary to Wieneke's (*Luther und Petrus Lombardus*, 144–45) suggestion, completely reject the use of the distinction *per modum voluntatis/nature* in Trinitarian matters, since he explicitly mentions a satisfactory interpretation for the idea of the Holy Spirit's emanation *per modum voluntatis*.

10. WA 9, 45–46. Luther's inference from the biblical idea of the human being created as the image of God to the proposition that the human soul is an image of the Trinity is by no means self-evident, even if it is, in the light of the long tradition of psychological analogy, neither considered far-fetched or at least not unintelligible to his contemporaries. On different interpretations of the psychological analogy in the late Middle Ages, see Kärkkäinen, "Interpretations of the Psychological Analogy."

11. WA 9, 20–21, 38. All translations are mine.

Furthermore, Luther uses a doctrinal formulation of the Fourth Lateran Council, which states that the divine essence does not generate, as a basis for disputing the universal validity of a semantic distinction between two meanings given to the attributes of the divine essence, one of them denoting the essence, the other the persons.[12] It is clear, therefore, that Luther, despite his programmatic note on scriptural authority in theological matters, in his practice of interpreting the *Sentences* continued to accept the formal authority of the Church and even that of Augustine.

The majority of Luther's notes on Book I of the *Sentences* consist of discussions on Trinitarian questions raised by Peter Lombard, which Luther deals with in a similar manner as his scholastic predecessors, above all d'Ailly and Biel. The names of God are, according to Luther, derived from creatures; they designate God only in an improper manner by means of similarity.[13] In his notes on *De vera religione* from the same period of time, Luther discusses Augustine's view that the similarity between God and creation is based on Christ as the creative *Logos*. According to Luther, Christ is the similarity itself that establishes the similarity between God, on the one hand, and the image of God in human beings and all the creatures, on the other.[14]

In good Augustinian manner, Luther stresses the ineffability of Trinitarian matters.[15] Nonetheless, he is not shy about using the semantic machinery of his predecessors to address the problems of Trinitarian theology. That is, for example, how Luther tries to solve the problems involving distinction 25, where quotations from Augustine seem to suggest that person is the same as essence. Luther notes that "person is a common name (*nomen commune*), whereas essence is a common thing (*res communis*)." Luther's wording resembles a distinction made by Pierre d'Ailly, according to which certain names of God, such as "person" and "*suppositum*," are classified as "common personal names." The source of confusion is that such names designate all three persons as common nouns and, due to the identity between essence and persons, the divine

---

12. WA 9, 34–35.
13. WA 9, 47, 58.
14. WA 9, 13–14.
15. WA 9, 20, 47.

essence as well. "Essence" names the divine essence common to all the persons, but does not designate the persons *qua* persons.[16]

A noteworthy feature in Luther's Trinitarian semantics is his interpretation of the traditional notion of Trinitarian appropriation (*appropriatio*). "Love" as a property of the Holy Spirit is appropriated to the third person on the basis of the biblical mode of speech; there are no logical reasons for such a procedure, by which "love" might also designate the common divine essence, which is in fact another acceptable use of the term for Luther.[17] He also uses the notion of appropriation to substantiate his rejection of Scotus's notion of formally distinct principles of generation and spiration in God. Like Pierre d'Ailly, he solves the related problems with the help of the appropriation of the will of God to the Holy Spirit.[18]

Luther also devotes considerable attention to another related theme: whether it is permitted to use the terms "God," "essence," and "wisdom" to denote both divine persons and the divine essence. In one case he seems to reject the use of the term "God" to denote the individual persons, since that would imply that there are three Gods and three objects of adoration. Later on he notes that it is allowed to use "God" in this way, calling on the authority of Pierre d'Ailly, who even considers such sentences as "there are three Gods" to be true, although he does not allow them to be used because of the possibility of heretical misunderstanding. There is also a very strong reason for allowing the application of the term "God" to the individual persons: the wording of the Nicene Creed. Without allowing such a use of language, the formulation "God from God" would became suspect. In distinction 5, Luther notes that on the grounds of such a use of language, one could argue against Peter Lombard's position that the Father did not beget the divine essence: if "God," "wisdom," and "light" can be predicated of individual persons, why not "essence"? He concludes that the philosophical reasons (*rationes*) are not decisive,

---

16. *WA* 9, 48. The end of the text ("Non autem sic est omnino de essentia, quia hoc est actu significans terminus") is a bit obscure. Wieneke (*Luther und Petrus Lombardus*, 128) maintains that Luther is simply identifying person with essence.

17. *WA* 9, 51; Kärkkäinen, *Luthers*, 50–52; Wieneke, *Luther und Petrus Lombardus*, 135.

18. See *WA* 9, 45–46; Pierre d'Ailly, *Quaestiones*, Book I, qu. 6.

but that the theological ones are: in this case the decree of the Fourth Lateran Council must guide the use of the terms.[19]

It should be noted that even if Luther did not allow "essence" to be used as a designation of the individual divine persons, in another context he notes that the Fathers, such as Augustine, sometimes use "nature" in a sense that makes it a "transcendental term." Luther apparently means that it can be used in the same way as *res* ("thing" or "entity") and other transcendental terms. According to traditional usage, *res* could be predicated either of the essence or of the persons; in this sense nature, too, could then be predicated of the persons. Luther is aware that this kind of usage contradicts distinction 5 of the first Book.[20]

Luther is inclined to limit the use of some attributes such as "wisdom" and "goodness" to denote only the persons of the Son and the Spirit. He is aware that Augustine did not make such a restriction, but used those terms as names of the divine essence also. On that matter Luther does not dare to contradict the Church Father. Nonetheless, he expresses his own opinion, which would be to treat those terms as relational, analogously to such terms as "father" and "son." This would imply that the divine Father could be called "wise" only in regard to having a Son, who is the wisdom of the Father. Similarly, the Father would be called "good" only through the Holy Spirit, who is his goodness.[21]

On the question of whether the procession of the Holy Spirit from the Father and the Son (*filioque*) is fundamental for the distinction between the persons of the Son and the Spirit, Luther seems to favor Pierre d'Ailly's view rather than Biel's. Luther ties the procession of the Spirit as love to the notion of the human soul as an image of the Trinity.[22] The

---

19. See *WA* 9, 34, 35–35, 5. It is too much to say, as Wieneke does (*Luther und Petrus Lombardus*, 117), that Luther is negating the distinction between essence and person; he merely applies Peter Lombard's idea that the divine essence is present in each of the persons (see *Sentences* I, dist. 5, chap. 1, no. 1), which makes it possible to say that "God the Father is the divine essence" (chap. 1, no. 3). If one applied the same idea to the Son, it would be entirely consistent to say that an essence begets an essence, although, according to Luther, this is obviously not acceptable. See *WA* 9, 35, 6–8.

20. See *WA* 9, 84.

21. See *WA* 9, 38; see also *WA* 9, 19; 20–21 (marginal notes on Augustine's *De Trinitate*). Luther argues that there is an inconsistency in Augustine's wording in different passages, but warns against rash statements because of the ineffability of the matter. See White, *Luther as Nominalist*, 196–200.

22. See *WA* 9, 46; Pierre d'Ailly, *Quaestiones*, I, qu. 8; Gabriel Biel, *Coll*, Book I, dist. 13, qu. un. A.

crucial role of the *Filioque* reappears in Luther's later works, although he never thoroughly discusses the problems concerning the distinction between the divine persons.[23]

The criticism of Scotus, then, seems to be his only emphatic comment in relation to the work of the Trinity toward the world, which was to become the main focus of Luther's Trinitarian theology in later years. Luther considers Scotus's position, according to which the enjoyment of one Trinitarian person without the enjoyment of another is not contradictory, as an almost heretical statement.[24] Luther's own statements on the matter are largely governed by the Augustinian principle of the indivisibility of the works of the Trinity *ad extra*.[25] However, this principle does not prevent him from ascribing some works of the Trinity to individual persons, such as the infusion of charity to the Holy Spirit.[26]

His anti-Scotist tones and use of semantic strategies mark Luther's notes on the first book as belonging distinctly to *via moderna*-style commentary. There are nonetheless some signs of a humanist return to the sources, above all to Augustine and the Bible.

TRINITY AND THEOLOGICAL PSYCHOLOGY

During the early Wittenberg years Luther's theology was gradually transformed into its mature, reformatory form. The transformation even concerned his theology of the Trinity to a degree. One of the topics where certain change can be observed is the use of the psychological analogy of the Trinity. In his early lectures Luther uses this doctrine as a given part of the traditional theology, although he frequently stressed the radical corruption of human mental powers caused by the Fall.[27]

In most cases the psychological analogy occurs in the analysis of spiritual life. After a description of the fallen state of the faculties of the soul, Luther explains how individual persons of the Trinity heal the diverse faculties by divine grace. The focus is therefore in a certain sense psychological rather than Trinitarian. Luther aims at elucidat-

---

23. Kärkkäinen, *Luthers*, 115–16. See also Knuuttila & Saarinen, "Innertrinitarische Theologie" and Bielfeldt, "Luther's Late Trinitarian Disputations."

24. See WA 9, 43: "error et heresi proxima sententia Scoti." On this view and the related late medieval discussions, see Kitanov, *Beatific Enjoyment*, 178–216.

25. See, e.g., WA 9, 39; 43.

26. See WA 9, 42.

27. Wieneke, *Luther und Petrus Lombardus*, 149–52; Kärkkäinen, *Luthers*, 85–87.

ing the powers of the soul and how they resemble the persons of the Trinity rather than the relationships between the Trinitarian persons. Consequently, the difference between the mental powers, on one hand, in their natural fallen state and, on the other hand, as renewed by grace, plays a vital role. Like his late medieval predecessors, Luther thought that without grace, the image of the Trinity is to be found in the human being only in a much diminished manner:

> These three powers of the soul, intellect, will and memory, remain even in the baptised in weakness and in a stall, where they continuosly need care.[28]

> First [temptation] concerns intellect, second affect and third memory, since none of these three is cured and sound in the moment of our baptism...These three evils meet the soul through sin, since by turning away from God the Father, the memory of the soul is weakened, from God the Son intellect is gone blind and from God the Holy Spirit the soul is inclined to evil and reluctant to good, since power is appropriated to the Father, wisdom to the Son and goodness to the Holy Spirit.[29]

Luther likes to link the Trinitarian persons to respective powers of the soul through appropriations, which he had already utilized in the early marginal notes in Erfurt.[30] The term "appropriation" is here to be understood in a technical sense. The term was considered to be an appropriation of a Trinitarian person, if it was not an exclusive property (like fatherhood) nor an equally common attribute of three persons (like divinity), but a common attribute which was particularly attributed to one of the Trinitarian persons.[31] In Wittenberg Luther developed further the idea of the appropriations being based on the language of the Scriptures, which was already present in his early marginal notes.[32] Along with the psychological analogy, the Trinitarian appropriations form the basis from which Luther several times in the early Wittenberg writings draws the persons of the Trinity in the descriptions of the renewal of mental powers by grace:

---

28. WA 55/2, 830.
29. WA 55/1, 716.
30. Kärkkäinen, *Luthers*, 85–86.
31. Ibid., 119; 125.
32. Jansen, *Studien*, 68; Kärkkäinen, *Luthers*, 118–26.

> The blessed Trinity performs a threefold enlargement of his living image, which is human being. Intellect is enlarged by learning and understanding, memory or substance or nature of the soul is enlarged by the virtue and power of grace and will is enlarged by joy and consolation.[33]

> None of us is not sick and wounded by these three vices [blindness of reason, desire of evil and hate of the good] of the first sin and therefore not in need of a doctor, who cures the three parts of the soul through power of the Father regarding the irascible part, through truth of the Son regarding the rational part and through sweetness of the Holy Spirit regarding the desiring part.[34]

> The Father wants that we look at Christ's humanity, and love him in return, but also that we think that he has done this all by his order and because of his most noble benevolence. Otherwise it is frightening to think of Christ. The power is attributed to the Father, the wisdom to the Son, and the benevolence is attributed to the Holy Spirit.[35]

Already at this stage it is evident that the psychological analogy is not an indispensable part of Luther's theological thinking, even if he uses it in a positive sense. In 1523/24 he seems to consciously ignore the topic in the interpretation of Gen 1:26.[36] In the late *Lectures on Genesis* Luther expresses suspicion of the doctrine because of some interpretations based on it. His target is a particular teaching that argues for the freedom of choice by appealing to the psychological analogy of the Trinity.[37]

Luther's remarks have been considered by many theologians, both Catholic and Protestant, as a rejection of the psychological analogy. The remark in the *Lectures on Genesis*, where Luther mentions the doctrine of the freedom of choice and the psychological analogy together, has gained special attention. Karl Barth considered it particularly insightful and a good reason for the rejection of the psychological analogy.[38] The problem with Barth's view is that Luther's awareness of the theories

---

33. *WA* 55/2, 59–60.
34. *WA* 1, 86.
35. *WA* 1, 274.
36. *WA* 24, 49.
37. *WA* 42, 45.
38. See Jansen, *Studien*, 172; Wieneke, *Luther und Petrus Lombardus*, 153.

which argued for the freedom of choice on the basis of the psychological analogy did not lead him to reject the analogy, but merely to sustain his judgment concerning it. One cannot even say whether Luther considered such arguments coherent.

However, it would be too much to say that Luther would have intentionally and unequivocally given up the long tradition and disagreed with Augustine. What is clear is that he gave up the doctrine of psychological analogy as an indisputable piece of tradition. However, Luther did not reject the language of analogies or vestiges of the Trinity in general. This has partly to do with the language of the Bible, from which he continually drew metaphorical expressions about God, in which psychological terms were attributed to individual Trinitarian persons. But Luther's analogies of the Trinity were not confined to biblical metaphors:

> It is as if Christ establishes a kind of divine school, where Father is the speaker, who produces the Son, the Son is the produced word and the Holy Spirit the listener.[39]

CATECHISMS AND THE TRINITY *AD EXTRA*

The expositions of the Apostles' Creed in the *Small* and *Large Catechism* present a version of Luther's Trinitarian theology, which is strongly focused on the salvation-historical work of the Trinity in the world. It is precisely this version that has been most widely regarded as articulating Luther's view of the Trinity. Among the writings of Luther, the catechisms have made the most enduring contribution to the theology of the Trinity, not least because of their inclusion into the *Book of Concord*. Consequently, a fair amount of interest has been devoted to them in scholarly studies.[40]

However, it would be a mistake to judge Luther's Trinitarian thinking in the catechisms in isolation from his other works. A comparison with the earlier catechism sermons reveal that while some themes of discussion had many parallels in his earlier sermons, other features look more like temporary peculiarities which do not form a permanent part of Luther's theological thinking. This last group includes the notion that

---

39. WA 59, 298. For Luther's use of vestiges of the Trinity, see Jansen, *Studien*, 192-94; Kärkkäinen, *Luthers*, 87-89.

40. See, for example, Jansen, *Studien*, 74-86; Peters, *Kommentar zu Luthers Katechismen II*; Herms, *Luthers Auslegung des Dritten Artikels*.

Luther did use the word "Trinity" in the *Large Catechism* and that he was also generally cautious in using the traditional Trinitarian terminology at that time.[41]

Among the permanent features of Luther's Trinitarian thinking which underlie the expositions of the Creed in the catechisms, first and foremost is the use of the Trinitarian appropriations. Luther divided the Creed into three parts, which he considered narrations of three works of the triune God, namely creation, redemption, and sanctification.[42] Furthermore, he understood each of these three works to be appropriated in a special way to one of the persons of the Trinity, although none of the persons were excluded in the absolute sense of any of the three works.[43]

This way of using the appropriations was not common in traditional Trinitarian theology, but for Luther it seems to have provided a way to incorporate his scripturally based theology into a more general framework of Trinitarian theology. The specific works of the individual persons were, according to Luther, derived from the Scriptures, as was also the whole content of the Apostles Creed. This seems to be the setting in which Luther's sayings about knowing God through his works should be understood.[44]

In the catechisms Luther also stated very clearly that knowing the Trinitarian God does not consist of mere affirmation of a correct doctrine on the relationships between the Trinitarian persons. True faith has necessarily a personal character: it includes the affirmation that God is not only the Godhead in himself, but also God *for us*. Although Luther brings out this idea often as a general notion of God and faith, in the catechisms it is expressly articulated in Trinitarian terms:

> Therefore the Ten Commandments do not succeed in making us Christians, for God's wrath and displeasure still remain upon us because we cannot fulfill what God demands of us. But the Creed brings pure grace and makes us righteous and acceptable to God. Through this knowledge we come to love and delight in all the commandments of God because we see here in the Creed how

---

41. Jansen, *Studien*, 85.

42. On Luther's division of the Creed into three parts according to the persons of the Trinity, see ibid., 23–35.

43. Ibid., 68.

44. Ibid., 59–72.

God gives himself completely to us, with all his gifts and power, to help us keep the Ten Commandments: the Father gives us all creation, Christ all his works, the Holy Spirit all his gifts.[45]

This quotation summarizes one fundamental strand in Luther's Trinitarian theology. The knowledge of God comes about in a Trinitarian form from the outset, first through the work of creation attributed to the Father, then through redemption attributed to the Son. Both of these are received through the gifts of the indwelling Spirit, who makes the work of the Trinity a reality *for us* through faith and incites us to love, which is the fulfillment of the law.[46]

In the final analysis, Luther's way of describing the salvific knowledge of God is not that far from a traditional view of the perfection of the image of the Trinity in acts of knowing and loving God.[47] The decisive factor is Luther's preference of a specifically biblical and theological conceptualization instead of a scholastic fusion of a philosophical psychology and the doctrine of theological virtues. Faith as a theological understanding and love as a theological will are faculties given through a process where the Father himself comes to abide in a believer as Son and Spirit. While theological faculties of attaining God, faith, and love on one hand presuppose the presence of the divine, on the other hand they imply a specific personal relationship with God.[48]

Although Luther described the presence and operation of the Trinity in the believer with the help of psychological terminology, he did not see the manifestation of the Trinity as being confined to the categories of the internal and the spiritual. One of the basic tenets of Luther's theology is to see the work of God as sacramental, bound to the external, corporeal reality. True to this understanding Luther joined the long tradition of exposing certain central events of salvation history as visible self-manifestations of the Trinity. In addition to Christ's incarnation as the visible manifestation of the Second Person, these included the baptism of Christ in Jordan, the Transfiguration and the miracles on the Pentecost Day.[49]

---

45. *BC*, Creed, Third Article, 68–69.
46. On faith and love, see Kärkkäinen, *Luthers trinitarische Theologie*, 102–12; 145–52.
47. On psychological analogy before Luther, see Kärkkäinen, "Interpretations."
48. Kärkkäinen, *Luthers trinitarische Theologie*, 146–49.
49. Jansen, *Studien*, 188–92; Kärkkäinen, *Luthers trinitarische Theologie*, 160–93.

THE TRINITY AND LUTHER'S LATE THEOLOGY

The developments in Wittenberg theology in the 1530s had some influence on Luther's late view of the Trinity. During the 1530s disputations were reintroduced in theology. Together with the growing worry about the emerging anti-Trinitarian movements, this resulted in a number of disputations on matters of Trinitarian theology, which form a distinctive contribution to Luther's work on the topic.[50]

Above all, the late disputations show that Luther did not simply abandon the importance of philosophical theology in Trinitarian matters. On the contrary, the Trinity (and Christology) shows up as a topic, as it had for centuries, when central questions concerning the philosophy of logic and language, as well as metaphysics, are discussed. Although Luther had already in his early disputation *Against Scholastic Theology* (1517) criticized the use of syllogistic reasoning in theology and carried on similar thoughts in his later disputations, such thoughts did not lead him to abandon the use of logic and disputations in theology altogether.[51] However, the main focus of the disputations was apologetic: the disputations were carried out in order to equip the students with arguments against those who denied the doctrine of the Trinity. In addition to the Scriptures, the main devices were found from philosophy, particularly from logic, and therefore Luther went back to the resources he had gained through his scholastic education.[52]

Some details of the disputations reveal that Luther still shared certain positions of the scholastic *via moderna*. For example, he criticized Scotus's use of formal distinction in intra-Trinitarian matters.[53] Generally speaking, he used the logical analysis he had learned from Pierre d'Ailly's commentaries. He also developed anew some topics of his scholastic youth, which were set in a new perspective after the definite break with the authority of the medieval councils. So we find him

---

50. Brecht, *Martin Luther 3*, 131–37. On Luther's Trinitarian disputations, see Helmer, *Trinity and Martin Luther*, 42–120.

51. Knuuttila, "Luther's View of Logic".

52. Helmer, *Trinity and Martin Luther*, 46–50; White, *Luther as Nominalist*, 181–230.

53. WA 39/II, 363–64; White, *Luther as Nominalist*, 222–23; 229; Helmer, *Trinity and Martin Luther*, 100–101.

advocating the doctrine that the divine essence generates, which was condemned by the Fourth Lateran Council.[54]

Luther did not only use the logical approach as an exercise. In the *First disputation against the Antinomians* Luther answers his opponents by devising a conceptual distinction, which sounds at the same time both traditional and innovative, and is closely tied to his reformatory views of God:

> Therefore, we distinguish between the Holy Spirit as "God in his divine nature and substance" and "given to us" . . . To sum up, insofar as the Holy Spirit is "God in his nature," he is lawgiver, without which law does not accuse of sin; insofar as he is gift given through Christ, he is our vivifier and sanctifier.[55]

By using this distinction, Luther tries to convince his opponents that their view that the Ten Commandments do not belong to the work of the Holy Spirit is mislead. The related part of the disputation hints at the unrealized potential of combining conceptual analysis and the new reformatory view of the Trinity, which Luther partly brought into the light in his last years.[56]

Still, perhaps the most profound contribution of late Luther is to be found in his lifelong devotion to the interpretation of the Bible. As a conclusion of his analysis of one of Luther's last publications in this field, *On the Last Words of David* (1543), Mickey Mattox has suggested that the aged Reformer became wary of the misuse of new exegetical devices, which had formed the basis for his own novel interpretation against the authorities of the medieval Church. Therefore he had turned towards a more straightforwardly Trinitarian interpretation of several biblical passages, such as 2 Samuel 23, which was the main topic of the treatise, and saw more hints of the Trinitarian doctrine than had either his medieval predecessors or some contemporary anti-Trinitarians such as Servetus. Even if he did not find exact precedents for his particular interpretations, Luther considered himself as the follower of the Trinitarian theology of the "dear" fathers and the medieval Church.[57]

---

54. WA 39/II, 288; Helmer, *Trinity and Martin Luther*, 107–13; White, *Luther as Nominalist*, 181–220.

55. StA 5, 256; 281.

56. For a more detailed discussion of the distinction, see Kärkkäinen, *Luthers trinitarische Theologie*, 134–41.

57. Mattox, "From Faith to the Text," 300–1. See also Mattox, "Luther's Interpretation."

Luther even accuses his adversaries Eck and Cochlaeus of sharing Servetus' heresy, since all of them maintain that the doctrine of the Trinity was not articulated until the early Church by John the Evangelist. Thus with similar argumentation Luther could oppose on such diverse fronts, which he saw as separating Scripture and dogma from each other in a wrong way.[58]

CONCLUSION

Luther's theology of the Trinity reveals perhaps more the many other fields of his thinking a strong urge for returning to the sources of true theology. From his earliest years on, these sources consisted of the Scriptures, but not of them alone, but also of the theology of the ancient Church, which formulated it into Trinitarian creeds and which was for the most part passed down in the Church up to his own time. Guided by such a vision, Luther provided the later Reformation with a treasury of a new kind of Trinitarian theology even if he did not ever collect his views into one systematic treatise.

---

58. WA 39/II, 290. See Helmer, *Trinity and Martin Luther*, 65–66. On other topics of Trinitarian theology in old Luther, see Helmer, *Trinity and Martin Luther*, 67–119.

5

Baptism

Eeva Martikainen

MARTIN LUTHER'S CONCEPT OF baptism is decidedly marked by his Trinitarian theology and understanding of salvation history. Its theocentricity is concrete, dynamic, and strongly rooted in history.[1] Creation and redemption are two different events, but redemption takes place among the creatures and through them. Since the finite can contain the infinite (*finitum capax infiniti*), God is immediately present in material reality (ubiquity). The relationship between the divine and human nature in Christ constitutes the model for this presence.[2] The material aspect of baptism, its mark and sign, is therefore not something inessential that could point to an essential spiritual event beyond itself; rather God is at work in the sign itself.[3] The hypothesis that baptism is an act performed by God must be seen in the context of the christological inter-penetration of creation and redemption.[4]

Luther's view of baptism was marked by clear continuity between the date of *De captivitate* (1520) and that of his catechisms (1529). The

---

1. WA 26, 505, 38–507, 16. See also Althaus, *Theologie Martin Luthers*, 297–317; Hermann, *Luthers Theologie*, 179–183; Jetter, *Taufe beim jungen Luther*; Grönvik, *Taufe in der Theologie Martin Luthers*, 12–54; Maurer, *Historischer Kommentar zur Confessio Augustana* II, 185.

2. Grönvik, *Die Taufe*, 24–40.

3. WA Tr, 4, 666, 7–10. no 5106: "*Signum philosophicum est nota absentis rei, signum theologicum est nota praesentis rei...*" WA 45, 174, 19–27. Grönvik, *Taufe*, 41, 55–65. Mannermaa, *Der im Glauben gegenwärtige Christus*, 88–89.

4. Grönvik, *Taufe*, 41–45.

former is one of the most important Reformation documents and the latter forms part of the normative Lutheran confessional writings. This continuity also applies to the way in which he understands the inner and outer work of the Spirit, to his concept of the total gift of divine communion to which human beings always have free access through faith, and to his explanation of *fides infantium*, the faith of children.

In his confession of 1528, Luther touched on baptism and a number of elements closely related to it, all of which are connected with faith. The article on faith also constitutes the substance of the framework within which Luther situates baptism. He states that he confesses his faith "bit by bit" before God and the whole world so that after his death no one could say whether Luther were alive now he would have taught this or that article differently.[5] This confession clearly points to the context in salvation history within which Luther situates baptism. Here he describes the working of the Trinity as God's giving of himself to humankind.[6] God gives himself in three ways: in creation, in Christ, and in the working of the Spirit both inwardly and outwardly. The external work of the Spirit consists of distributing the work of Christ in word and sacrament, and the internal work is the faith that is kindled in human beings who receive the gift rightly and are made them into new persons. The train of all of Luther's baptismal theology is clearly expressed in his understanding of the gift of baptism as the total gift of God's presence and of salvation. Because God gives himself holistically to human beings, baptism implies new life with all its aspects: Forgiveness of sins, communion with God, and the fruits produced by the baptized can be specifically mentioned here. The relation between baptism and the church is also clearly expressed.

In his sermons on baptism (1530), Luther emphasizes that being baptized means being in Christ. Baptism constitutes communion and participation, because all the baptized share in Christ and his goodness.[7] This understanding of the presence of God has an eschatological reference and implies that baptism as God's work is comprised of the whole of time with its promise. It anticipates eternity and simultaneously receives its fulfillment in eternity. There is a fundamental agreement among

---

5. WA 26, 499, 15.

6. WA 30 I, 44, 28–45, 13; Jansen, *Studien zur Luthers Trinitätslehre*, 68–69.

7. WA 31/I, 167, 27–31; Elert, *Abendmahl*, 8; Peters, *Kommentar zu Luthers Katechismen II*, 41–42, 218–20; Lutz, *Unio*, 291–92.

scholars that Luther understood baptism as a unique and unrepeatable sacrament. It is given only once and must not be repeated.

GOD'S OMNIPRESENCE AS A PREREQUISITE FOR HIS SAVING PRESENCE IN BAPTISM

Luther's thinking, characterized by a Trinitarian understanding of salvation history, is of fundamental importance for his baptismal theology: God's omnipresence in creation forms a kind of prerequisite for his saving presence in the sacrament of baptism. This helps explain the strong emphasis on the element and the sign which a later, idealistic tradition has often found objectionable. In Luther's view, God must not and cannot be brought to a place where he was not already present anyway. Creation and baptism are both seen as direct works of the God who is present.

As early as 1519, Luther describes baptism as a new birth or new creation.[8] The new creation brought about by Christ and baptism re-establishes communion with the Creator. The person who is recreated in baptism is still a person created by God, though he is someone who has turned away from God. And God's coming in the elements of the sacrament demonstrates that God comes in baptism to his own possession.[9] A new determination of the relationship between God and the outward, material world is characteristic of Luther, who does not conceive of God and the material world as two isolated entities, which must first be brought into a relationship. Luther sees these as a unity. Luther's view of reality implies a radical break with any ontology based on discrete things and places. God is not tied to any fixed point, and the whole of space is equal before him.[10] God is directly present in creation and, at the same time, he demonstrates that he is the sovereign Lord in relation to creation.[11] Luther's statement about the omnipresence and working of God in creation also corresponds to the main concern in Luther's baptismal theology and influences his understanding of creation, Christology, and sacraments. Nowhere does Luther see the spiritual-divine in isolation or separated from the bodily-concrete. God is at work in the finite and

---

8. WA 2, 728, 1; 729, 3.
9. Grönvik, *Die Taufe*, 22–29.
10. Metzke, *Sakrament und Metaphysik*, 41.
11. WA 23, 139, 18–19.

the earthly. He who fills heaven and earth is not distant but near and present.[12]

Luther's view of God and the world thus also implies for the sacraments that the same God, who is present everywhere in the material world as Creator meets us in the sacraments, in the outward elements, in order to give of himself and therein is his gift to human beings. Both in creation and in baptism, therefore, God is acting through outward elements, and in both cases God is acting through his word. So the omnipresence of God in creation does not exclude his special presence in baptism, preaching, and Holy Communion. Instead, his omnipresence forms the background and, one might say, is a prerequisite for his being present preaching and sacrament. Christ himself is omnipresent and not tied to any place or outward thing. Although the body of Christ is everywhere, we will not for that reason so easily eat or drink or grasp it. God's right hand is certainly everywhere but at the same time nowhere and beyond our grasp. "There is a difference between his presence and your grasping."[13]

Although the whole triune God is present and acting in baptism, baptism is still seen primarily as the work of the Holy Spirit. The Spirit has a special function in distributing the gift of Christ and applying salvation of which baptism with preaching and the Holy Communion are a part. On this basis, no later or additional question arises for Luther about how the Spirit could be given still greater emphasis in connection with the sacrament.

THE OUTWARD WORK OF THE HOLY SPIRIT IN BAPTISM: WORD AND WATER

In baptism, as in salvation as a whole, God acts through outward means. Just as with Christ's humanity, so too in baptism, the water and the word we find something external through which God himself acts. In the Large Confession of 1528, the connection Luther sees between Christology and the understanding of baptism can be readily identified.[14] It must be mentioned of course that he underlines a difference between the acquisition of salvation and the imparting of salvation. However, both in

---

12. *WA* 23, 131; Metzke, *Sakrament und Metaphysik*, 27.
13. *WA* 23, 149, 31–34.
14. Grönvik, *Taufe*, 34; Prenter, *Spiritus Creator*, 5, 26.

Christ's incarnation and in baptism, God comes to human beings and acts in relation to them. Both are God's work: in both "the Christ event" and "the baptismal event" God himself is the actor. Both cases concern a "treasure which he gives us and which faith grasps."[15]

Moreover, Christ and baptism are also the same because, according to the principle "Abuse does not destroy the essence but confirms it," both are still works of God even without faith.[16] "Indeed, my faith does not make baptism, but receives baptism."[17] Human beings are given a share in Christ's unique work through baptism. The view that God's work is performed through outward means and his presence comes about in the midst of the external is of central importance for Luther's Christology and teaching about baptism. Here, the work of Christ is incorporated into the work of the Spirit. In baptism, the Spirit comes "to us and the suffering of Christ in us brings about and bestows blessedness."[18] This concept is also evident in the Smalcald Articles in which Luther discusses the various forms of the Gospel. God is rich in grace and causes the Gospel to come to people in different ways.[19]

The theoretical quantification of *pro nobis* determines Luther's interpretation: it is God himself who is for us. Baptism is therefore not a projection of a human decision, nor is it by nature information about a distant God; rather God himself is really present in the outward sign and is acting here on behalf of human beings. Luther's understanding of the word and the sacraments is initially marked by his attributing to the word, namely, the Gospel, the same status as the sacraments, namely equal means of grace. The word is understood sacramentally, meaning that it is the real presence of God himself. Christ comes to human beings in sermons as well as in the sacraments. For Luther, the concept "word" means the creative, direct, self-giving presence of God himself. Word is thus understood in the category of God's presence and not the other way around. Against this background, Luther sees the relationships between baptism and the sermon and Holy Communion, but also the various functions of the word in baptism.

15. WA 30/I, 216, 31–34.
16. WA 30/I, 219, 27.
17. WA 30/I, 218, 30–31.
18. WA 26, 506, 10–12.
19. WA 50, 240, 27–241, 3.

This understanding of baptism as God's work also demonstrates Luther's view that God's concrete action in relation to humankind takes place through ordinances that God himself has willed and instituted. The fact that God is "there for you" means precisely his presence in the forms of the Gospel in which he offers and gives himself to human beings so that he can be received through them in faith. Since God is bound to his word and promise, human beings are freed from the task of seeking God everywhere. The terms "sign," "word," and "promise" all show themselves in baptism to be all strongly related to the present: Christ is present *hic et nunc* and gives us the kingdom of heaven. But at the same time there is also a pointer to the coming physical death and the coming bodily resurrection.

THE INNER WORK OF THE SPIRIT IN BAPTISM: FAITH AS SHARING IN CHRIST

The difference between the outward and the inward work of the Spirit is clearly expressed in Luther's Large Confession (1528). First, he describes the work of the Father and of the Son and then the work of the Spirit, which consists of giving human beings a share in Christ's work.[20] Luther's unified, closed conception of baptism and faith also proves to be an expression of his Reformation theology as a whole. In particular, we must recall his statements about faith itself, which is never complete, and his view that faith is concerned repeatedly with the works and promises of God. If this concern is ignored, one loses sight of the whole of Luther's evangelical doctrine of justification; this would be the equivalent of returning to Luther's penetrating questions and temptations during his monastic struggle. By means of the view that, in baptism, human beings receive a total gift and communion with God to which they always have free access, Luther is able to overcome both the scholastic and the enthusiastic approach.

Luther's view of infant baptism and of a child's faith corresponds to his view of baptism and faith as a whole. In his arguments for infant baptism, it is the reasoning that begins from an overall conception, which proves decisive. With regard to the fides infantium we should note that what is constitutive for faith is that it is allowed to be "being-in-the-hand-of-Christ," which naturally does not exclude but rather includes

---

20. WA 26, 506, 7–12.

that, for adults who have an awareness of their own, conscious listening also plays a natural and important part.

In baptism, newborn children receive their own faith, according to Martin Luther's teaching. This teaching was also incorporated into the Large Catechism and thus forms part of the authoritative tradition of the Lutheran church.[21] Based on the evidence, there is no question that Luther understood faith, including the faith of children, to be God's work and God's gift. And yet the question does arise of what Luther meant by these words. How does God give faith and what does God give when he gives human beings faith?

Since baptism is God's work and gift, baptizing people cannot add anything to this, nor is any kind of addition needed. Even in *De captivitate* we can find several passages where Luther speaks about the gift of baptism being preserved indestructibly for the whole of a person's life. The passage in which he compares baptism with a ship that cannot sink has become a classic.[22] There, Luther directs his attention to the

---

21. BSELK 702-3; WA 30 1, 218. The study by Karl Brinkel published in 1958 (*Die Lehre Luthers von der fides infantium bei der Kindertaufe*), became fundamental to the discussion of baptism and children's faith. According to Brinkel's thorough investigation, it is generally accepted that Luther's main teaching on children's faith remained unchanged until the 1540s. However, Brinkel's view of the importance of Luther's statements on children's faith in the overall context of Lutheran theology has been subjected to considerable criticism. One of Brinkel's results was his claim that Luther's understanding of children's faith fit perfectly into the reformer's theology as a whole. Brinkel maintained that, by means of the word of God, God tied himself through faith to the child and thus gave to the child faith. The child heard and received God's word because a child is not yet able to reject it. Hence, *fides infantium* is a pure gift of God, which only becomes a reality in the child because God speaks to the child and thus a new child stands before God. So Brinkel understood the faith of the child as being addressed by God with the child being unable to reject God's word. Paul Althaus rejected Brinkel's theory soon after the book appeared. Althaus considered that the reformer's statements on infant faith do not fit the overall context of his real Reformation theology of the faith. Althaus also strongly criticized Brinkel's concept of children's faith as a gift from God. The emphasis on God's work threatened to annul the human-personal reality of faith. Althaus' view that the statements on *fides infantium* were not appropriate to the Reformation was shared by many scholars. Althaus and subsequently many other scholars emphasized that what was characteristic of Luther's Reformation concept of faith was that faith was understood as a "personal act" in which the will, insight, and activity of human beings had a place of their own. According to Althaus, Luther's endeavor to cling to the practice of infant baptism in the church was really in contradiction to the Reformation concept of faith. The discussion is found to a large extent in Huovinen, *Fides Infantium*, 1-21.

22. WA 6, 529, 22-32.

fact that not only does baptism remain unchanged but also the "strength of baptism" (*vis baptismi*) remains unchanged. Hence, baptism not only continues to be God's conditional promise or offer that is always open to human beings, it also continues to have the same effective character with its "strength" and "truth." So Luther's basic argument can be summarized in the statement that "baptism never loses its validity." Human beings can never rid themselves of baptism, of its sign, and certainly not of its "real effect." Therefore *signum*, *vis*, and *res* continue to be realities in the life of the baptized; these realities are always present and do not merely constitute potential possibilities.[23]

In order to understand Luther's intention, attention must first be paid to his view that baptism is effective. In baptism, God's name makes "pure, holy, indeed, nothing but divine people."[24] With its promise and its total gift, baptism continues to exist permanently for repeated, new reception in faith. A Christian must learn throughout life that baptism promises and bestows victory over death and the devil, forgiveness of sins, God's grace, Christ as a whole and the Holy Spirit. What human beings require is not a supplement but reception: a life in baptism and resulting from baptism. In order for a Christian to be totally justified, it is necessary for the Holy Spirit to continue its sanctifying work in the person right up until death.

If "faith returns to, or remains in, God's promise which is given to the baptized," then the "salvation" which has always been and is present becomes indestructible again. So Luther understands the indestructible gift of baptism to mean that its *signum*, its *vis*, and its *res* always remain realities in the lives of human beings. In persons who have lost their faith, the power of the sacrament performs its "alien work" (*opus alienum*), whereas in the believer it does its "own work" (*opus suum*).[25] Without faith the sacrament brings the recipient "great harm." By way of explanation, it should also be recalled that Luther raises this objection specifically to defend the doctrine of *fides infantium*. In his view, at baptism children receive their faith as a gift from God. Therefore, for

---

23. WA 6, 535, 10–14: "Ita semel es baptisatus sacramentaliter, sed semper baptisandus fide, semper moriendum semperque vivendum. Baptismus totum corpus absorbuit et rursus edidit: ita res baptismi totam vitam tuam cum corpore et anima absorbere debet et reddere in novissimo die indutam stola claritatis et immortalitatis."

24. WA 37, 642, 35–643, 6: 643, 32–38.

25. WA 6, 526, 5–10; WA 11, 452, 29–33.

them this baptism is "no harm" but rather a benefit. This idea also sheds light on Luther's view that the gift of baptism is indestructible. Just as God gives faith to the child and thus a blessing is part of baptism, so God and his "truth" can also cause faith to return to the unbelievers and the alien work to become baptism's own work. Just as God, from whom human beings never wander off, always remains God or the Almighty and the Actor, so baptism is always present and at work in the life of the baptized.[26]

On the whole, Luther interprets the efficacy of baptism a uniform way. Baptism is the personal work of the triune God, that is, God himself is the real actor in baptism. The act of baptism consists of the sign (*signum*) and the word. The latter can be presented in three forms that belong unconditionally and organically together: command (*institutio*), baptismal formula (*nomen Dei*), and promise (*promissio*). Word and sign are aspects of one and the same reality, which brings about salvation. God is present in baptism and imparts his grace through it, which is both his favor (*favor*) and his gift (*donum*). Baptism is both *extra nos* and *in nobis*. However, faith is not a structural component of baptism but the *medium receptionis*. Nor is faith the product of human achievement; it is brought about by God's promise.

INFANT BAPTISM: SHARING IN THE WHOLE KINGDOM OF GOD

In his sermon for the third Sunday after Epiphany in the year 1524, Luther opposed the view of the Moravians who claimed that children receive a share in the kingdom of God by being "brought to the Gospel" and are taken into the Christian community, but that children did not share in eternal life. In contrast, Luther believed that, through baptism and the faith that is given to them, children receive "the whole kingdom of God" or true participation in eternal life.[27]

26. WA 26, 165, 7-16. See also Huovinen, *Fides Infantium*, 66-74.
27. WA 17/II, 81, 32-82, 8. Luther describes the situation as follows: "Es hilfft auch nicht, das sie das reich Gott's dreyerley scheyden. Eyn mal sey es die Christliche kirche, das ander mal das ewige leben, zum dritten das Euangelion. Und darnach sagen, die kinder werden zum hymel reich getaufft, auff die dritten und ersten weyse, das ist, sie werden getaufft, nicht das sie da durch selig seyen und vergebung der sunden haben, Sondern sie werden ynn die Christenheyt genomen und zum Euangelio bracht. Das ist alles nichts geredt und aus eygenem dunckel ertichtet. Denn das heysst nicht yns hymelreich komen, das ich unter die Christen kome und das Euangelion höre, wilchs

With his criticism of the Moravians who spoke in three different ways about the kingdom of God, Luther wants to emphasize that children really become "blessed" when they receive God's kingdom. So *fides infantium* does not mean merely coming to church or to the word of the Gospel, but it means "living" and real "being-in-the-kingdom-of-heaven." God's word and Christ's blessing, in fact, do not treat the baptized like an insensitive "block" or "lump," but rather give the child the promised blessings. In this way Luher emphasizes the participation brought about through the child's faith when he states that children receive the "true kingdom of heaven."[28]

The real participation of children's faith in Christ is also articulated by Luther in a number of "figurative" expressions in which he presents the way Christ related to the children who were brought to him. It is hardly a coincidence that he regularly emphasizes the concrete, "physical" nature of Christ's work. "At the same time, he commands us to bring the children to him, [Matt 19:14], he takes them in his arms, kisses them and says that the kingdom of heaven is theirs."[29]

Christ's blessing, the laying on of hands and the embracing and kissing of the children have great importance. That is precisely how the children receive "the true kingdom of heaven." For Luther, this gift also implies that the children become truly blessed. "For through being brought and coming to Christ they become blessed by his embracing and blessing them and giving them the kingdom."[30] Thus, the faith of the children means that the children really become holy and blessed. They do not receive this holiness without their own faith, which is given to them. So regeneration takes place not just as an effect of baptism without the child's own faith. Both baptism and faith are necessary: baptism

---

auch die heyden thun kunden und on tauffe geschicht. Solchs heyst auch nicht yns hymel reich komen, du redest vom hymelreich auff die erste, ander odder dritten weyse, wie du wilt. Sondern das heysst ym hymelreich seyn, wenn ich ein lebendig gelied der Christenheyt byn und das Euangelion nicht alleyne höre, sondern auch gleube. Sonst were eyn mensch eben ym hymelreich, als wenn ich eynen klotz und bloch unter die Christen wurffe, odder wie der tcuffel unter yhn ist. Darumb taug dis gar nichts."

28 WA 17/II, 83, 24–28: "Wöllen wyr sagen, sie seyen on eygen glauben gewesen, so sind die vorigen spruch falsch: Wer nicht gleubt, der ist verdampt etcete. So wird auch Christus liegen oder spiegelfechten, da er sagt, das hymelreich sey yhr, und wird nicht mit ernst vom rechten hymelreich reden."

29. WA 26, 157, 7–8.

30. WA 26, 157, 35–36: "Denn durchs brengen und komen zu Christo werden sie so selig, das er sie hertzet, segenet und das reich gibt."

brings about faith and in this way the child receives God's righteousness and holiness.

In order to understand Luther's view it is important to remember that children not only receive the characteristic of holiness itself when they become holy, but they also receive God's own holiness. In baptism they receive simultaneously faith and "the Spirit," that is, the Holy Spirit or God himself. Instead of receiving only a supernatural effect of grace, the child participates in God's own self. In the letter about re-baptism, Luther expresses this idea in a passage a comparing the child's faith with the faith of John the Baptist before he was born. Christ speaks at baptism through the mouth of the priest as he once spoke through John's mother's mouth. Luther asks: "Since he is present there, speaking and baptizing himself, why should not the faith and the Spirit also come into the child through his speaking and baptizing, as he entered there into John?"[31]

The justification of human beings can therefore never be based on created gifts. For the same reason, grace should not be understood as habitual. God's gifts never become inherent human characteristics upon which people can "build." Although Luther rejects the teaching about *habitus*, he still maintains the real character of God's gifts. It is precisely this approach of Luther's that is evident in his interpretation of the Letter to the Romans (1515/1516) in which he also presents God's gifts as real entities. On the one hand Luther rejects the idea that the faith given in baptism is a habitual characteristic but, on the other hand, he emphasizes the real character of this gift at the same time.

Luther clearly assumes that faith is given to human beings through baptism, including to infants. He also states that human beings should not imagine that they "personally" please God, even on the basis of this gift, that is, on the basis of their own qualities. Human beings who place their trust in the supernatural gifts they have been given construct their own righteousness and try in that way to please God "without Christ." But Luther clearly emphasizes that human beings really have this faith (*fidem habere*).[32]

---

31. WA 26, 156, 32-40.

32. WA 56, 298, 27-31: "Ut sunt nunc multi, qui ex operibus fidei etiam sibi faciunt opera legis et Literae, dum accepta fide per baptismum Vel penitentiam iam personaliter etiam ipsi sine Christo Deo placeant, Cum Utrunque sit necessarium Scil. fidem quidem habere, Sed tamen Christum adhuc simul inaeternum habere, in tali fide mediatorem."

Thus, Luther understands *fides infantium* as a real gift that God gives to a child. In baptism the child receives the "strength of baptism." This "absorbs" the child's whole body and soul and grants him/her a real share in God's grace. But Luther does not speak just in the abstract about baptism and the child's faith being real gifts. His true intention is expressed only when he spells out what the content of this gift means. The content of a child's faith as God's real gift is none other than what baptism also gives to the child, namely, a share in God.

Throughout the different periods of his writings, it is typical of Luther's baptismal teaching that the gift of baptism means participating in God, indeed being united with God. This is clearly expressed in his earliest writings on baptism. In his sermon of 1519 on the sacrament of baptism he states: "The honorable sacrament of baptism helps you in that God unites himself with you in it and becomes one with you, forming a gracious, comforting bond."[33]

The teaching on baptism in *De captivitate* is also structured around the idea that baptism brings about a real union between the baptized and Christ. Here it is also clear that Luther considers the effects of baptism in scholastic theology to be too "weak" and "powerless." For him, the gift of baptism resides not only in an abstract effect; but it also constitutes a real union with Christ.[34] The profound and "complete" event of baptism consists of its really linking the baptized with Christ's death and resurrection.[35]

There are other central passages on baptism in Luther's writings, which also treat the gift of baptism as a real link with God or as a real

---

33. WA 2, 730, 20-22: "Das hilfft dir das hochwirdige sacrament der tauff, das sich gott daselbs mit dyr vorpindet und mit dyr eyns wird eyns gnedigen trostlichen bunds."

34. WA 6, 534, 6-17: "Consepulti enim sumus Christo per baptismum in mortem, ut, quemadmodum Christus resurrexit ex mortuis per gloriam patris, ita et nos in novitate vitae ambulemus. Hanc mortem et resurrectionem appellamus novam creaturam, regenerationem et spiritualem nativitatem, quam non oportet allegorice tantum intelligi de morte peccati et vita gratiae, sicut multi solent, sed de vera morte et resurrectione. Non enim baptismus significatio ficta est . . . fides vere sit mors et resurrectio hoc est spiritualis ille baptismus, quo immergimur et emergimus."

35. WA 6, 534, 18-26: "Quod ergo. . . Hac ratione motus vellem baptisandos penitus in aquam immergi, sicut sonat vocabulum et signat mysterium, non quod necessarium arbitrer, sed quod pulchrum foret, rei tam perfectae et plenae signum quoque plenum et perfectum dari, sicut et institutum est sine dubio a Christo. Peccator enim non tam ablui quam mori debet, ut totus renovetur in aliam creaturam, et ut morti ac resurrectioni Christi respondeat, cui per baptismum commoritur et corresurgit."

gift to human beings. In the Large Catechism, Luther speaks repeatedly about baptism as a "treasure" or "medicine," which God gives or administers to the baptized. "And so you see clearly that it is not a work we do but a treasure which he gives us and which faith grasps, just as the Lord Christ on the cross was not a work but a treasure contained in a word and presented to us and received by faith."[36]

This passage from the Large Catechism also shows that Luther understood the gift as a real gift given to human beings. Christ is certainly present in the word or "contained in the word." Christ's presence does not "stop" at the instrumental word but becomes a "treasure" given to us through the mediation of the word. Similarly, the gift of baptism is also a treasure, which God gives and which human beings grasp and therefore possess in faith. That is exactly how Luther understands the gift of baptism when speaking of the faith of children. On the one hand, the child receives its own faith through baptism and, on the other, precisely through this faith the child comes to Christ himself. So the child does not depend on an instrument received through faith; rather, the child is united directly with Christ. This is the argument Luther always follows when interpreting the Children's Gospel (Mark 10:13–16).

The child certainly receives his or her own faith through the Church, which exists in history and its means of grace, but then the child does not remain only "in the lap of Christendom," but comes directly to Christ. When children believe the word of Christ, they believe the effective word, which gives them the kingdom of heaven.

---

36. *WA* 30 1, 216, 31–34. See also *WA* 30 1, 215, 14; 216, 15; 217, 25.

6

Eucharist

JARI JOLKKONEN

For Luther the significance of the sacraments was indisputable, yet the same cannot be said of all Luther researchers. Around the turn of the twentieth century, both romantic theology and liberal Protestantism emphasized the subjective dimension of faith to the extent that these had great difficulty understanding why Jesus had to go and institute outward rituals such as baptism and the Eucharist.

Theologians such as Friedrich Schleiermacher, Adolf von Harnack, and Wilhelm Dilthey either overtly or covertly represent the notion the Lutheran Reformation carried out a de-sacramentalization program (*Entsakramentalisierung*). It was maintained that the Reformation led Christianity away from the narrow Roman Catholic sacramentalism bound to materialistic-magical thinking, freeing it up to become merely an inner religion (*Verinnerlichung und Vergeisterung der Religion*).[1] The awkward fact however is that only second to his writing about the doctrine of justification Luther wrote the most about the Eucharist. This was explained away as either a blunder or a remnant of the past: Luther took the first steps away from sacramentalism but did not by any means to give it up altogether.

The school that had adopted the Kantian criticism of metaphysics and was existentially oriented also had felt very little interest in Luther's sacramental theology. Gerhard Ebeling, a famous Luther researcher,

---

1. See, for example, Peters, *Realpräsenz*, 10–22.

virtually bypassed the sacraments altogether in his general surveys on Christianity (1959) and Luther's theology (1964).[2]

But a quick glance at the oldest and most respectable confessional texts of the Lutheran Reformation, such as the Large and Small Catechisms by Luther in 1529 and the Augsburg Confession by Philipp Melanchton in 1530, open up a different world. They reveal that 1) Luther and his supporters considered the proper understanding and celebration of the Eucharist of crucial importance and 2) they waged a passionate battle over this on two fronts.[3]

In all three confessional texts a stand is taken on both the Roman Catholic and Reformed emphases, even though the articles dealing with the Eucharist are clearly directed more against the Reformed concept. While Luther had criticized the doctrine of transubstantiation, he still adhered to the traditional sacramental realism of the church, according to which, by the power of the Word of God and his promise, Christ's body and blood are really present in the bread and the wine when the priest pronounces the words of consecration. In receiving Holy Communion the Christian is forgiven his or her sins, is united with Christ, and receives, for the strengthening of faith, a concrete sign of his participation in the communion of saints and eternal life. The real presence is a consistent outcome of the Incarnation. By the work of the Holy Spirit and by the power of the Word of God, Christ's presence continues in the sacraments.[4]

Ulrich Zwingli, Johannes Oecolampadius, and Andreas Karlstadt, supporters of a more radical form of Reformation, developed a new concept of the Eucharist, called symbolistic or spiritualistic, according to which it was a commemorative meal where the congregation is reminded of Christ sitting at the right hand of the Father. Christ's body is not in the

---

2. Ebeling, *Das Wesen des christlichen Glaubens* and *Luther: Einführung in sein Denken*. See more Saarinen, *Gottes Wirken*.

3. The original texts of the *Confessio Augustana* (CA), *Der Grosse Katechismus* (GK) and *Der Kleine Katechismus* (KK) see *Bekenntnisschriften der Evangelisch-Lutherischen Kirche* (BSELK). Large Catechism in *BSELK* 545–733 (or *WA* 30 I, 125–238) and Small Catechism in *BSELK* 501–44 (or *WA* 30 I, 239–425).

4. Luther defends the doctrine of real presence especially in the following antispiritualistic writings: *Wider die himmlischen Propheten von den Bildern und Sacrament*, 1525 (*WA* 18, 62–214); *Dass diese wort Christi 'Das ist mein Leib' noch fest stehen: wider die Schwarmgeister* (*WA* 23, 68–320); *Von Abendmahl Christi, Bekenntnis*, 1528 (*WA* 26, 261–509).

bread but in heaven. The Holy Spirit brings him close to the believers in a spiritual way. The Eucharist is rather a symbol in which believers confess their faith and strengthen their mutual fellowship. Even though Luther also considered the Eucharist a meal of fellowship in the congregation, this angle on the matter is given less attention in the catechisms as a consequence of their anti-spiritualistic nature.[5]

The traces of the dispute are visible both in Luther's Catechism and in the Augsburg Confession. In the train of thought followed in these two works, the doctrine of justification *sola gratia, sola fide*, and *solus Christus*, necessarily calls for sacramental realism. According to the third article of the Augsburg Confession, God himself carries out reconciliation in Christ and according to the fourth article (considered the core of the Confession) we accept this reconciliation through faith. In order that faith would not become a new human act of merit, but remains God's gift, it will have to come from outside of people, through the proclaimed Word and the visible Sacraments. It is therefore that the fifth article states that the Holy Spirit produces saving faith "through the Word and the sacraments, as through instruments," not without them.[6] Luther expressed the same even more emphatically: "Amongst us the Holy Spirit is not present in any other way than in the bodily sense, that is, in the word, the water, Christ's body and his saints."[7]

In the Large Catechism Luther justifies the decisive role of the sacraments in God's plan of salvation using the old differentiation between Christ's merit (*meritum Christi*) and its personal distribution (*distributio meriti*). The fact of reconciliation is based on the cross, yet the cross does not enter into the mouth of the receiver of salvation. The Word and the Sacraments are needed in order to share that fact with new generations: "For although the work is accomplished and the forgiveness of sins acquired on the cross, yet it cannot come to us in any other way than through the Word. But now the entire Gospel and the article of the

---

5. On the Cathechisms antispiritualistic nature, see, e.g., Peters, *Kommentar zu Luthers Katechismen IV*; Wengert, "Luther's Cathechisms," 54–60.

6. CA V in *BSELK*, 58: "Ut hanc fidem consequamur, institutum est ministerium docendi evangelii et porrigendi sacramenta. Nam per verbum et sacramenta tamquam per instrumenta donatur spiritus sanctus, qui fidem efficit, ubi et quando visum est Deo, in his, qui audiunt evangelium."

7. *WA* 23, 193, 31–33. All translations are mine unless otherwise noted.

Creed: I believe in a holy Christian Church, the forgiveness of sin, etc., are by the Word embodied in this Sacrament and presented to us."[8]

In the Augsburg Confession the sacraments are also fundamental from the viewpoint of the apostolicity and unity of the church. Next to the proclamation of the pure gospel, another necessary sign of the true church is the administration of the sacraments in a proper way (*recte*). It follows then that conflicting notions of the correct understanding and celebration of the Eucharist result in schism, division in the church. These are not simply matters concerning the technical administration of the liturgy in accord with a handbook of a church but about understanding the Eucharist in a broader context.

What then was meant by the "proper" celebration of the Eucharist? This essay aims to explicate what Martin Luther understood by the Eucharist and its proper celebration. Thus both doctrinal viewpoints and concepts dealing with the practice of the Mass need to be taken into consideration.

Several studies have been published on Luther's doctrine of the Eucharist, primarily in the area of systematic theology.[9] In addition, his liturgic reform dating back to the 1520s has been debated on to this very day.[10] In those studies more in the sphere of practical theology, there has been special interest placed on the question of what should be thought of Luther's decision to remove the Roman Canon Prayer (*canon missae*). Some contend that the decision was justified but there are more of those who claim that Luther's resolution was liturgically clumsy, even when thinking of it from his own theological viewpoint. I myself tend to favor the latter option. It is my desire to combine the systematic and practical dimensions since, at the heart of the matter, in the Eucharist itself doctrine and practice are interlinked.

---

8. *BSELK*, GK, Abendmahl, 31.

9. See, for example, Peters, *Realpräsenz*; Sasse, *This is My Body*; Cleve, *Luthers nattvardslära*; Hilgenfeld, *Mittelalterlich-traditionelle Elemente*; Hardt, *Adorabilis & Venerabilis Eucharistia*; Lessing, *Abendmahl*; Simon, *Messopfertheologie Martin Luthers*.

10. See for example Vajta, *Theologie des Gottesdienstes bei Luther*; Meyer, *Luther und die Messe*; Messner, *Messreform Martin Luthers*.

GOD AS SELF-GIVING LOVE

Before we can answer what Luther taught about the Eucharist, we need to ask what he taught about God. The underlying factor in the Reformator's doctrine of the Eucharist and his practice of the Mass is the doctrine of God as self-giving love (*agape*). While the rich medieval spirituality emphasized the question of how people can love God properly and purely, in his early commentaries on the Psalms, Luther turned the question completely around: "This it means to be God: not to receive good but to give it" (*hoc est esse Deum: non accipere bona, sed dare*).[11] God is an active giver of good things, not a passive receiver of them. This concept of God directs all his thinking, also on the Eucharist. Using expressions corresponding to those in his commentaries on the Psalms, Luther defines the Eucharist as a testament, which is a gift given by God, not received by him (*non beneficium acceptum, sed datum*).[12]

The close union between the image of God and the doctrine of the Eucharist will later be dealt with in its Trinitarian context. In the Large Catechism Luther combines the metaphor of the gift and the doctrine of Trinity when he summarizes the message of the Apostles Creed: "The Father bestows upon us the entire creation, Christ his completed work and the Holy Spirit all his gifts."[13]

The Reformor employs almost identical phrases when he summarizes the entire account of Christianity, using this against the spiritualistic concept of the Eucharist in his work *Von Abendmahl Christi* (*Confession Concerning Christ's Supper*). For our topic, this text is especially significant, not only because it deals with the doctrine of the Eucharist but due to its personal nature. Luther meant the book to be his theological testament in a situation where, because of extreme pain, he believed he would soon die:

---

11. *WA* 4, 269, 25–26. Luther comments here on Ps 116:12 (How can I repay the Lord for all his goodness to me?).

12. *WA* 6, 364, 17–21: "Nu meynn ich, ßo wir die vorigen ding recht vorstandenn habenn, das die meß nit anders sey, den eyn testament unnd sacrament, darynnen sich gott vorspricht gegen uns unnd gibt gnad und barmhertzickeit, ßo wirt sichs nit fugen, das wir ein gutt werck odder vordienst solten drauß machen, den ein testament ist nit beneficium acceptum, sed datum, es nympt nit wolthat von uns, ßondern bringt uns wolthat."

13. *BSELK*, GK, Glaubensbekenntnis, 69.

> These are the three persons and one God, *who has given himself to us all wholly and completely, with all that he is and has*. The Father *gives himself to us*, with heaven and earth and all the creatures, in order that they may serve us and benefit us. But this gift has become obscured and useless through Adam's fall. Therefore the Son *himself subsequently gave himself* and bestowed all his works, sufferings, wisdom, and righteousness, and reconciled us to the Father, in order that restored to life and righteousness, we might also know and have the Father and his gifts. *But because this grace would benefit no one if it remained so profoundly hidden and could not come to us, the Holy Spirit comes and gives himself to us also, wholly and completely.* He teaches us to understand this deed of Christ which has been manifested to us, helps us receive and preserve it, use it to our advantage and impart it to others, increase and extend it. He does this both inwardly and outwardly—inwardly by means of faith and other spiritual gifts, *outwardly through the gospel, baptism, and the sacrament of the altar, through which as through three means or methods he comes to us and inculcates the sufferings of Christ for the benefit of our salvation* . . . In the same way I also say and confess that in the sacrament of the altar the true body and blood of Christ are orally eaten and drunk in the bread and wine, even if the priests who distribute them or those who receive them do not believe or otherwise misuse the sacrament. It does not rest on man's belief or unbelief but on the Word and ordinance of God.[14]

The text brings out the unity between the image of God and the doctrine of the Eucharist. The Eucharist instituted by Christ reflects the love of the triune God. In the Eucharist the grace of God comes to the present moment and is distributed personally to each individual. Without the Eucharist the fruits of Christ's reconciliatory work remain in the past. If the Word and the Sacraments do not communicate God's love to new generations, the Christian faith will be narrowed down to an ideology or a moral system.

THE SACRAMENT OF UNITY AND LOVE

Since the Eucharist reflects God's self-giving love, it also has a horizontal dimension in Luther's theology. The Eucharist unites the Christian with Christ and his saints. But it also creates communion among people attending the Eucharist.

---

14. WA 26, 505, 38–506,12. Translation from *LW*, Italics mine.

The Lutheran Franz Pieper and the Roman Catholics Joseph Ratzinger and Louis Bouyer maintain that Luther somehow reduced the Eucharist to a supper for the forgiveness of sins of an individual.[15] We may also receive this impression if we only read the Catechism or the disputed writings of 1520. Nevertheless this viewpoint does not do justice to Luther's concept of the Eucharist. For example, the Eucharist is also a meal of thanksgiving, of the confession of faith and communion.[16]

The nature of communion in the Eucharist is vividly present in Luther's sermon on *The Blessed Sacrament of the Holy and True Body of Christ and the Brotherhoods*, 1519. Luther starts the sermon unambiguously by stating that the significance or effect of this sacrament is the communion of all saints.

According to Luther the Eucharist is a visible sign of the union of all Christians with Christ and other Christians. It is like a visible proof and seal of belonging to the Kingdom of God, whose head is Christ, and whose citizens include both saints still struggling in this world and saints who have already reached home. According to the Reformer, the old name of the Eucharist *communio*, and its derivation *communicatio*, portrays its contents very well, meaning doing something together and sharing gifts. Through the Sacrament of the Altar all the good from Christ and his saints will become shared property. Similarly, one person's anxiety, suffering and sin will belong to everyone:

> The significance or effect of this sacrament is the communion of all saints. From this it derives its common name *synaxis* or *communio*, that is, fellowship. And the Latin *communicare*, or as we say in German, *zum sacrament gehen*, means to take part in this fellowship ... This communion consists in this, that all the spiritual possessions of Christ and his saints are shared with and become the common property of him who receives this sacrament. Again all sufferings and sins also become common property; and thus love engenders love in return and mutual love unites.[17]

15. Pieper, *Christian Dogmatics*; Ratzinger, *Theologische Prinzipienlehre*, 273–76; Boyier, *Eucharist*, 388.

16. See Peura, "Church as Spiritual Communion," 93–131.

17. StA 1, 273, 16–24: "Die Bedeutung odder das werck disses sacraments ist gemeynschafft aller heyligen, drumb nennet man es auch mit seynem teglichen namen Synaxis oder Communio, das ist gemeynschafft, vnd Comunicare auuf latein heyst dis gemeysachfft empfahen, wilchs wir auff deutsch sagen zum sacrament gehen, vnd kumpt daher, das Christus mit allen heyligen ist eyn geystlicher corper." StA 1, 274, 15–18: "Dysse gemeynschafft steht darynne das alle geystlich gutter Christi vnnd seyner

This communion taking place in love is a reciprocal sharing both between Christ and the Christian and among Christians. Christ gives Christians all good things, his grace, holiness, and righteousness, making them partakers of both his life and suffering. Therefore at the Eucharist both the bread and the wine are distributed, elements which symbolized life and suffering in the Old Testament.[18] Christians give Christ their own anxiety, misery, angst, and sin. This sharing is not only vertical but is to take place among people as well. Those in communion with one another are to give all their good things to be shared and respectively own the wants and needs of others. In this sense the Eucharist has a strong ethical dimension, similar to baptism:

> Christ with all saints, by his love, takes upon himself our form (Phil. 2:7), fights with us against sin, death, and all evil. This enkindles in us such love that we take on his form, rely upon his righteousness, life, and blessedness. And through the interchange of his blessings and our misfortunes, we become one loaf, one bread, one body, one drink, and have all things in common. O this is a great sacrament, says St. Paul, that Christ and the church are one flesh and bone. Again through this same love, we are to be changed and to make the infirmities of all other Christians our own; we are to take upon ourselves their form and their necessity, and all the good that is within our power we are to make theirs, that they may profit from it. That is real fellowship, and that is the true significance of this sacrament. In this way we are changed into one another and are made into a community by love. Without love there can be no such change.[19]

In his sermon of 1519 Luther uses surprisingly strong expressions concerning the change of the elements of the Eucharist. Some researchers say these expressions are to be interpreted as symbolic.[20] Luther's expressions are, however, real not just symbolic. The "changing" of the bread and the wine is spoken of in many Early Church liturgies and written about by theologians as far back as a thousand years before the doctrine of transubstantiation. The Reformer can also talk about the "change" of

---

heyligen mit geteyllet vnd gemeyn werden dem, der dyss sacrament empfeht, widderrumb alle leyden vnd sund auch gemeyn werden vnd alsso liebe gegen liebe antzundet wirdt vnd voreynigt."

18. *StA* 1, 280, 5–11.

19. *StA* 1, 278, 34–279,12. Translation from *LW*.

20. Althaus, "Luthers Abendmahlslehre," 5.

the bread and the wine despite his criticism of the doctrine of transubstantiation. In his thinking the "change" taking place in Christians on the one hand and the "change" of bread and wine on the other hand are not disconnected, but belong together. While the congregation's change and growth into a community of love becomes possible on the basis that the bread and the wine "change" to Christ's real body and blood, yet the Eucharist was not instituted for naught but for the very reason that the congregation might "change" and grow into a community of love. Both are real and require the other:

> Besides all this, Christ did not institute these two forms solitary and alone, but he gave his true natural flesh in the bread, and his natural true blood in the wine, that he might give a really perfect sacrament or sign. For just as the bread is changed into his true natural body and the wine into his natural true blood, so truly are we also drawn and changed into the spiritual body, that is, into the fellowship of Christ and all saints and by this sacrament put into possession of all the virtues and mercies of Christ and his saints.[21]

The nature of the Eucharist, that it is public and serves to enhance fellowship, also has its own practical consequences regarding those who intend to partake of it. According to Luther, a Mass officiated by a priest for his own devotion is in conflict with the nature of the Eucharist as communion.[22] On the other hand he also rejected the notion of arranging the Eucharist in a private home without a minister. Parents are to teach the gospel to their families, but the Eucharist was instituted as a public remembrance of Christ and as the meal of church communion so the one officiating it is to be a minister ordained into public office.[23] The

---

21. *StA* 1, 279, 31–280, 4: "Vbir das alles hatt er disser zwo gestalt nit bloss nach ledig eyngesetzt, sondern seyn warhafftig naturlich fleysch yn dem bort, vnd seyn naturlich warhafftig blut yn dem weyn geben, dass er yhe ein volkomens sacrament odder zeychen gebe. Dann zu gleych als dass brot yn seynem warhafftigen naturlichen leychnam vnd der weyn yn seyn naturlich warhafftig blut vorwandelt wirt, alsso warhafftig werden auch wir in den geystlichen leyp, das ist yn die gemeynschafft Christi vnd aller heyligen getzogen und vorwandelt vnd durch diss sacrament yn alle tugende vnd gnad Christi vnd seyner heyligen gesetzt." Translation from *LW*.

22. *WA* 8, 513, 29–514, 3; *BSELK*, 418–19; *WA* 39 I, 134–73.

23. See for example *WA* Br 7, 339, 18–32: "Dass aber ein Hausvater die Seinen das Wort Gottes lehret, ist recht und soll so sein; den Gott hat befohlen, dass wir unser Kinder und Haus sollen lehren und ziehen, und ist das Wort einem iglichen befohlen. Aber das Sacrament ist ein offenbarlich Bekenntnis und soll offenbarlichen berufene

communion nature of the Eucharist requires that both a congregation and an ordained minister be present.

CRITICISM OF THE SCHOLASTIC DOCTRINE OF THE SACRIFICE OF THE MASS

Luther engaged in disputes concerning the Eucharist on two fronts. At the onset of the Reformation, in the early 1520s, he discussed the doctrine of transubstantiation, the distribution of wine to lay people as well as the sacrificial nature of the Eucharist with the Catholic Scholastics of his time. The sacrificial interpretation of the Mass offended Luther the most. It was to him a "most ungodly abuse."

The increase in the sacrificial nature of the Mass has gone through a great many phases and it has included many models. According to St Augustine each sacrifice and the act of offering (*offere*) includes four parts or components: 1) the recipient or the one to whom the sacrifice is given (*cui offeratur*), 2) the donor or the one who gives (*a quo*), 3) the gift or what is given (*quid*), as well as 4) the beneficiary (*benefitor*) or the one for whom it is given (*pro quibus*).[24] It is to be noted that the Mass can be understood as a sacrifice in various ways. In the Middle Ages there were many patterns as to who or what was the recipient, the subject, the gift or the beneficiary.[25]

According to Thomas of Aquinas, celebrating the Eucharist is both a sacrament and a sacrifice. The Eucharist can be seen as a sacrifice for three reasons. First, it is the representative image of Christ's suffering; secondly, in it the Lord's suffering is jointly remembered; finally, it com-

---

Diener haben, weil dabei stehet, als Christus sagt, man soll es tun zu seinem Gedächtnis, das ist, wie St. Paulus sagt, zu verkundigen oder predigen des Herrn Tod, bis er komme, und daselbst auch spricht, man solle zusammenkommen, und hart straft die, so sonderlich ein iglicher für sich selbs wollt des Hernn Abendmahl gebrauchen... Dann es ein gar anders umb ein ein offentlich Ampt in der Kirchen und umb ein Hausvater uber sein Gesind, darumb sie nicht zu mengen sind noch zu trennen." See also WA Tr 5, 6361; WA Br 7, 338, 7; WA Br 5, 528; 6, 143, 12; 7, 143, 12.

24. Augustine, *De trinitate* 4, 14 (*MPL* 42, 819–1098): "Ut quoniam quatuor considerantur in omni sacrificio: cui offeratur, a quo offeratur, quid offeratur, pro quibus offeratur."

25. See, for example, Simon, *Messopferlehre Martin Luthers*, 9–79; Senn, *Christian Liturgy*, 253–63; Iserloh, "Abendmahl," 90–103.

municates the fruits of Christ's passion to those partaking of it.[26] Luther would not have had difficulty accepting such a view.

Later in the Middle Ages, especially among the Nominalists, the notion of the sacrifice, however, gained more and more anthropocentric emphases. It was taught that Christ's death reconciled us from original sin, but to reconcile for daily sins we need the sacrifice of the Mass. The more the Eucharist gained an independent sacrificial position beside the sacrifice of Christ, the more strongly it seemed to be in conflict with the New Testament, according to which Christ's sacrifice was once for all, complete and adequate (Heb 10:10). The more the priest was emphasized as the active officiator of the sacrifice, the more passive role was afforded to the sacrificial offering of Christ. The more teaching was offered on how the fruits of the sacrifice of the Mass were to benefit absent parishioners and those in purgatory, the more instrumental value was conferred upon the Eucharist.

The Second Council of Lyon had defined the officiation of the Eucharistic sacrifice as one way to bring relief to souls in purgatory.[27] This strengthened the position of the Votive Masses, where the parishioner purchased a Mass from a priest on behalf of a reason or a person. The priest celebrated the Votive Mass alone joining the intercessory prayers to the Canon Prayers of the Mass. The Mass, administered in Latin and partially in an inaudible voice, left the parishioners with the role of a silent audience; thus their presence was not particularly necessary.

Luther strongly resisted the pattern where the priest was interpreted as offering up the sacrifice, God was the recipient, Christ's body and blood were the gift, and parishioners, absent and in purgatory, were the beneficiaries. The problem was worsened by the fact that the Mass could be purchased from a priest.

26. *ST* III, q.73, a.4: "Dicendum quod, hoc sacramentum habet triplicem significationem. Unam quidem respectu praeteriti: inquentum scilicet est *commemorativum Dominicae passionis*, quae fuit verum sacrificium, ut supra dictum est. Et secundum hoc nominatur 'sacrificium.'" See also *ST* q.79, a.7, r: "Dicendum quod hoc sacramentum non solum est sacramentum, sed etiam est sacrificium. Inquantum enim in hoc sacramento repraesentatur passio Christi . . . habet rationem sacrificii; inquantum vero in hoc sacramento traditur invisibilis gratia sub visibili specie, habet rationem sacramenti." Also *ST* III, q.83, a.1, r: "Dicendum quod duplici ratione celebratio hujus sacramenti dicitur immolatio Christi. Primo . . . Celebratio autem hujus sacramenti est imago quaedam et repraesentativa passionis Christi quae est vera eius immolation . . . Alio modo quantum ad effectum passionis."

27. *DS* 856; *DS* 940; See also *DS* 1304 and 1743.

Criticism of the implicit doctrine of the sacrifice of the Mass and of the image of God it called for came out early in Luther's 1518 sermon on the Eucharist. According to the central claim of the sermon, God is not a tax collector or an avenger, who expects outward deeds and sacrifices from people, but rather a savior and a giver of gifts, who desires faith from the heart and a confident trust. The real communicant is a person who confesses his or her sins and unworthiness and who believes that grace is bestowed gratuitously in the Eucharist. The expressions describing God, "not needy" and "generous," indicate that in the sacrament of the Eucharist God is the giver of the gift, not its recipient: "God does not need (*non indicus*) any of your good things, but he will come to you and bestow upon you generously (*largus*) of his own good supply."[28]

Luther openly attacked the doctrine of the sacrifice of the Mass in three of his early writings, 1520–21.

According to him the doctrine of the sacrifice of the Mass presents an altogether false image of God. In his work *The Misuse of the Mass* (*De abroganda missa privata*), Luther emphatically declares that the one who considers the Mass a sacrifice wants to reconcile and placate God. And the one who wishes to reconcile God must consider him to be angry, expecting placation (*iratum et implacatum*). Anyone believing in an irate God thus expects from him more anger than love, more malevolence than good. So the theologians of the sacrifice of the Mass have confused the entire Christian faith because "they have turned divine love into anger, made the Father an enemy, created hell of heaven, traded the completed work of reconciliation for an incomplete task."[29] They seem to believe in a god who has in his anger closed the gates to heaven and

---

28. *WA* 1, 330, 33–34: "Deus tuus est bonorum tuorum non indigus, sed bonorum suorum largus in te venit ad te."

29. *WA* 8, 441, 20–33: "Deinde, cum sacrificant, necesse est, cogitent deum placare. Velle autem deum placare est eum iratum et implacatum credere. Credere autem iratum est expectare iram potius quam charitatem, mala potius quam bona. At Eucharistiam salubriter accepturis necesse est credere deum summa charitate iandudum placatissimum ultro donare id, quo nihil habet charius, ita ut nihil eque pugnet adversus Eucharistiae fructum, atque haec sacrilega opinio papistarum et nocentissima conscientia deum esse iratum et hoc sacrificio placandum, qui, nisi summe esset placatus et amantissimus, tantas suoas opes nec exhibet, nec effunderet. Vides ergo, ut sacrifices isti, verius carnifices, suo sacrificio nos docent incurrere horrenda et pericula et omnia bona in mala, vivifica in mortifera, salutifera in damnabilia, certa in incerta, fidem in dubium, sacuratem in paverom, breviter, ipsam divinam charitatem in iram et amorem in odium, patrem in hostem, coelum in ingernum et summa in infirma verter, omnia miscere, confundere et perturbare." See also *WA* 8, 444, 38–445, 3.

opened the doors to hell, not because of people's sins or the neglect of the Ten Commandments but because God Himself is "a tyrannical judge and a tax collector."[30]

According to Luther the doctrine of the sacrifice of the Mass also distorts the doctrine of justification, as it gives the impression that celebrating the Mass, partaking of it or purchasing one is a meritorious act, by which God has mercy on people and receives them to his bosom; thus the uniqueness of Christ's death, gratuitous grace and the significance of faith are all bypassed. Luther considered the doctrine of the sacrifice of the Mass such a serious distortion that he hoped it would become the main theme for an ecumenical council.[31]

It is true that Luther also criticized the doctrine of transubstantiation. In modern research, Luther's criticism is however sometimes afforded a disproportionately large emphasis. To Luther the doctrine of transubstantiation was more useless than false. To him it was not a heresy but a theologically and pastorally useless effort to explain Christ's sacraments by means of Aristotelian philosophy.

Luther presented four counter-arguments to the doctrine. According to him the language of the Bible does not call for transubstantiation. The church lived quite well for 1,200 years without this term. If believers worshipping the Eucharistic elements were to be protected against idolatry, transubstantiation was a poor and useless means for doing this: simple believers understand correctly that they worship Christ present at the Eucharist (not the bread as such), but they will never understand the explanation of the sacraments by means of Aristotelian metaphysics. Besides, someone might digress to worship the accidents of bread and wine despite the doctrine of transubstantiation. Finally, philosophy may well serve theology, but divine revelation cannot be submitted to the bondage of a currently fashionable philosopher.[32]

Since theology was to be independent of philosophy, Luther thought it was safer to explain Christ's presence in the elements on the basis of the Chalcedonian Christology. "Just as each thing is in respect to Christ, so it is also in respect to the sacraments." In the consecrated wafer

---

30. WA 8, 467, 7–10: "Ex quo ulterius sequitur coelum esse clausum et infernum paratum homini summa iniquitate dei, nempe non propter peccata hominis, neque propter non impleta mandata dei, sed propter tyrannicam et arbitratiam exactionem dei."

31. See *Smalcald Articles*, II, 10 in *BSELK*.

32. WA 6, 508–10.

both the substance of bread and of Christ's body are present together, as are Christ's human and divine natures present together in the Person of Christ. "If philosophy does not comprehend this, faith will."³³

PRACTICAL CONSEQUENCES OF THE CRITICISM DIRECTED AT SCHOLASTICISM

The Roman Catholic Johannes Eck defended the distribution of mere bread to the lay people using John 6:51: "If anyone eats of this bread, he will live forever," while the Reformed Zwingli rejected the real presence with another verse from the same gospel: "It is the Spirit who gives life; the flesh profits nothing" (John 6:63). Luther contended that John's Gospel had to be considered, but it could not have a decisive position for the doctrine and practice of the Eucharist, because it was a matter of dispute whether those verses spoke about the Eucharist.³⁴

According to Luther, in the interpretation of both the doctrine of the Eucharist and the practice of the Mass, decisive importance was to be placed on the accounts of the institution of the Lord's Supper in the New Testament. The basis for assessing whether a Mass was proper was the first Eucharist instituted by Christ: "The Mass is the more Christian, the more it resembles the first Mass officiated by Christ."³⁵ The gospel accounts of the institution shows how the Eucharist is to be properly celebrated (*recht halten*) and how it is to be understood correctly (*recht vorstahn*). They are an absolute minimum; they have nothing extra, nothing unnecessary. They also have everything adequately, missing nothing that belongs to the perfect integrity, use, or efficacy of the sacrament.³⁶

---

33. WA 6, 511, 34-39: "Sicut ergo in Christo res se habet, ita et in sacramento. Non enim ad corporalem inhabitationem divinitatis necesse est transsubstanciari humanam naturam, ut divinitas sub accidentibus humanae naturae teneatur. Sed integra utraque natura vere dicitur 'Hic homo est deus, hic deus est homo'. Quod et si philosophia non capit, fides tamen capit. Et maior est verbi dei autoritas quam nostri ingenii capacitas."

34. WA 6, 502, 7-13.

35. WA 6, 523, 25-26: "Missa quanto vicinior et similior primae omnium Missae, quam Christus in caena fecit, tanto Christianor." See also StA 1, 290, 31-32.

36. StA 1, 291, 12-18: "Wollen wir recht mess halten vnd vorstahn, so mussen wir alles faren lassen, was die augen vnd alle synn in dissen handel mugen zeygen vnd antragen, es sey kleyd, klang, gesang, tzierd, gepett, tragen, heben, legen odder was da geschen mag yn der mess biss das wir zuuor die wort Christi fassen vnd wol bedecken damit er die mess volnbrach vnd eyngesetzt vnd vns zuuolnbringen beuolhen hatt dan darynnen ligt die mess gantz mit all yhrem wessen, werck, nutz vnd frucht on wilche nichts von der mess empfangen wirt." WA 6, 513, 9-11: "Nihil enim in his omissum,

Thus the rite divinely instituted by Christ entails bringing forth the bread and the wine, giving thanks, blessing these elements, breaking the bread and distributing the consecrated gifts.[37] Everything else is a later addition or human tradition. Apart from the Canon Prayer of the Mass, Luther nevertheless did not remove the other parts of the Roman Mass, preserving the Liturgy of the Word nearly unaltered. In 1523 in the renewed Order of the Mass, *Formula missae*, Luther kept the sections, such as the Psalm Introit, the Kyrie, the Gloria, the Collect Prayer, the Epistle, the Gospel, the Gradual, the Alleluia, the Creed, the Sanctus, the Agnus Dei and the Communion Hymn. According to him these parts gave proof of the original purity of the early church, beautified the celebration of the Eucharist and imparted the word of God both in a read and sung form among the people.[38]

Luther was both doctrinally and liturgically a traditionalist, yet his theology of the Eucharist led to the change of some practices concerning the Mass.[39] As a consequence of Luther's protest, Votive Masses were abolished. This question was not about a harmless detail but had significant spiritual and economic consequences. To give an example: in the church of a small town the size of Wittenberg with a population of some 2,500, as many as 8,994 Masses were administered under the sponsorship of a certain foundation during 1519, which makes an average of 24 Masses per day.[40] Many priests made a living from Votive Masses. Thus the critique of the Reformation took away their livelihood. Apart from Votive Masses, Private Masses were also discontinued, which the priest administered without the congregation for his own devotion, even though they did not include such abuse as did the Votive Masses.[41]

The second change was to begin to distribute the two elements to the congregation as well. Luther did not consider the distribution of mere bread, or the Eucharist in one kind, wrong as such. From the Words of

---

quod ad integritatem, usum et fructum huis sacramenti pertinet, nihilque positum, quod superfluum et non necessarium sit nobis nosse." See also WA 6, 512, 33–34.

37. WA 12, 206, 17–18: "Nam hoc negare non possumus, Missas et communionem panis et vini ritum esse a Christo divinitus institutum."

38. See, for example, WA 12, 206, 23–207, 9; 37, 27–29.

39. On Luther's liturgical traditionalism, see more for example Schultz, "Luthers Liturgische Reformen," 247–75; Senn, "Reform on the Mass," 35–52.

40. Junghaus, *Wittenberg als Lutherstadt* and "Luther on the Reform of Worship".

41. On medieval liturgical practices, see Cabié, *Church at Prayer*.

Institution one could draw the conclusion that Christ had left the matter to discretion. To be exact, Luther's protest had been directed at the magisterium of the church *denying* the distribution of the wine to the parishioners, as Luther believed it did not have that right. The Words of Institution unequivocally indicate that Christ also distributed the wine to each and everyone, which was reinforced by the patristic sources to be in accord with the practice of the early church.[42] Concerning the issue of the chalice for the laity, Luther's stand became stricter. Back in the early 1520s he supported the idea that during the phase of transition all could act according to their consciences. At the end of the 1520s he stated that the congregation had received enough instruction on the matter so the distribution of the bread alone did not need to be allowed any longer.

Thirdly, the minister began to read the Words of Institution in a loud voice to the congregation, at first in Latin, but later in the vernacular as well. Traditionally, Luther regarded the Words of Institution as words of consecration directed towards the elements. But they were also words of promise, including a promise of Christ's presence and the forgiveness of sins. Therefore they were to be read or sung aloud so that every person would be able to hear them and believe them.[43] The Lutheran specialty was that they were also used as the words of distribution. As the receiving of the Eucharist called for faith, it also called for the presence and participation of the believer.

Fourthly, Luther removed the entire Canon Prayer of the Mass from its proximity to the Words of Institution. This Canon Prayer, to be read prior to the distribution of the Eucharist, consisted of some twelve prayers. The majority of the Eucharistic prayers of the Eastern Church were named after the church fathers and they often proceeded in accordance with the contents of the Creed, the emphasis being on the remembrance of God's saving deeds.[44] On the other hand, the origin of the Canon Prayer is obscure. Nor does it have a consistently proceeding sequence. The prayers emphasize supplication and the sacrifice which is offered up by the congregation.[45]

---

42. StA 2, 273, 1–15; WA 6, 507, 6–13; WA 10 II, 11–41.

43. WA 12, 212, 17–26.

44. Original texts, see for example Brightman, *Liturgies Eastern and Western*; Hänggi and Pahl, *Prex Eucharistica*. English translations see Jasper and Cuming, *Prayers of the Eucharist*.

45. See, for example, Wegmann, "Genealogie," 212: "Jede Rekonstruktion des römischen Kanons bleibt hypotetisch." Also Rudolf Stählin, "Die Geschichte," 36: "Die

On the other hand, in a great many liturgical disputes, based on his sacramental realism, Luther held on to traditional Roman Catholic practices. He accepted elevation, bowing, incense, and other forms of adoration directed towards the elements. These were natural consequences of his sacramental realism. Since Christ is present in the bread and the wine as really as he was in the manger at Christmas, in the house of Peter's mother-in-law, and on the cross on Calvary, it is appropriate to show him worship and adoration in the Mass. Yet Luther deemed it important that they not be made compulsory. While on the earth, Christ did not demand outward acts of worship, though he did not reject them either. Christ taught faith in God and love toward our neighbors. Faith has the decisive role in this as well, since both God and people in high places are shown respect using the same gestures.[46]

Luther preserved the old Roman Catholic tradition whereby the communicant receives the Eucharist kneeling. He also quite deliberately held on to the Catholic practice where the priest distributes the wafer directly to the communicant's mouth rather than into the hand. While Luther was hiding in the Castle of Wartburg, some of his supporters had started to demand that the wafer be placed in the communicants' hands because Christ had said in the Words of Institution "Take and eat" and Luther had in fact written that the praxis of the Mass had to be arranged exactly on the basis of the institution account. After returning from his hide-out in Wartburg, Luther put an end to the dispute in his eight sermons titled "Invocavit." If the sign of a good Christian was that he or she takes the wafer in the hand, in that case "even a pig would pass for a good Christian as it can receive the wafer with its trotter."[47] Luther considered it quite possible to distribute the wafer to each person's hand, but out of respect for the sacrament he preserved the old tradition in Wittenberg; the wafer was distributed to the communicants' mouths.

Geschichte des römischen Ritus in den Jahrhunderten nach Hippolyt liegt völlig im Dunkel." More on the development of the Mass see Jungmann, *Missarum solemnia*.

46. On the adoration of Christ in the Eucharist, see *Vom Anbeten des Sakraments des heiligen leichnahms Christi* (WA 11, 417–57).

47. WA 10 III, 46, 9–14: "Do werd jr felen, lieben freünde, dann wann jr jo guote Christen für allen andern gesehen wolt sein, Das jr das sacrament mit den henden angreyfft und darzuo beydergestalt nemet, So seydt jr mir schlecht Christen: mit der weyße künde auch wol ein Saw ein Christen sein, sie hette jo so eynen grossen ryessel, das sie das sacrament eüsserlich nemen künde." See also WA 10 II, 24, 14–16.

DISCUSSION ON THE REMOVAL OF THE CANON PRAYER OF THE MASS

Luther removed almost the entire *canon missae* prayer read before the Eucharist. The underlying reason was found in the wording of the prayer, which in Luther's words "sounded and smelled like a sacrifice."[48] The solution was a radical one as the prayer was and is the heart of the Mass, parallel to the distribution of the elements. Several theological and liturgical revelations of Luther's have been later adopted across denominational borders, yet the amputation of the Eucharistic prayer has raised critical discussion.

As early as 1930 when his book came out, Yngve Brilioth assessed that Luther was lucid and deep in his doctrine of the Eucharist, but as a liturgist was impractical. He thought that by removing the prayers from the mere Words of Institution Luther destroyed the liturgy of the Eucharist, leaving a mere torso.[49] William D. Maxwell said that Luther's way of dealing with the Canon was "negative, illogical and subversive" and that even Luther's own theology would not have demanded that removal. Luther's solution has also been criticized by a great many researchers in different churches.[50] Many felt Luther over-emphasized the pedagogic dimension of the Mass, which meant that prayer and thanksgiving were overshadowed. By emphasizing the mere Words of Institution as a formula of consecration and by removing the prayers around these words Luther was more papal than the Pope himself. Luther went all the way to the end of a path which was problematic from the start.[51]

A more positive assessment has been given by Bryan D. Spinks[52] and representatives of confessional Lutheranism Oliver Olson, Gottfried Krodel, and Armand Boehme.[53] These were joined by Dorothea Wende-

---

48. WA 12, 212, 14–22

49. Brilioth, *Eucharistic Faith*, 110–16 and *Nattvarden*, 183.

50. Maxwell, *An Outline of Christian Worship*, 73–79.

51. See, for example, Schmidt-Lauber, *Die Eucharistie*, 84–89; Jenson, *Christian Dogmatics*, 337–66; Pfatteicer, *Commentary*, 183; Parvio, "Ehtoollisliturgian ongelmia," 118–34; Kotila, *Liturgian lähteillä*, 103–18; Reed, *Lutheran Liturgy*, 336–37; Brand, "Luther's Liturgical Surgery"; Lathrop, "Prayers of Jesus," 158–73; Senn, "Martin Luther's Revision," 101–18 ; Pfatteicher & Messerli, *Manual on the Liturgy*, 242.

52. Spinks, *Luther's Liturgical Criteria*, 16–41.

53. Olson, "Contemporary Trends," 110–57; Krodel, "Great Thanksgiving," 12–26; Boehme, "Sing a New Song," 96–116.

bourg, a German professor, who in her 1997 inauguratory presentation set out to strongly support Luther's solution, deeming it exemplary.

Wendebourg stated that Luther's solution was a necessary liturgical consequence of his doctrine of justification. The Words of Institution are to be clearly separated from the surrounding prayers, because the Words of Institution are about God's act (*actio Dei*) whereas the prayer is the congregation's act (*actio ecclesia*). In the Western Mass the ascending, (anabatic, sacrificial) dimension threatens to override the descending (katabatic, sacramental) dimension. In her evaluation of the current liturgical movement where the worship service is seen as an offering of thanksgiving, instead of being God's gift, Wendebourg finds the same problematic anthropocentric development to hold true. Luther both adhered to the Western liturgical tradition and made the necessary alterations by disentangling the Words of Institution from the surrounding prayers. The reading of merely the Words of Institution thus consistently expresses the Lutheran doctrine of justification.[54]

It can be stated in Luther's defense that the Canon of the Mass is ambiguous as a text. Luther was unable to go beyond the distorted sacrificial interpretations of his time in his reading of the Canon, nor could he reach the "original" interpretation of the Canon, which might have been more acceptable to him. On the other hand, the Canon of the Mass includes parts from such different times that one may wonder if it has actually got an original interpretation. At any rate there are good grounds to consider Luther's resolution too extreme—one of them being his own doctrine of justification which does not render this removal necessary.

However, Wendebourg's theses have a few problems. First, Luther's critique of the Canon was not directed at the prayer itself but at the wording of the prayer. It is a specific wording that "sounded and smelled like a sacrifice." This also comes out conversely. In the *Formula missae* he expressly preserved the Preface he approved of, which was also part of the Canon Prayer. Secondly, Luther's theology does not contain a polarity between God's promises and human prayers. Luther says that what God specifically promises, people are to pray for. This is plainly stated in the explanation to the Lord's Prayer in the Large Catechism: "Just as the

---

54. See Wendebourg, "Den falschen Weg," 437–67 and her response, "Noch einmal 'Den falschen Weg,'" 400–440.

name of God is in itself holy, we pray nevertheless that it may be holy among us."⁵⁵

Thirdly, the Words of Institution themselves call for the context of prayer. According to the account of the institution, Jesus took bread and "gave thanks to God," meaning that he read an ordinary Jewish table grace. The Christian prayer of the Eucharist has risen out of the Words of Institution. It would be anachronistic to think that Jesus took the bread and read the Words of Institution from a synoptic gospel. If, as does Luther, we view the first Eucharist the norm for the celebration of the Mass, then after the bringing forth of the bread and the wine comes giving thanks to God and remembering his good deeds in prayer. Thanksgiving logically means that something good has happened to people. Thanksgiving and the whole liturgy is a reaction to God's saving action. In this sense, too, the prayer of the Eucharist fits well with Luther's own doctrine of justification.

The mechanical separation of God's act and that of the congregation in the liturgical event would lead to both practical and theological problems. In the liturgy God's and the congregation's acts are concentric and interpenetrating. When we study the phenomenon of the Mass with the five senses, we only perceive the congregation's offering of thanksgiving and human actions: *people* pray, read the Bible, sing hymns, consecrate the bread and the wine and distribute the sacrament. From the viewpoint of the promise in God's word, the thanksgiving offered by the congregation becomes God's act.⁵⁶ To use the famous principle of St Augustine: the congregational offering of thanksgiving is the element that God's word attaches itself to and penetrates. On the basis of God's own promise he is present and works in and through the act of the congregation. If we said that this matter concerns God's and people's cooperation, we would be quite right.

In hindsight we might speculate that had Luther known more about the divinely centered and more descending, katabatic, sacramental prayers of the Eastern Church, he might have replaced the Canon Prayer with one of these—or reconstructed a new one. For good reason, many Lutheran churches have ended up with such solutions today.

---

55. BSELK, GK, Vater unser, 5–19 and 49–50.

56. Here I agree with [Braaten and] Jenson, *Christian Dogmatics*, 341–42 and his other writings on the theme.

WHY DOES A CHRISTIAN NEED THE EUCHARIST?

When the Reformation was just starting, many people felt it was a liberation movement. The new doctrine and the new practice awakened spiritual enthusiasm among ordinary people. But in such a movement too, it is a short way from the ecstasy of freedom to indifference.

The preface to the Large Catechism vividly reveals that even Luther had become disappointed in regard to his expectations. In this preface, instead of condemning the Papists or those supporting the radical form of the Reformation, Luther strongly criticized ministers who had sided with the Reformation. He objected to their misinterpreting the freedom of the gospel and giving in to spiritual sloth. He felt that was why many parishioners had been led to an incorrect understanding. They worked out that the new interpretation of the gospel would make confession and the Eucharist voluntary or unnecessary for Christians.

In addition, the spiritualistic view of the sacrament held by the radical wing of the Reformation and even Luther's own early emphasis on the significance of faith included elements which meant that it was but a short step to the depreciation of the sacraments. If faith alone will save, why do we need confession and the Eucharist?

In the *Large Catechism* Luther presents three reasons why the Christian is to partake of the Eucharist. One is to attend the Eucharist because of Christ's command, because of the promise included in it, and because of one's own need.

First the Christian is to partake of the Eucharist because Christ Himself instituted it and he told Christians to celebrate it often. According to Luther, salvation is received by faith, but faith also entails obeying God's will and Christ's command.[57] Secondly, the Christian needs to come to the Lord's Table because Christ attached to it the promise of the forgiveness of sins and of eternal life. The Eucharist offers people what God's word promises. Of course, God is present in nature and even under each stone, but as Savior and "God to me personally" he can only be found in the Mass, where the gospel is proclaimed and the Eucharist administered.[58]

According to Luther even people's own anxieties lead them to the Communion table. They can fall into despair or become proud or indif-

---

57. WA 30, I, 228, 7–35.
58. WA 30 I, 230, 24–38.

ferent. In both, people run the risk of losing saving faith. The Christian constantly falls, needing forgiveness.[59] Yet, by human anxiety Luther does not merely mean guilt from sins of commission. The issue is more broadly the sphere of life where people live. In addition to guilt, for example sickness, loneliness, fear of death, depression, or experience of the futility of life feel like the powers of evil threatening faith and all human existence.[60]

THE ISSUE OF POST-CONSECRATION AND THE HANDLING OF POST-COMMUNION ELEMENTS

The facts concerning how the elements are handled in the Mass and thereafter reveals a great deal concerning what is believed about the Eucharist and what is taught about it. In his last years of life, Luther participated in two debates about how the Eucharistic elements were to be handled in practice. Researchers have paid surprisingly little attention to these two. These debates dealt with post-consecration, that is, what should be done in case the supply of consecrated wafers or wine would become exhausted in the middle of the distribution as well as the handling of the post-communion consecrated elements. Are they ordinary bread or the body of Christ?

The problem of post-consecration is well illuminated by an incident in 1545 in the town of Friesnietz. Pr Adam Besserer assisted in the distribution of the Eucharist on the Third Sunday in Advent. The number of communicants was known beforehand, as they had to come to confession prior to the Mass. So the exact number of wafers was reserved for the Eucharist.

When distributing the Eucharist to the last communicant Besserer noticed that the wafers had run out. For some reason he had misplaced one of them. He resolved the problem by fetching an unconsecrated wafer from the host box after which he distributed that wafer. Soon afterwards the misplaced wafer was found and put back. Now Besserer made a second and even more fatal error: he slipped the consecrated wafer back into the host box among the unconsecrated wafers.

---

59. *WA* 30 I, 231, 14–232, 29.

60. Here I agree with Peters, *Kommentar zu Luthers Katechismen IV*, 176–77, who writes: "Er fügt die 'Furcht des Tods, Anfechtung des Fleischs und Teufels' hinzu, in welchen es nicht um die Dimension der 'Schludfrage', sondern um den Bereich der 'Machtfrage' geht."

This became a scandal and Besserer was suspended from office. The theologians at Wittenberg University were asked for counsel on whether this was a matter of abuse and if so, what sanctions should be taken. Together with Johannes Bugenhagen, Luther replied in a letter dated January 11, 1546 only six weeks prior to his death.

The reply from Wittenberg was unambiguous. Luther considered that the way the minister handled the matter was abuse. As Besserer returned the recovered consecrated wafer to where the unconsecrated wafers were kept, he indicated that he held the consecrated and the unconsecrated wafers to be the same thing. This, to the theologians of Wittenberg, was not only a sign of pastoral negligence but nothing other than godlessness.[61] Dispensing with a consecrated wafer could be explained away as carelessness, placing it back among the unconsecrated wafers was already deliberate. Possibly the theologians of Wittenberg were aggravated by a rumor according to which Besserer at first defended his act, claiming that there was no specific difference between the consecrated and the unconsecrated wafers.[62]

In Luther's opinion Besserer confessed with his action that he was a Zwinglian and a denier of Christ's real presence. Therefore he deemed it self-evident that the minister in question was to be removed from office and excommunicated: "Let him go to the Zwinglians!"[63]

The issue of the handling of the post-communion consecrated elements raised a heated correspondence between Wittenberg and Eisleben in the summer of 1543. A minister from Eisleben by the name of Wolferinus thought that the consecrated Eucharistic elements were merely ordinary elements (*mera elementa*) after the Mass, which is why they did not need to be handled as sacraments. He based his action on the slogan he had learned from the Reformers, according to which he claimed that the sacraments did not exist outside the sacramental act itself (*nullum sacramentum extra actionem sacramentalem*).

Wolferinus had learned this slogan from the theologians of Wittenberg. To begin with, the words were developed to criticize and

---

61. *WA* Br 11, 258, 5–7: "Primum non est negligentia, Sed nequitia Eaque insignis istius Diaconi, Qui contemptor Dei et hominum abusus est hostias consecratas ad non consecratas pro eodem habere."

62. See *WA* Tr 6, 179, 16–17.

63. *WA* Br 11, 258, 7–10: "Ideo simpliciter est ejiciendus extra nostras Ecclesias. Vadat ad suos Zuinglianos. Non est opus, ut carcere teneatur homo alienus a nobis, cui nihil etiam iuranti credendum est."

reject such Catholic traditions of popular piety where the sacraments were used for purposes other than those for which Jesus had instituted them. According to the idea behind these words, the sacrament was correct only in the proper usage, that is, in use according to Jesus's intent, not in such things as healing leprosy with baptismal water or blessing fields with hosts. Wolferinus went too far in reaching conclusions on this doctrine of *in usu* by thinking that the real presence ends the moment the Mass is over.

Luther protested strongly against this in his two letters, and was also joined in this by Bugenhagen.[64] He thought it was a scandal that the priest in question saw fit to mix the consecrated bread and wine with the unconsecrated elements after the Mass. The Reformer asked who the priest had learned this from and whose example he was following.

Luther rebuked Wolferinus for arousing, in general, with his incorrect use, speculation over the duration of the real presence, which was both dogmatically and pastorally "a scandalous and detrimental issue."[65] First, it was dangerous to claim to know for certain when the real presence ended. Secondly, the disrespectful behavior of the said minister harmed the congregation's sense of faith and aroused offence and sophistry. Soon the claim of Zwinglianism echoed: "You sound Zwinglian and I am beginning to believe that you are involved in their insanities."[66]

While urging Wolferinus to get back in line, Luther also exposed the normal use of Wittenberg, according to which the clergy or the last communicants finished all the elements. This is how no further pastoral or theological problems evolved: "You can well do as we do, that is drink and eat the rest of the elements with a few communicants, so that no hurtful or detrimental questions would arise about the duration of the

---

64. See *WA* Br 10, 336–41 (Luther's and Bugenhagen's Letter to Simon Wolferinus in Eisleben, 4.7.1543) and *WA* Br 10, 348–49 (Luther's second Letter to Simon Wolferinus, July 20, 1543).

65. *WA* Br 10, 340, 16–22: "Non nos a te, sed tu a nobis haud dubie habes, quod Sacramenta sint actiones, non stantes factiones. Sed quae est ista singularis tua temeritas, ut tam mala specie non abstineas, quam scire te oportuit esse scandalosam, nempe quod reliquum vini vel panis misces priori pani et vino? Quo exemplo id facis? Non vides certe, quam periculosas quaestiones movebis, si tuo sensu abundans contendes, cessante actione cessare Sacramentum?"

66. *WA* Br 10, 340, 22–23.

sacramental act, questions you will choke on if you do not soon come to your senses."⁶⁷

Luther reminded Wolferinus that he had learned the concept of *in usu* from the theologians of Wittenberg (not the other way around) but applied it incorrectly. The Reformator's train of thought reflects the concept according to which the Eucharist is both a created reality (*factus*) and an act (*actus*). In an ontological sense the consecrated bread is a new essence or element (*factus*) and eating it is an act.

In the second letter Luther defined the sacramental act broadly, so that apart from the consecration and the communion, also the remaining elements were to be finished. This was both theologically the safest and pastorally the most expedient usage: "Thus we are free and safe from all unsolved questions, gnawing at the conscience and offensive to it."⁶⁸

LUTHER'S POSITIVE UNDERSTANDING OF SACRIFICE

In the field of Luther research, a Protestant paradigm prevailed for a long time, according to which Luther unequivocally rejected all kinds of talk about the sacrifice of the Mass, as that was considered to represent Roman Catholicism and false religiosity.⁶⁹ It is true that Luther strongly criticized the then current concept of the Mass as a sacrifice. Nevertheless, our image of Luther is not clear enough. The New Testament often speaks in a positive sense of the sacrifice and of sacrificing, and Christians are admonished to offer God spiritual sacrifice (Rom 12:1; 1 Pet 2:5; Heb 13:15–16). Luther does the same. In his 1520 sermon on the Eucharist, for example, he claims "it is not only permissible but also useful to call the Mass a sacrifice."⁷⁰ How are these disparate points to be explained?

In the 1980s researchers such as Juhani Forsberg and Robert Jenson noticed that Luther also had an alternative theology of the sacrifice.⁷¹

---

67. WA Br 10, 341, 37–41: "Poteris enim ita, ut nos hic facimus, reliquum Sacramenti cum communicantibus ebibere et comedere, ut non sit necesse, quaestiones istas scandalosas et periculosas movere de cessatione actionis sacramentalis, in quibus tu suffocaberis, nisi resipiscas."

68. WA Br 10, 348, 13–33.

69. See Wislöff, *Abendmahl und Messe*.

70. *StA* 1, 303, 11–13: "Auß welchen worten wir lernen, das ... nach der meyß ist es leydlich, yha nuetzlich, das wir die meß ein opffer heyssen".

71. Forsberg, "Rukous tekona," 29–41; [Braaten &] Jenson, *Christian Dogmatics*, 351–52.

The Roman Catholic Reinhardt Messner in his dissertation in the 1990s contemplated, without prejudice, if Luther could also be a theologian supporting the sacrifice of the Mass (*Theologe des Messopfers*).[72] Finally, Wolfgang Simon in his massive study proved that Luther had an alternative theology of the sacrifice of the Mass. According to Simon, Luther did discard the interpretation of such a doctrine of the sacrifice of the Mass where the priest sacrificed the body and blood of Christ for the benefit of absent, live, parishioners and for those dead in Purgatory. Despite this, according to Simon one could find from Luther the doctrine of the sacrifice of the Mass.[73]

In Luther's thinking a sacrifice always has a reactive, or as Simon puts it, an "aposterior" nature. The sacrifice of the Mass cannot be an act whereby people aim to do their best to make God love them but it is always a reaction in which people respond to the saving deed already accomplished by God. A reactive act calls for faith: by believing in God's once for all saving deed on the cross, people confess God to be God, who acts first and who wills good things to them.

First, according to Luther, the Mass is called a sacrifice on the basis of the gifts of food and money, to be brought to the celebration and to be distributed among people: "We need to differentiate very clearly what we sacrifice and what we do not. The word 'sacrifice' has no doubt come about and kept its status in connection with the Eucharist, because during the Apostles' time, when certain Old Testament traditions were still observed, Christians brought together food, money, and other useful things to be divided to those in need, in connection with the Mass."[74]

---

72. Messner, *Messereform Martin Luthers*, 172-85.

73. See Simon, *Messopfertheologie Martin Luthers*, especially 262-389 and 699-712.

74. StA 1, 299, 15-300, 5: "Derhalben die weyl nu fast alle welt auß der messe hatt ein opffer gemacht . . . ßo muessen wir hie weyßlich unterscheydt haben, was wir hie opffern oder nit opffern. Es ist on allen zweyffel das wort 'opffern' in der meß da her kummen und bißher blieben, das zu den zeytten der Apostolen, da noch ettlich ubung des alten testaments ganghafftig waren, die Christen zusammen trugen essen, gellt und nottdurfft, wilchs neben der meß wart außgeteyllet den duerfftigen, wie ich gesagt habe, als wir noch leßen Act. iiij. das die Christen vorkaufften allis was sie hetten und brachtens fur die fueß der Apostolen, die liessens dan außteyllen unnd geben auß dem gemeynengut eynem yglichen was eer bedurfft. Szo leret nu der heylig Apostel S. Pauel, das man allis essen und wes wir brauchen sollen mit beeten und gottis wort gebenedeyen, und got darumb dancken, da her kompt das Benedicite unnd Gracias ubir tisch. So war der prauch des alten testaments, wen man gott danckt ubir den enpffangenen, guetter, das man sie empor hub mit den henden gegen gott, wie do stett ym gesetz Mosi:

Underlying this way of speaking is the tradition of the early christians to bring food and money to the Mass as gifts of God's creative work. Some of these were given to people suffering from want and some were set aside for holy use in the Eucharist. The giver would be a well-to-do parishioner, the gift is the shared wealth or property, the recipient and the beneficiary is the parishioner in need. Such a sacrifice is a social one because the communication of the gift takes place among people. The term does not refer to sacrifice but to the gifts of creation brought forth and the prayers attached to them.

According to an old tradition, the bread and the wine to be used at the Eucharist were separated from among the gifts (though this tradition gradually faded). According to Luther the bread and the wine as gifts of God's creative work were a part of the offering of thanksgiving. At the beginning of the Eucharistic liturgy they were brought forth and offered as signs of the congregation's gratitude. But as soon as they were consecrated, they became the sacrament, which was not sacrificed to God but distributed to people as God's gift.[75]

Secondly, Luther speaks about the sacrifice in the sense that in the Eucharist the congregation is giving and offering itself to God. In this case the one sacrificing is not only the priest ordained into office but also each Christian baptized into the common priesthood through baptism, meaning the entire congregation. And furthermore the sacrificial gift is not Christ's body and blood but the whole persona of the Christian: Christians give God themselves, their will, their thanksgiving and praise.

Such a concept comes out especially in the work *Misuse of the Mass*. Apart from praying and teaching, the intrinsic task of the priesthood is to offer sacrifice. In the New Covenant, sacrifice however concerns all Christians not only priests. Since in the New Testament the priesthood is made common by naming all baptized believers "the holy and royal priesthood", therefore sacrificing is also common, and belongs to every-

---

drumb haben die Apostell auch alßo auffgehaben, gott gedanckt, und speyß und was die Christen zusammen trugen mit dem gottis wort gebenedeiet. Auch Christus selbs, wie S. Lucas schreybt, hub den kilch auff und danckt got, tranck und gab den andern, ehe er das sacrament und testament eynsetzet."

75. WA 6, 525, 1–3: "Panis enim et vinum antea offeruntur ad benedicendum, ut per verbum et orationem sanctificentur. Postquam autem benedictus et consecratus est, iam non offertur sed accipitur dono a Deo."

one.⁷⁶ Since sacrificing is the task of the common priesthood, it follows then that the status of donor belongs to the entire congregation.

What does Luther mean by giving of oneself? In the New Covenant sacrificing is above all spiritual: to this belongs the mortification of the sin in oneself, private and communal prayer, the thank offering in the divine service (*sacrificium laudis*) as well as sacrificing oneself, that is, giving oneself to be used by God as an object of his work (*seipsum offere*). Ultimately the last item includes the following of the suffering Christ, that is, the entire Christian life based on faith and love.⁷⁷

These concepts of sacrifice are presented, for example, in a sermon on the Eucharist of 1520. When by gift we mean sacrament, Christ in the bread and the wine, people cannot be benefactors nor can God be the recipient. It is just the other way around: in the sacrament "God gives us everything." But it is acceptable to call the Mass a sacrifice when by gift we mean thanksgiving in the divine service and giving of oneself.⁷⁸ In the Mass people can be ascribed to the position of donor and God the position of recipient when the gift means a thanksgiving rising from faith and Christians' offering themselves.

---

76. WA 8, 420, 8–15: "Paremus et alterum aeque fortem et pergamus testimonia adducere de sacerdotio novi testamenti et eius officio! Paulus Rom. XII 'Obsecro vos per misericordiam Dei, ut exhibeatis corpora vestra hostiam sanctam, viventem, placentem Deo, rationabile obsequium vestrum'. Hic negare nemo potest, quin sacerdotale officium describat, quod est offere seu exhibere hostiam et rationabilem cultum, hoc est, ut non pecora irrationalia, sicut legis sacerdotes, sed *se ipsos offerant*. Quare hic locus sacerdotes facit. At *communiter omnibus Christianis* dicitur. *Omnes enim suo corpora offere debent Deo in hostiam sanctam et rationale sacrificium*." Italics mine.

77. WA 8, 420, 17–24: "Habemus ergo hoc loco Pauli auctoritate non solum, quod sit sacerdotium et qui sacerdotes novi testamenti, sed et quod sit eorum officium et sacrificium, nempe *se ipsos mortificare et offere in hostiam sanctam*, quo verbo simul universa legis sacrificia mystice interpretatur. Sic enim et Christus, summus sacerdos, prior sese sacrificavit, factus omnibus filiis suis sacerdotibus exemplum et sequantur vestigia eius." Italics mine.

78. StA 1, 302, 3–12: "Drumb sollen wir des worts 'opffer' wol warnhemen, das wir nit vormessen, etwas gott zu geben yn dem sacrament, ßo er uns darynnen alle dingk gibt. Wir sollen geystlich opffern, die weyll die leyplichen opffer abgangen und in kirchen, kloester, spital guetter vorwandelt seyn. Was sollen wir den opffern? *Uns selb und allis was wir haben mit gleyssigem gepeet*, wie wir sagen 'dein will geschehe auff der erden als ym hymel', Hie mit *wir uns dargeben sollen* gottlichem willen, das er von und auß uns mache, was er wil noch seynem gottlichen wolgefallen, dartzu yhm *lob und danck opffern* auß gantzem hertzen fur sein unaussprechliche suesse gnade und barmhertzickeit die er uns in dißem sacrament zugesagt und geben hat." Italics mine.

Luther's *On the Babylonian Captivity of the Church* makes a corresponding distinction between the sacrament and the sacrifice. According to Luther people give and sacrifice *prayers* to God but not the Mass, the sacrament (*non Missa sed orationes offerantur Deo*). When the Scholastic doctrine of the Mass as a sacrifice understands the consecrated elements to be the people's gift, Luther in a way replaces them with prayer. The Eucharist descends whereas prayer ascends. The Eucharist is a sacrament and a testament which comes from God to us (*a Deo ad nos*) through the service of the minister and it requires faith. On the other side, prayer is a sacrifice and a good deed, which rises from our faith to God (*a fide nostra ad Deum*) through the service of the minister and it requires hearing.[79] Luther can thus easily accept a constellation where people are understood as being in the position of donors and God that of a recipient. The sacrifice in this is not the sacrament but the intercessory prayer.

Thirdly, Luther calls the Mass a sacrifice because in it "Christ sacrifices us." "We learn from these words that we do not sacrifice Christ but Christ offers us. It is in this very sense that it is not only permissible but also useful to call the Mass a sacrifice, not for the Mass itself, but because we sacrifice ourselves with Christ."[80] In the cult of Christianity, prayer, thanksgiving, praise, and self-sacrifice are thus not brought directly to God but everything takes place through Christ.[81] This concept is seen in the closing formula of the Collect and Eucharistic prayers: *per Iesum Christum Dominum nostrum* or *per ipsum et cum ipso et in ipso*.

The idea of the two subjects of giving, Christ and the congregation, as part of Luther's third model, is not unique within the history of theology. Both the modern liturgical movement as well as present-day Roman Catholic theology stress the doctrine of Christ as a primary subject of

---

79. WA 6, 526, 13-18.

80. StA 1, 303, 11-15: "Auß welchen worten wir lernen, das wir nit Christum, sondern Christus uns opffert, und nach der meyß ist es leydlich, yha nuetzlich, das wir die meß ein opffer heyssen, nit umb yret willen, sondern das wir uns mit Christo opffern." See also Simon, *Messopferlehre*, 298-300.

81. StA 1, 302, 27-303, 7: "Das ist wol war, solch gepeet, lob, danck und unser selbs opffer sollen wir nit durch uns selbs fur tragen fur gottis augen, sondern auff Christum legen und yhn lassen dasselb furtragen, wie S. Pauel leret Heb. xiij. Lasset uns altzeyt gott opffern ein opffer des lobes, wilchs ist die frucht der lippen, die yhn bekennen und preyssen, und das allis durch Christum, den darumb ist er auch ein priester, wie ps. 109. sagt 'Du bist ein ewiger priester nach der weyße Melchisedech', das er fur uns bittet ym hymel, unser gepett und opffer emphehet, und durch sich selb, als ein frumer pfaff, fur gott angenhem macht."

the liturgy. Christ is not only the object of the liturgy celebrated by the congregation but also a subject who works in and through the liturgy of the congregation.

Despite his strong criticism directed at the doctrine of the sacrifice of the Mass, Luther has his own positive theory of the Mass as a sacrifice. The Mass can be called a sacrifice in the sense that 1) in connection with the Mass Christians give of their earthly goods to their needy fellowmen, and 2) they give to the Heavenly Father as a spiritual sacrifice their will, thanksgiving, praise and their entire persons as well as 3) they give themselves in Christ, through him, and with him. The bread and the wine can in themselves as good gifts of creation be considered the visible signs of the spiritual sacrifice of thanksgiving among Christians.

7

Faith

Olli-Pekka Vainio

All too often Martin Luther's spiritual struggle is summarized in the claim that Luther "wanted to find a merciful God," and the solution to this search was the doctrine of justification by faith alone. Even though this claim is not totally false, it gives too limited a view of what was going on in the mind of this Augustinian monk. Luther is depicted thereby as a person pathologically interested in his feelings of guilt, a picture repeated in the film *Luther* (2004) in which Joseph Fiennes' character shakes and cries like Gollum from *The Lord of the Rings*. This trajectory leaves us with a picture of the Christian religion that is overtly individualistic, subjectivist, even irrational, and of little value for society as whole. If justification is understood as merely a change of person's status before God, we have secured the objective side of salvation *outside of us* but we are still lacking a coherent account of how this faith affects our internal and communal life. How should we understand the nature of faith *in us*?[1]

The purpose of this article is to describe how Luther understood the nature of faith. Naturally, "justification by faith alone" is the center of Reformation theology, but I am afraid that we have become so accustomed to this phrase that it betrays both the originality and the traditionality of Luther's idea. In the following discussion, I will first examine

---

1. This view could be easily augmented in the following way. The reverse side of guilt is the question of performing good works. What a good should I strive for? How are good works to be performed so that they are genuinely good? This opens a more communal view into Luther's inner struggle.

how Luther understands the apprehension and application of Christ's righteousness; then, I will show what consequences the union with God has for Christian life; and finally, I will address how Christian life is to be understood as a progressive growth in grace and holiness.

WHY FAITH JUSTIFIES?

What does it mean when we say that faith justifies? The standard Lutheran answer is that because faith receives the merit of Christ. But this just pushes the problem further away. Why does faith receive the merit of Christ?

For Luther, the ultimate basis for an individual's salvation lies in Christ's person and his work. As Sammeli Juntunen argues in a greater detail in this same volume, the personal union and the communication of attributes in the person of Christ are the prerequisites for the salvation of the human race. As the true God, Christ destroys the powers and principalities that hold creation captive; as the true Man Christ also embodies this victory in his own person. Luther depicts this act with two opposite concepts of annihilation and creation, which can be attributed to God alone as acts peculiar to divine nature.[2] Salvation is, however, incomprehensible to us outside the human form of Christ in which God has manifested himself. Nevertheless, incarnation does not take place only because of cognitive comprehensibility, but because Christ's acts and obedience in his assumed nature create the form of righteousness, which is reckoned to us in faith.[3] In later Lutheranism it was the matter of debate whether the righteousness of faith that is reckoned to us is God's essential righteousness or Christ's obedience.[4] The Formula of Concord (1580) offered a solution that brought together these views by claiming that it is "the righteousness of the person of Christ" (FC III, 55–58) that genuinely expressed Luther's view on this issue as well. From this formulation it follows that righteousness is now bound to the person of the incarnated and risen Christ. Luther expresses this as follows.

---

2. *WA* 40/I, 441, 1–11. See also *WA* 40/I, 442, 3–7, 21–24.

3. *WA* 40/I, 78, 3–79, 6; 78, 24–26. *WA* 40/I, 64, 22–65, 18.

4. Andreas Osiander (1498–1552) claimed that the righteousness that avails *coram Deo* is God's essential righteousness. Other Lutheran theologians, however, accused Osiander of dismissing the role of satisfaction and Christ's work, and emphasized Christ's merit as the formal righteousness.

> Therefore, Christ, who is divine Power, Righteousness, Blessing, Grace, and Life, conquers and destroys these monsters—sin, death, and the curse—without weapons or battle, in His own body, and in Himself (*in suo corpore et Semetipso*) ...[5]
>
> Therefore I have conquered the Law by double claim: first, as the Son of God, the Lord of the Law; secondly, in your person (*in persona vestra*), which is tantamount to your having conquered the Law yourselves.[6]

Because Christ suffers and shows obedience to the will of his Father in his assumed human form, this enables his merit to be applicable to us. In faith a happy exchange (*commercium admirabile*) takes place in which the parties involved (individual human being and God) are mutually entangled with each other's attributes, so that a person's sin, damnation, death, and all his evils are transferred to Christ, and the righteousness of Christ is transferred to the believer.[7] Believers still feel the effects of sin in their lives until the end of their earthly life, but God no longer imputes the punishment to them.[8]

Resulting from the christological basis of justification, the mode of participation, and the happy exchange, salvation is now bound ontologically to the person of Christ. In other words, Christ *himself* is the righteousness of the Christian. The belief in Christ brings forth the union of Christ and consequent sharing of his merits and righteousness. The proclamation of the Gospel thus has to deliver both the cognitively understood information about what Christ has done for human beings (*gratia*) and Christ himself, the gift (*donum*).[9] The cognitive understanding of the mercy of God and the possession of the gift together form an indivisible entity, since mercy becomes effective only through the gift, namely, Christ's real presence, and mercy is what makes the gift recognizable.

With this christological foundation in place, we may return to our initial question about what it is that makes faith the medium of salva-

---

5. WA 40/I, 440, 21–23. Translation from *LW* 26, 282.
6. WA 40/I, 566, 14–17. Translation from *LW* 26, 370–71.
7. WA 40/I, 454, 9–455, 6; 454, 19–455, 30.
8. WA 40/I, 273, 2–9, 19–29.
9. On the mutual order of *gratia* and *donum*, see Risto Saarinen's article in this volume. Mercy here means the objective foundation of salvation, Christ's salvific acts and the forgiveness of sins. The gift means Christ's effective, salvific, and vivifying presence. WA 40/I, 236, 15; 72, 28–29.

tion? Although everything is ready on God's side, there has to be an application of what Christ has done on the human side. This participation in Christ's merit is depicted by the concept "apprehending Christ" (*apprehendere Christum*). The key to Luther's understanding of the nature of faith lies in the use of the verb *apprehendo*.[10]

The word *apprehendere* was a standard concept in scholastic philosophy with which Luther become familiar during his studies. A standard division between the faculties of the human mind was made by St Thomas Aquinas, who claimed that there are appetitive (*appetitivus*) and apprehensive (*apprehensivus*) faculties.[11] Appetitive faculties include the acts of will, whereas apprehensive faculties are connected with knowledge and understanding. For Luther too, *apprehendo* means intellectual apprehension, understanding, and comprehension. However, the term has a deeper meaning whereby the object of knowledge becomes the property of a knowing subject.[12]

Luther's understanding of apprehension can be characterized as follows: the Gospel is the good news about a merciful God, who acts in order to save the fallen human race by sending his Son to redeem the world. This news is genuine news to humans, since they are not naturally aware of God's mercy. The Holy Spirit reveals God to the terrified sinner as a loving and forgiving father.[13] The intellectual and cognitive apprehension of the good news means knowing God who gives himself to and on behalf of sinners. This proclamation of the Gospel evokes faith in the sinner, which grasps and possesses (*apprehendit*) Christ. The mode of this apprehension is to be understood in terms of Aristotelian epistemology, which Luther uses and develops further when he speaks of Christ as the form of faith. Aristotle claimed that in the act of know-

---

10. See, e.g., WA 40/I, 164, 18–21. The verb *apprehendo* appears in the *Commentary* over 300 times. In some studies, Luther's notion of faith is summarized in the formula "faith that apprehends Christ" (*fides apprehensiva Christi*). Luther uses this formulation in WA 39 I, 45, 21–22: "Haec est autem fides apprehensiva (ut dicimus) Christi, pro peccatis nostris morientis, et pro iustitia nostra resurgentis." For more on this formulation, see *Huovinen, Fides infantium*, 157–70.

11. *ST*, I, 79–80.

12. Huovinen (*Fides infantium*) has demonstrated how the notion of "infused faith" (*fides infusa*) forms a pair with the idea of "apprehending faith" (*fides apprehensiva Christi*). *Fides infusa* depicts the actual effects of God in the human being, while *fides apprehensiva* is disposed toward the object of faith.

13. WA 40/I, 602, 5–603, 2; 602, 18–603, 13.

ing, the form of the object of knowledge is transferred into the knower.[14] According to Aristotle, when we think about horses, for example, the object of the intellect is the form (*eidos, forma*) of the horse as the form is actualized in a particular horse. However, this entails the same form being actualized in the observer's mind, while the object retains its form; in other words, the horse does not lose its form (and consequently cease being a horse) when we perceive it. But how this is possible? What do we actually perceive and what is it that we receive in the act of perception? This was an essential question in medieval philosophy and the cause of great debate, because Aristotle's texts did not give an exact answer to this question. Without going into the details of the medieval discussion, the general view was that human thought and intellect re-enact the rational structure of the world and somehow become identical with the world, while objects in the world still retain their inherent structure. As a solution, philosophers thus supposed the existence of a particular intelligible species (*species intelligibilis*) or a secondary form, which is identical with the form of the object, while remaining distinct from it.[15]

Luther builds his notion of faith as apprehension on this medieval theory, while giving it a new interpretation. Luther interprets Aristotle in ontologically realistic terms to mean that Christ is not present in the mind of the observer merely in the sense of *species intelligibilis*, but as the actual form. Thus, when the human intellect focuses on Christ in the Gospel, it apprehends and owns Christ, and consequently Christ is made the form of the human intellect. In this apprehension the believer does not possess the intelligible species of Christ, but possesses Christ himself. This means that Christ is presence in the believing person cannot be understood in terms of the redirection of the human faculties or as new psychological and anthropological entities alone. Instead, Life and Bliss bestowed by Christ are not entities separate from his person but are divine attributes.[16]

One crucial result of this is that faith becomes essentially a divine act in human person. In the union with Christ the corrupted human will is annihilated and created anew by Christ so that in faith, the ap-

---

14. See Spruit, *Species Intelligibilis*, 37–38, 45–46; See also Aristotle *De anima* 424a17.

15. Spruit, *Species Intelligibilis*, 47.

16. See Mannermaa, "Über die Unmöglichkeit," 390.

petitive and apprehensive faculties merge.[17] Therefore, the person believes in Christ because Christ himself is not only an object of faith, but also the subject of faith.[18] The faith that saves is a new divine reality in the human being, Christ, who takes over both the intellect and other faculties of the soul.[19]

Salvific faith for Luther is ultimately an act that eludes exact definition or explanation, although Luther may use an elaborate conceptualization to make his point. What distinguishes Luther from later generations is his use of mystical language and metaphors. Instead of using approaches similar to later "orders of salvation" (*ordo salutis*) in which numerous stages or phases of faith were listed, Luther refers to biblical pictures, such as a branch re-joined to a tree or christological scenes where believer and Christ are represented as one person (*quasi una persona*).[20] Luther sees salvation as one act that joins multiple elements, which mutually both enable and require each other.

> Here it is to be noted that these three things are joined together: faith, Christ, acceptance or imputation. Faith takes hold of Christ, and has Him present, enclosing Him as the ring encloses the gem. And whoever is found having this faith in Christ who is grasped in the heart, him God counts as righteous.[21]

THE UNION WITH LOVE

Participation in Christ in faith generates participation in the Trinity as well (2 Pet 1:4). The union with Christ entails becoming one with God—

---

17. WA 40/I, 282–88. Here Luther explains Gal 2:20 ("I live; yet not I, but Christ lives in me").

18. WA 40/I, 545–46; 610; WA 40/II, 178–79. See also Hays, *Faith of Jesus Christ*.

19. Christ's status as the form of the faith means that the mind of the believer and the mind of Christ share the same form. WA 40/I, 650, 21–32: ". . . per omnia de Deo cogitant, ut in corde affectus est, habent eandem formam in animo quam Deus vel Christus."

20. WA 40/I, 285, 24–286, 21. See also WA 40/I, 285, 5–286, 1. Although the union with Christ is real, the substances are not absorbed into one another. See Peura, "Der Vergöttlichungsgedanke," 179–80.

21. WA 40/I, 233, 16–24: "Est et hic notandum, quod ista tria, Fides, Christus, Acceptio vel Reputatio, coniuncta sunt. Fides enim apprehendit Christum et habet eum praesentem includitque eum ut anulus gemmam, Et qui fuerit inventus cum tali fide apprehensi Christi in corde, illum reputat Deus iustum." Translation from *LW* 26, 132.

who is Love.²² Here we must return to the concept of form and how Luther reconstructs the trends of medieval theology. Some branches of scholastic theology held the view that human love was totally corrupted by the Fall so that love still follows the "order of love" (*ordo caritatis*) instituted and inscribed into the hearts of humankind in the creation, whereby human love is always inclined toward the greater and better object.²³ A top of this order is, of course, the highest good (*summum bonum*), that is, God. Human beings can use this natural disposition to good so that it evokes the love of God and fullfils the first commandment, at least in minimal fashion. When a person does everything that is within his or her powers (*facere quod in se est*), God infuses his grace into this person.²⁴

Luther, however, does not think that this genuinely reflects the biblical account of salvation. Human love may follow the order of love in some matters but employing it in relation to God is problematic because human intellect and will are corrupted by evil desire.²⁵ In spiritual matters it is love that may lead one away from God, or even worse, against God (*contra Deum*). Hence, merely an accidental change in the human faculties of the soul is not enough because people are in need of more substantial change.²⁶ Further theological argument against the *ordo caritatis* is that it makes faith secondary while love is the primary medium of salvation. In scholastic language this was expressed in the concept "faith formed by love" (*fides charitate formata*).²⁷ Using this model as a framework, Luther claims that it is not faith formed by love that saves, but faith formed by Christ (*fides Christo formata*). Our formal righteousness (*iustitia formalis*) is not love, but faith—Christ—himself.²⁸

---

22. WA 40/I, 182, 4–5, 15–16.

23. On Luther's *critique of ordo caritatis*, see Raunio, *Summe des Christlichen Lebens*, 57–59, 76–87, 121, 123.

24. According to Luther, *facere quod in se est* means that a person could fulfill the Law with his or her own powers, and is thus able to acquire *meritum de congruo*. This provides grace, which makes the person worthy of eternal life (*gratia gratum faciens*), and eventually leads to reception of *meritum de condigno*. See, e.g., WA 40/I, 220, 4–10, 13–16, 22–29; 227, 21–25; 228, 18–21; 230, 19–20; 291, 16–20.

25. WA 40/I, 293, 18–294, 22.

26. WA 40/I, 461, 16–24.

27. WA 40/I, 164, 15–19; 422, 14–22.

28. WA 40/I, 197, 7–198, 2; 229, 2–13; 369, 1–6; 363, 8–364, 2; 370, 6–11; 371, 1–4; 372, 8–12. Luther uses interchangeably the expressions "Christ" and "faith." See and

Such are the dreams of the scholastics. But where they speak of love, we speak of faith. And while they say that faith is the mere outline but love is its living colors and completion, we say in opposition that faith takes hold of Christ and the He is the form that adorns and informs faith as color does the wall. Therefore Christian faith is not an idle quality or an empty husk in the heart, which may exist in a state of mortal sin until love comes along to make it alive. But if it is true faith, it is a sure trust (*fiducia*) and firm acceptance (*assensus*) in the heart. It takes hold of Christ in such a way that Christ is the object of faith, or rather not the object but, so to speak, the One who is present in the faith itself (*in ipsa fide Christus adest*). Thus faith is a sort of knowledge (*cognitio*) or darkness that nothign can see. Yet the Christ of whom faith takes hold is sitting in this darkness as God sat in the midst of darkness on Sinai and in the temple. Therefore our "formal righteousness" (*formalis iustitia*) is not a love that informs faith; but is faith itself, a cloud in our hearts, that is, trust in a thing we do not see, in Christ, who is present especially when He cannot be seen.

Therefore faith justifies because it takes hold of and possesses this treasure, the present Christ. But how He is present—this is beyond our thought; for there is darkness, as I have said. Where the confidence of the heart is present, therefore, there Christ is present, in that very cloud and faith. This is the formal righteousness on account of which a man is justified; it is not on account of love, as the sophists say. In short, just as the sophists say that love forms and fulfills faith, so we say that it is Christ who forms and trains faith, so we say that it is Christ who forms and trains faith or who is the form of faith. Therefore the Christ who is grasped by faith and who lives in the heart is the true Christian righteousness, on account of which God counts (*reputat*) us righteous and grants us eternal life. Here there is no work of the Law, no love; but there is an entirely different kind of righteousness, a new world above and beyond the Law. For Christ or faith is neither the Law nor the work of the Law.[29]

But does this mean that faith and love are essentially opposed? If justification is by faith alone, what role is there left for love? Pope Benedict XVI expressed this concern in his speech at the Vatican general audience on November 19, 2008. For the Pope, Luther's understanding of

---

compare WA 40/I, 229, 2, 13, 18, 25; 232, 24; 363, 9; 364, 12; 368, 31; 369, 24; 408, 7. See also Mannermaa, "Hat Luther eine trinitarische Ontologie?"

29. WA 40/I, 228, 28–229, 30. Translation from *LW* 26, 129–30.

justification is correct "if it is not opposed to love."[30] In order to answer this question we need to clarify what we mean by "love" in this context: what is the nature of love, and what is love supposed to do? The Pope wants first of all to safeguard Christianity against libertinism. He writes: "Christian freedom is not libertinism; the liberation of which St. Paul spoke is not liberation from good works." In other words, justification by faith should not be taken to mean that love and good works are not obligatory for Christians. Apparently, Luther never meant this by his formulation. On the nature of faith, the Pope writes in a way that shows a remarkable affinity with Luther's views.[31]

> Being just simply means being with Christ and in Christ. And this suffices. Further observances are no longer necessary. For this reason Luther's phrase: "faith alone" is true, if it is not opposed to faith in charity, in love. Faith is looking at Christ, entrusting oneself to Christ, being united to Christ, conformed to Christ, to his life. And the form, the life of Christ, is love; hence to believe is to conform to Christ and to enter into his love. So it is that in the Letter to the Galatians in which he primarily developed his teaching on justification St Paul speaks of faith that works through love (cf. Gal 5: 14).[32]

Being united with Christ and entrusting oneself to him is the essence of faith, which also brings about the union with divine love. According to the Pope: "It is the same vision, according to which communion with Christ, faith in Christ, creates charity. And charity is the fulfillment of communion with Christ. Thus, we are just by being united

---

30. Benedict XVI, *General audience on Wednesday November 19, 2009*. All the subsequent citations of the Pope are from this same source.

31. The affinity is not merely imaginary and it has natural explanation. Benedict's theology is deeply influenced by Augustine, as Luther's thought was as well. Additionally, the statements in *Fides et Ratio*, for example, indicate a less rigid support for Thomism, which allows more sympathetic treatments of other philosophical systems among modern Catholicism reflecting thus the central criticism of Luther regarding the abuses of selfsupported, unbiblical, philosophies. Benedict's Thomism resembles to some extent the one of Radical Orthodoxy and its claims that Aquinas's philosophical account of truth needs theological basis. See Rowland, *Ratzinger's faith*, 27–28.

32. Compare this to Luther's words in WA 40/I, 283, 34–284, 28: "Abiding and living in me, Christ removes and absorbs all the evils that torment and afflict me. This attachment to Him causes me to be liberated from the terror of the Law and of sin, pulled out of my own skin, and transferred into Christ and into His Kingdom, which is a kingdom of grace, righteousness, peace, joy, life, salvation, and eternal glory. Since I am in Him, no evil can harm me." Translation from *LW* 26, 167.

with him and in no other way." Hence, the Pope denies that human works have justifying power because everything that is needed for salvation is included in the person and the work of Christ in whom we are united through faith. Because the union with Christ essentially means becoming one with divine love, it cannot be said that Luther's view is "opposed to love." This love is not human endeavour to reach heaven by natural powers alone, but a participation in Christ who enables the good works. Additionally, love does not function as a medium of salvation since Christ alone suffices.[33]

REGENERATION, SANCTIFICATION, AND THE GROWTH IN GRACE

Shortly before his death, Richard John Neuhaus (1936–2009), a Lutheran minister who later became Catholic and one of the most politically influential Christians of recent decades, wrote about his experience as a young seminarian one of whose professors taught, "the phrase *growth in grace* is a contradiction in terms."[34] From the professor's point of view, if forgiveness is absolute, then there is no need for growth. If some kind of growth is required, does that not spoil the unmerited grace? Does the grace not become dependent on the growth? But how can we motivate holiness, which is clearly a part of Christian life?

Lutheran spiritual life is typically depicted through the dialectics of the Law and the Gospel. The Law shows the sins of a person and when the sinner realizes that he has not fulfilled the requirements of the Law, God's wrath start to terrify him breaking the human self-righteousness. The solution to this problem is the Gospel, which freely promises God's mercy.[35] This dialectical model has been somewhat problematic in the history of Lutheranism because it has produced forms of life that are

---

33. Luther's comments in his *Commentary on Galatians* on the passages in the Bible where it seems that deeds are meritorious (e.g., Gen 4:3). This way of speaking is, according to Luther, possible because faith truly makes a person's deeds righteous. The special example of this is Abraham, who is diffused by faith so that the deeds are no longer done by the sinner, but the righteous person. Faith is like divine nature in the person of Christ; the whole is made truly holy because of the participation in divinity so that the faith and deeds form a composition (*compositio*). It is thus possible to say that deeds are salvific, although they are salvific only because of the faith that makes them so. WA 40/I, 412–19.

34. Neuhaus, "On loving the Law of God," 61.

35. WA 40/I, 505, 17–27; 506, 20–28; 506, 34–507, 14.

clearly against the basic intention of the Gospel, namely, the libertinism and antinomianism the Pope warned against.[36] Another unwanted result is spiritual laxity, which is produced by the fear of self-righteousness. If all my deeds are totally sinful, even spirituality (praying, reading the Scripture, singing, praise, charity, and so forth) is tainted with evil desires that spoil these practices. Thus, the spirituality can develop into the worst kind of hypocrisy, and then the only deed resembling in the slightest something good is to expose the hypocrisy of the practice. Naturally, there results a rather destructive form of spirituality, whose closest dialogue partners can be found among radical postmodern deconstructive theology. If freedom from the Law means liberation from obeying God's commandments or the deconstruction of Christian spirituality, then we have come a long way from Luther's original intentions.

The strength of Luther's idea of the distinction between Law and the Gospel is that it can effectively soothe a troubled conscience as the Gospel turns eyes to God's mercy. However, the danger lies in its reductive reading of spiritual reality. Christians are not either complacent or despairing (a complacent person should receive the annihilating treatment of the Law, and a despairing one should be comforted by the Gospel). But surely Christian life does not boil down to perpetual and radical oscillation between these two extremes, as Neuhaus rightly points out in his essay.[37]

If we take Luther's understanding of Christ's presence in faith as the center of spiritual life and progress, the dialectics of the Law and the Gospel find their natural and rightful place, and the dangers and fears of Pelagianism and self-righteousness are avoided as well. In other words, if the person of Christ is the center and the *forma* of justification, then the *materia* (the purely human endeavors and deeds) lose their justifying function. The human faculties as *materia* are nothing when compared to *forma*. This is because it is the form that gives matter its essence. Thus,

---

36. For example, Reinhard Hütter (*Bound to be Free*, 134–35) speaks of "the antinomian fallacy" of mainline Protestantism and argues that recent Roman catholic moral theology has in effect expressed Luther's views more authentically than Lutherans themselves.

37. Neuhaus, "On Loving the Law of God," 63. The dialectical spirituality also makes it hard to understand whether there can be real, non-sinful, self-love if everything that is in Christians is sinful.

the change that takes place in the conversion has no merit for the form; Christ now calls the shots, not the matter.[38]

Traditionally, the essence of justification in Lutheran theology is described as an imputation of Christ's merit. Luther's aforementioned notions, however, seem to suggest that this interpretation does not address every detail of the issue. Yes, justification is based on God's mercy and Christ's work outside of us, which is made our own through imputation. But the question that follows is the same as one regarding why faith justifies: why is it the imputation that applies Christ's merit? Luther seems to think imputation takes place because Christ is present in the individual through faith.[39] As was already noted, Luther does not consider different elements of justification as being separable. Justifying righteousness involves the apprehension of Christ in faith, not merely imputation of righteousness (*pura reputatio*), which Luther explicitly denies.[40] Thus, Luther distances himself from the strictest interpretations of forensic justification.[41] Justification involves participation in Christ. But what is the relation between apprehending Christ and actually becoming righteous?

Luther argues that justification entails that one is "being formed;" a person is born again as a new creature (*nova creatura*). Something has changed in the person. All of this takes place without human merit, as does the natural birth of individuals.

> Therefore we come to these eternal goods—the forgiveness of sins, righteousness, the glory of the resurrection, and eternal life—not actively but passively. Nothing whatever interferes here; faith alone takes hold of the offered promise. Therefore just as

---

38. I have dealt with the charges against Pelagianism, subjectivism and mysticism in my "Christ in us and for us." See also Mannermaa, *Christ Present in Faith*, 23–31; Juntunen, *Der Begriff des Nichts*, 347–53.

39. WA 40/I, 233, 1–5: "...fides quae includat Christum et habeat eum praesentem ut in einer Zang ein edlenstein. Qui fuerit inventus tali fide apprehensi Christi, illum reputat deus iustum."

40. WA 40/I 372, 8–11: "Non est pura reputatio, sed involvit ipsam fidem et apprehensionem Christi passi pro nobis, quae non levis res. Sic vides, quod sine operibus propter peccata manentia et peccata oportet illam habere reputationem quae fit propter Christum, in quem credimus." Luther juxtaposes verbal (*verbaliter*) and actual (*realiter*) change. Verbal change implies only outward transformation while actual change transforms the mind and the will as well. See WA 40/II, 179.

41. An example of strict version is Matthias Flacius's view. See Vainio, *Justification and Participation*, 109–17, and Nüssel, *Allein aus Glauben*, 90–91.

> in society a son becomes an heir merely by being born, so here faith alone makes (*efficit*) men sons of God, born of the Word, which is the divine womb in which we are conceived, carried, born, reared, etc. By this birth and patience or passivity (*patientia et passione*) which makes us Christians we also become sons and heirs. But being heirs, we are free of death and the devil, and we have righteousness and eternal life. This comes to us in a purely passive way; for we do not do anything, but we let ourselves be made and formed (*fieri et formari*) as a new creation through faith in the Word.[42]

On the other hand, while Luther stresses the reality of change, he also stresses the distinct nature of justification and faith, and good works and love.

> Therefore this gloss is to be avoided as a hellish poison and we must conclude with Paul: By faith alone, not by faith formed by love, are we justified. We must not attribute the power of justifying to a "form" that makes a man pleasing to God; we must attribute it to faith, which takes hold of Christ the Savior Himself and possesses Him in the heart. This faith justifies without love and before love.[43]

But isn't this exactly the teaching the Pope warned against? Here again we must take notice of the use of the word "love". Luther here opposes love as a *human deed* to faith, stressing that this love does not have the "faculty of justification". In later Lutheranism it became common to treat justification and good works in different articles; Luther himself states that "The fact that Christ gives commandments and teaches, or actually interprets the law in the Gospels does not belong to the *locus* of justification but to the *locus* of Good Works."[44] This is supposed to clarify the means and method of justification so that good works are not considered meritorious, although the ability to perform them is included in the effective nature of justification. Sometimes this idea is paraphrased by saying that justification and sanctification are distinct but not separated. Usually in Lutheran theology, it has been more important to emphasize the distinction rather than the unity of these acts. Nevertheless, in *Von*

---

42. WA 40/I, 597, 19-29. Translation from *LW* 26, 392. See also WA 40/I, 596, 12-597, 13; 599, 8-600, 4; 597, 14-23; 600, 16-20.

43. WA 40/I, 239, 30-240, 16. Translation from *LW* 26, 137.

44. WA 40/I, 568, 25-27.

den Conciliis und Kirchen (1539), Luther emphasised that Christ must be both *gratia* and *donum*. Removing *donum* from the heart of soteriology leads to a make-believe Christian life in which grace is spoken about merely in a outward manner, yet the person keeps on sinning; there is no call to a new life.[45] Both justification (the forensic side) and sanctification (the effective side) take place simultaneously because Christ is the source of both. The righteousness present in a Christian consists of imputed righteousness and renewal begun in the individual through the presence of Christ. However, this renewal cannot be considered the believer's own meritorious act, since it is a form of participation in God's love, which affects the new birth. In this context, Luther uses the metaphor of becoming a good tree. When the nature of the tree is changed, it can bear good fruit according to its new nature.[46] Accordingly, a Christian who has been justified and renewed can now perform deeds that are good in God's sight.[47] In this limited sense justification is connected with becoming righteous, although justification is based on the presence of the gift, Christ, in the sinner, not on this change as such. Justification as the imputation of alien righteousness is needed until death since the Christian is still sinful, albeit in a state of constant renewal.[48]

Justification is the beginning of life-long renewal. The Holy Spirit illuminates and renews the Christian day by day so that it becomes easier to love God and to love neighbor.[49] Since this renewal remains imperfect

---

45. WA 50, 599–600. This was the original Roman accusation against Lutheranism, which was repeated in the twentieth century, see, e.g., Denifle, *Luther*. Daniel M. Bell has examined implications of different understandings of forgiveness for liberation theology. He convincingly argues that the effective form of forgiveness only functions as a counternarrative to the story of violence (he does not, however, refer to Luther in his work). This is one example where Luther's original ideas of justification could have practical use. See Bell, *Liberation Theology*, 177–95.

46. WA 40/I, 401, 30–402, 20.

47. WA 40/I, 265, 29–36; 287, 2–5, 19–23; 402, 1–11, 13–17; 404, 1–6, 17–18; WA 40/II, 66, 1–6, 14–22, 30–32.

48. WA 40/I, 233, 8–234, 5; 235, 1–236, 2. See also WA 40/I, 233, 25–234, 23; 235, 15–236, 16; 236, 26–32; 40/II, 86, 4–8, 13–19.

49. WA 40/I, 400, 31–402, 22; 40/II 168, 15–17. The regenerates have the form of Christ (*forma Christi*). WA 40/I, 649, 19–30; 650, 13–651, 15. See also WA 40/II, 177, 4–178, 5; 178, 16–19; 179, 33–35; 180, 22–30. This means actual renewal in the believer. New skills of evaluation (*iudicium*), new will, new mind, new movements of the mind (*motus animi*), new affects of love and the faculty to do outward good works result from this renewal. The Spirit infuses these new affects in the mind of the believer. WA 40/I, 572, 2–11; 574, 2–13; 578, 11–579, 6; 572, 16–31; 574, 23–575, 12; 578, 34–579, 17; WA 40/II, 124, 27–30; 177, 4–178, 5; 178, 16–179, 23.

until death, the Christian needs justification as an imputation of Christ's righteousness in order to maintain the certainty of salvation. Yet the absolute nature of imputation does not mean that growth in grace is a contradiction in terms. Luther writes about how Christians are called to become "more perfect day by day."[50] Nevertheless, this notion has been a problem in Lutheran theology. Sometimes it has been interpreted as growth in understanding of God's grace instead of ethical improvement. This interpretation, which emphasizes the declaratory nature of justification, seems to go against the assurances that Lutheran grace does not lead to the downplaying of sanctification.[51] The well-known principle in Lutheran theology is the claim that the Christian is simultaneously righteous and a sinner (*simul iustus et peccator*). This means that, from God's point of view the believer is totally holy, while the believer's viewpoint, one is totally a sinner; the *simul*-principle thus expresses the idea of forensic justification trying to cut away the wings from all kinds of self-righteousness. Eric Gregory aptly summarizes Augustinian fears regarding progress and growth:

> Augustinians are usually nervous with the language of habituation given their strong doctrine of grace (there is no ascent without the prior descent) and their strong doctrine of sin (the perpetual ruptures of the will in obeying moral demands placed upon us in any given moment). Indeed, for Augustine, habit (*consetuedo*) tends to solidify vice rather than promote virtue. Too much trust in virtue can lead one to take credit for what does not belong to you and also to imagine that a life of virtue becomes easier with time.[52]

Keeping these fears in mind, we may inquire how Luther balances this picture. Luther speaks about growing in grace so that the believer is not considered within the *simul*-framework only.[53] The believer is now

50. WA 40/I, 536, 20-537, 20. I am grateful to Rev. Juha Virta for sharing his thoughts on this issue.

51. Bruce Marshall has dealt with this problem in his article "Justification as Declaration and Deification." Marshall argues that Luther's Trinitarian theology keeps these two aspects of salvation together despite the fact they are sometimes considered as opposed to each other.

52. Gregory, *Politics and the Order of Love*, 68–69. Gregory also convincingly argues that there is no need to set habituation against confession as "protest against false virtue affirms the life of virtue in response to God."

53. See Saarinen, "Pauline Luther" and "Klostertheologie" for more detailed expositions of Luther's notion of will, desire and *simul*-principle.

partly sinner and partly righteous, and he should become less of a sinner and more righteous.[54] If the partial aspect is taken to mean only cognitive growth and increasing understanding, for example, then the transformative and communal sides of justification become incomprehensible. Of course, one aspect of growing in faith is deeper knowledge of God and his mercy. This becomes visible in trials and sufferings in which spiritual maturity is needed and also strengthened. For Luther it is important that growth and progress are first and foremost a question of one's relationship to God. Yet this also affects the progress in daily life and one's relationship to other beings. Christians should become more and more like Christ although they will never reach perfection and will suffer from all kinds of weaknesses till the ends of their lives. Yet the Spirit does not leave the Christian in an idle state but drives a person to do good deeds, which are sometimes visible, sometimes invisible to human eyes. These "fruits of the Spirit" (*fructus Spiritus*) are clearly not fruits of a person in a natural state, but fruits of the person who is joined together with the triune God.[55] The fruits grow as the result of hearing the word of God, which joins us with Spirit, who affects new virtues, such as Faith, Hope, Love, and Patience.[56]

This striving should not be considered meritorious as such so that one ends up guaranteeing salvation through growth. Instead, Christians are called to grow in holiness, not because they attain salvation this way but because they have already received salvation freely; the motivation for good works is not the Law and fear of punishment, but gratitude and joy. The Law does not provide power to do good although it provides the framework that Christians are obliged to follow as they seek how to live. In this sense Lutherans, and other like-minded Christians, can cite Psalm 119—which unashamedly praises God's commandments—with a clear conscience. The Law is not an enemy, which it would be if we were

54. WA 40/I, 537, 21–34.
55. WA 40/II, 116, 30–31; 351, 29–35.
56. WA 40/I, 351, 36–352, 18: "Cum igitur Concionator sic praedicat, ut verbum non frustretur suis fructibus, sed efficax sit in auditoribus, Hoc est, cum sequitur Fides, Spes, Charitas, Patientia etc., Ibi Deus subministrat Spiritum et operatur virtutes in auditoribus. Simili modo Paulus hic dicit Deum subministrasse Spiritum Galatis et operatum fuisse virtutes in eis, Quasi dicat: Deus non solum effecit per praedicationem meam, ut crederetis, sed ut etiam sancte viveretis, multos fructus fidei faceretis et mala pateremini. Item eadem virtute Spiritus facti estis ex avaris, adulteris, iracundis, impatientibus, hostibus etc. largi, casti, mites, patientis, amantes proximorum."

tied to strict Law-Gospel dialectics, but a friend, even the object of deep gratitude and praise.[57]

The Christ-centered picture offered here also secures three important aspects in growth in faith. First, if Christ is not the central agent in the acts of justification and sanctification, then we easily end up in the anthropocentric view of sanctification and natural co-operation in faith becomes difficult to understand without allusions to Pelagianism. Second, growth in faith is not a jungle-like growth, but more like a garden. Because Christ is the form of faith, the observance of Christ's example and will structures the actual content of the Christian life. Again, if Christ is removed, then the human being becomes central. Finally, growth must take place within objective sacramental framework so that Baptism and Eucharist hold the central place in spirituality. Naturally, this sets Christian life in communal context.[58] Thus, one is directed away from oneself to others and God.

---

57. See also Hütter, *Bound to Be Free*, 134–44 and Gilbert Meilaender's essay "Hearts Set to Obey."

58. See the articles of Jolkkonen and Martikainen in this volume. For an ecclesiological point of view, see also Peura, "Church as Spiritual Communion."

8

Theology of the Cross

Kari Kopperi

THE THEOLOGY OF THE cross (*theologia crucis*) is an essential theme in Martin Luther's theology.¹ Generally speaking, the theology of the cross concentrates on God's revelation in the crucified Jesus Christ and his suffering. Quite often Luther's theology of the cross has been connected with the idea that God is known in opposites or with the idea of annihilation of the human being as a part of the justification process. The theology of the cross has been considered a summary of his theology or a key to understanding his concepts of theology, revelation, epistemology, and the relation between theology and philosophy. Luther's theology of the cross has been an inspiring source for several approaches in modern theology as well.²

---

1. Many studies have been written about the subject, most of them in German language, but there isn't much of anything in English. The most widely known study on the theology of the cross is von Loewenich's *Luthers theologia crucis* (1929, English translation *Luther's Theology of the Cross*, 1976). Other important studies in English are McGrath, *Luther's Theology of the Cross* and Forde, *On Being a Theologian of the Cross*.

2. One of the first modern approaches was *Theology of the Pain of God* (1946) by the Japanese theologian Kitamori Kazoh. Perhaps the best known work is Jürgen Moltmann's challenging study *Der gekreuzigte Gott* (1972, English translation *The Crucified God*, 1973). The theology of the cross has also been a fruitful concept for several approaches in contextual theology: Latin American liberation theology, Indian Dalit theology (Devasahayam, *Frontiers of Dalit Theology*) and western feminist theology (Trelstad, "Way of Salvation in Luther's Theology," 236–45). Sometimes the theology of the cross has been used as a key in ecumenical discussions. See, e.g., Vercruysse, "Luther's Theology of the cross," 2–11; Kärkkäinen, "Salvation as Justification and Theosis," 74–82.

If we want to study carefully Luther's theology of the cross we must pay special attention to his disputation in Heidelberg in 1518, where the theology of the cross is a central issue.[3] In my understanding Luther's definition of the theology of the cross in theses 19–21 of the Heidelberg Disputation should be read in the light of his theology of love, as it is presented in the final theological thesis (28). I shall start my study with a short introduction to the text and the context of the Heidelberg Disputation and will then shift to its research history and its theology of the cross. In the third section, which is the main part, I will be analyzing the Heidelberg Disputation from the perspective of Luther's theology of love. This analysis includes also a review of Luther's understanding of the relationship between theology and philosophy in the Heidelberg Disputation.

THEOLOGY OF THE CROSS: TEXT AND CONTEXT

Most theologians know that the theology of the cross is an essential theme in Martin Luther's theology and therefore presume that Luther uses the concept frequently. The truth is that Luther makes use of the concept of *theologia crucis* very rarely. During spring 1518 he uses the concept in four separate texts, but afterwards he refers to it only occasionally. Thus, sometimes it has actually been supposed that the theology of the cross had only been a temporary theme in Luther's thinking and he had rejected it later.

Nevertheless, most scholars agree on the idea that the concept of the theology of the cross contains the very core of Martin Luther's theology. Luther uses the concept rarely as a technical term, but similar words and concepts appear frequently in his texts from his earliest writings to the latest lectures on Genesis. One of the best known formulations is his statement, "the cross alone is our theology (*crux sola est nostra theologia*)."[4]

Luther's Heidelberg Disputation, especially theses 19–21, offers the clearest definition of the theology of the cross. If we consider only the

---

3. The best critical editions of the Heidelberg Disputation are: for the theological theses: *StA* 1, 200, 4–212, 20; *WA* 1, 353–65; for the philosophical theses: *WA* 59, 409–26. An English translation, which does not contain the explanations of the philosophical theses, is found in *LW* 31, 39–58. All the subsequent translations of the text are from this source.

4. *WA* 5, 176, 32–33.

theses directly related to the concept of *theologia crucis* we might fall short of the point and interpret the theology of the cross separated from its relevant context, a mistake unfortunately quite common in Luther research. My research led me to the conviction that theses 19–21 containing definition of the theology of the cross should be read in the context of Luther's theology of love presented in thesis 28..[5]

The historical context also plays an important role in understanding the aim of Luther's Heidelberg Disputation. After Luther had posted his 95 theses in Wittenberg in 1517, the Augustinian Eremites were challenged in the debate concerning indulgences. They wanted to discuss the subject and the first opportunity was the friary's triennial meeting in Heidelberg. Luther held an important office within his order and therefore he would have joined the meeting in any case, but now he was asked to prepare theses for a public disputation to be held in connection with the meeting. Luther was asked to address the theological core questions of the time and his theological teaching.

Luther prepared twenty-eight theological theses and twelve philosophical theses for the disputation. He was clearly concentrating on his main theological interests and therefore we find theses on a large range of theological essentials (law, merits, grace, liberty of the will, theology, philosophy, the cross, glory, love of God and man, etc.).[6] Surprisingly there is no thesis related to the burning issues of the day, such as indulgences or the papal office. Luther's theses were received mainly positively, especially younger monks and humanists appreciated Luther's ideas and the order in general agreed with Luther; only a few older theologians, for example his former teacher Bartholomäus von Usingen, were not satisfied.[7]

---

5. StA 1, 207, 25–209, 5; 212, 1–19.

6. In the Heidelberg Disputation Luther presents his sharp criticism in a very polemic way and is using synecdoches. He is also speaking in a very narrow theological/soteriological sense and therefore does not see anything good in Aristotelian philosophy. In other texts the picture is wider and he sees some positive aspects in Aristotelian philosophy as well.

7. For the historical context of the disputation, see esp. Bauer, "Die Heidelberger Disputation Luthers," 233–68, 299–329; Brecht, *Martin Luther. Sein Weg*, 198–230; Clemen, "Beiträge zur Lutherforschung," 100–11; Delius, "Der Augustiner Eremitenorden im Prozeß Luthers," 22–42; Scheible, "Luthers Heidelberger Thesen," 121–26; "Die Universität Heidelberg und Luthers Disputation," 309–29; Wicks, *Cajetan und die Anfänge der Reformation*, 48–56; "Roman Reactions to Luther," 521–62.

THEOLOGY OF THE CROSS:
A BRIEF SURVEY OF ITS INTERPRETATION

The modern understanding of Martin Luther's theology has been deeply influenced by the nineteenth century Neo-Protestant theology, as Risto Saarinen has demonstrated. According to him, Neo-Protestant interpretations are heavily dependent on the German Neo-Kantian philosophy of the nineteenth century, which was very influential in German theological thinking and therefore intensely affected Luther-research also. Neo-Protestant theologians, such as Albrecht Ritschl and Wilhelm Herrmann, were convinced that in his Reformation theology Luther had rejected the scholastic metaphysical and ontological form of Christian religion and presented a totally new theological understanding (*theologisches Erkenntnisprinzip*) of Christian faith. This new understanding stressed the personal and ethically orientated relationship between God and the human being and liberated itself from all medieval ontological thinking.[8]

On closer examination, it becomes evident that this had repercussions on the interpretation of Luther's theology of the cross as well. Many scholars were convinced that Luther's Heidelberg Disputation was a good example of this new kind of theological thinking. It seems to me, however, that many interpretations of Martin Luther's theology of the cross and his Heidelberg theses are based more on modern theological presuppositions than on Luther's own theological writings. In the following research history, I shall stress three interconnected points: (1) The origins of the twentieth century interpretations of Luther's *theologia crucis* are rooted in nineteenth century Neo-Protestant theology. (2) Walther von Loewenich, who seems to reject the Neo-Protestant interpretation, claims that Luther's *theologia crucis* presents exactly the main theological idea of the Neo-Protestant theology. (3) The Neo-Protestant tradition culminates in the existential interpretation of Luther's theology in the thought of Gerhard Ebeling and his students.

---

8. Saarinen, *Gottes Wirken*. One of the reasons why Neo-Protestant scholars come to develop a very modern interpretation of Martin Luther's theology was the post-Enlightenment theological and philosophical situation in Germany. Theologians were challenged in the post-Kantian nineteenth century academic discussion, where all traditional metaphysical statements were considered to be old-fashioned. Moxter and Dalferth, "Protestant Theology: Germany," offer a good description of Protestant theology in Germany.

The modern understanding of Martin Luther's theology has often been marked by an ahistorical approach to his writings and in this respect Luther's Heidelberg Disputation is no exception. Ebeling, zur Mühlen, and several others have, for example, argued that Luther's criticism of Aristotle and his negative assessment of the theology of glory (*theologia gloriae*) proves his rejection of scholastic metaphysics and especially the Aristotelian ontology. According to this line of interpretation Luther focused his theses 19-21 in the Heidelberg Disputation against the scholastic comprehension of being. Therefore, when he states in thesis 19 "That person does not deserve to be called a theologian who looks upon the invisible things of God as though they were clearly perceptible in those things which have actually happened (*per ea quae facta sunt*),"[9] he is interpreted to be criticizing the scholastic belief that knowledge of God is possible by the principle of the analogy of being (*analogia entis*). Accordingly, scholars have claimed that Luther's criticism of the medieval theology concentrated on the scholastic theological and philosophical doctrines, based on the principles of Aristotelian metaphysics. In modern German Luther-research this pattern of scholastic theology is sometimes labeled "substance-metaphysics."[10]

One of the main difficulties of these modern interpretations of Luther's theology of the cross is that they rely on the philosophical and theological presuppositions implied in precedent studies, such as the works of Albrecht Ritschl, Wilhelm Herrmann, and Otto Ritschl. According to Albrecht Ritschl, Luther broke with the metaphysical tradition of the medieval scholastic theology and presented a new theological epistemology (*Erkenntnistheorie*), which is transcendental in its nature and does not concentrate on God's being or substance, but on God's influence (*Wirkung*) in this world.[11] Albrecht Ritschl's Luther-interpretation

---

9. StA 1, 207, 2-3.

10. See, e.g., Von Loewenich, *Luthers Theologia crucis*; Ebeling, *Luther*, 89, 259-62, 266-67, 271-75; Ebeling, *LuSt I*, 173; *LuSt II, 1*, 32-33; *LuSt II, 2*, 325-27, 436; *LuSt II, 3*, 1-2, 19, 23, 71-72, 479-81, 514, *LuSt III*, 327-28, 479-81; Joest, *Ontologie der Person bei Luther*, 118-30; Zur Mühlen, "Luthers Kritik am scholastischen Aristotelismus," 59-62; "Heidelberger Disputation Martin Luthers," 194-99; "Kreuz," 762-63. See also Ruokanen, *Hermeneutics as an Ecumenical Method*, 72-83, 110-15; Juntunen, *Begriff des Nichts bei Luther*, 11-19, 416-26; White, *Luther as Nominalist*, 60-81, 302; Grane "Erwägungen zur Ontologie Luthers," 188-98.

11. A. Ritschl, *Christliche Lehre von der Rechtfertigung*, 141-216; *Theologie und Metaphysik*; Saarinen, *Gottes Wirken auf uns*, 9-42; "Gottes Sein—Gottes Wirken," 103-19; Mannermaa, *Paralleeleja*, 55-61; "Grundlagenforschung der Theologie Martin

had a determining influence on Luther-research before the First World War. His son Otto Ritschl, for example, saw in Luther's concept of *theologia crucis* the monkish ideal of humility in Christian life. The concept therefore could not be linked with Luther's true theology, as it featured a remaining element of medieval catholic theology and consequently needed to be considered a preliminary stage of Luther's Reformation theology.[12]

Walther von Loewenich's famous study *Luthers theologia crucis* (1929) brought about a slight change in Luther-research. He demonstrated that the "theology of the cross is a principle of Luther's entire theology, and it may not be confined to a special period in his theological development." According to von Loewenich, Luther's theology of the cross is a "distinctive principle of theological knowledge (*theologisches Erkenntnisprinzip*) that corresponds exactly to the Apostle Paul's theology of the cross" and it "offers a characteristic of Luther's entire theological thinking".[13] "It is the distinctive mark of all theology" and "a specific kind of theology."[14]

A closer analysis reveals that von Loewenich's study, although it seems to oppose to the Neo-Protestant view, it did not change the standard interpretation of Luther's theology. In fact, his analysis of Luther's theology of the cross is compatible with the Neo-Protestant theology of the nineteenth century and with the transcendental theology of early twentieth century.[15] While the nineteenth century Neo-Protestant scholars thought that Luther had invented a new theological epistemology (*Erkenntnistheorie*) and that his theology of the cross belonged to his pre-reformatory thinking, von Loewenich asserts that it is precisely the *theologia crucis* that describes the main ideas of the new theological epistemology which the Neo-Protestants suggested. Von Loewenich's interpretation is rather implicit in his *Luther's theologia crucis*, but his study *Luther und der Neuprotestantismus* (1963) presents his position more

---

Luthers und Ökumene," 22–26; "Theosis als Thema der finnischen Lutherforschung," 12–18; *Christ Present in Faith*, 1–9; "Itse ihmisen hyvä tahto on läsnäoleva Kristus," 67–74; Martikainen, *Doctrina evangelii*, 85–94; *Doctrina*, 5–21; Peura, *Mehr als ein Mensch?*, 9–45; Raunio, *Summe des christlichen Lebens*, 21–38.

12. O. Ritschl, *Dogmengeschichte des Protestantismus II*, 40–3, esp. 42–43.

13. Von Loewenich, *Luthers Theologia crucis*, 12–13.

14. Ibid., 17–19.

15. See, e.g., R. Seeberg, *Lehrbuch der Dogmengeschichte IV/1*; E. Seeberg, *Grundzüge der Theologie Luthers*.

clearly.[16] In scientific Luther-research, von Loewenich's book became a standard work on Luther's theology of the cross, and his influence can be seen in the studies of Eduard Ellwein, Edmund Schlink, Rudolf Malter, and Daniel Olivier.[17]

This line of interpretation culminates in the existential interpretation of Luther's theology in the school of Gerhard Ebeling. Ebeling maintains that Luther's criticism of the scholastic theology was focused on the medieval substance-metaphysics and on the Aristotelian ontology. He concludes that Luther's Reformation theology replaced them with a modern relational ontology and existential view on Christian theology.[18]

Since the 1960s Ebeling's interpretation has been dominant especially in German Luther-research. If we consider various interpretations of the Heidelberg Disputation, there are two prominent examples of this tradition. In Wilfried Joest's *Ontologie der Person bei Martin Luther* the Heidelberg Disputation and especially Luther's theology of the cross play a central role. Joest thinks that Luther's concept of the theology of glory refers to all theological and philosophical systems that include metaphysical statements or the principle of analogy as means to describe the relation between God and the world. According to Joest, Luther's theology of the cross deviates from the medieval theological and philosophical system which is based on Aristotelian ontology and especially on the concept of *analogia entis* (analogy of being). Joest believes that with his theology of the cross Luther develops a new theological ontology grounded on the notion that the essence of the human being is not based on some kind of specific substance but on the relation to God and the human's position before God (*coram Deo*).[19]

Karl-Heinz zur Mühlen shares Joest's viewpoint to some extent, but in his analysis of the Heidelberg Disputation he draws a significant and crucial conclusion, suggesting that medieval theology was bound to

16. Von Loewenich, *Luthers Theologia crucis*, 11–17, 54–72, 86–95, esp. 14–15, 65, 71–72; *Luther und der Neuprotestantismus*, 140–43, 157, 313–15, 420–25, esp. 424–25.

17. See Ellwein, "Die Entfaltung der theologia crucis in Luthers Hebräerbriefvorlesung," 382–404; Schlink, "Weisheit und Torheit," 1–22; Malter, *Das reformatorische Denken und die Philosophie*; Olivier, "Der verborgene und gekreuzigte Gott," 55–60.

18. Ebeling, *LuSt* 1, 24; *Luther*, 274–75; "Zu Luthers Wirklichkeitsverständnis," 424.

19. Joest, *Ontologie der Person bei Luther*, 118–19. The interpretations of Ebeling and Joest were criticized already by Grane, "Erwägungen zur Ontologie Luthers," 188–98. See also Juntunen, *Der Begriff des Nichts bei Luther*, 416–18.

Aristotelian ontology while Christian theology is marked by an eschatological perspective, rejecting all ontological thinking. Zur Mühlen sees no connection between Christian eschatology and Aristotelian ontology. He concludes that Luther's Reformation theology was directed against Aristotelian philosophy and especially against Aristotelian ontology. Zur Mühlen is following an earlier tradition of interpretation but he formulates the point sharper than anyone before him.[20]

Zur Mühlen represents well the dominant Luther-interpretation of the twentieth century. This attitude is aptly described by Carl Braaten and Robert Jenson: "one should ignore all ontology found in Luther; faith is purely an act of the will with no ontological implication."[21] This line of interpretation has been continued through to the latest studies of Alister McGrath, Theodor Dieter, and Hubertus Blaumeiser, which, however, also contribute several important clarifications and critical comments.[22]

The preceding survey indicates that the Neo-Protestant tradition of interpretation has been very influential in modern Luther research. The idea that Luther rejected Aristotelian ontology and presented a new epistemological method for scientific theology has become a dominant presupposition in modern Luther-research and its interpretation of Luther's Reformation theology.[23]

I am convinced that this line of interpretation cannot lead to accurate conclusions, when analyzing the texts of a sixteenth century theologian. Although Luther criticized the scholastic theology of his time and

20. Zur Mühlen, "Luthers Kritik am scholastischen Aristotelismus," 79; "Die Heidelberger Disputation Martin Luthers," 196.

21. Braaten and Jenson, *Union with Christ*, viii–ix.

22. McGrath, *Luther's Theology of the Cross*; Dieter, "Amor hominis—amor crucis," 241–58; *Philosophischen Thesen der "Heidelberger Disputation" Luthers*; *Der junge Luther und Aristoteles*; Blaumeiser, *Martin Luthers Kreuzestheologie*. At the end of this overview of the research history, it is important to mention some scholars who have contributed valuable points and/or fruitful theological interpretations to the understanding of Martin Luther's theology of the cross: Bornkamm, *Das bleibende Recht der Reformation*; "theologischen Thesen Luthers," 130–46; Vercruysse, "Theology of the cross at the time of the Heidelberg Disputation," 523–48; "Gesetz und Liebe," 7–43; "Luther's Theology of the cross," 2–11; "A Theology of the cross and the Church as Sacrament," 453–70; Gerhard O. Forde's book *On Being a Theologian of the Cross* contributes an important study on the theme for English-speaking world, but offers hardly anything new for the academic discussion compared to the above-mentioned studies.

23. See esp. Mannermaa, "Itse ihmisen hyvä tahto on läsnäoleva Kristus," 67–74; *Paralleeleja*, 52–69; Martikainen, *Doctrina*, 5–21; Saarinen, *Gottes Wirken auf uns*; Peura, *Mehr als ein Mensch?*, 9–45.

especially Aristotelian metaphysics, we must bear in mind that he had a scholastic education and background. The influence of Neo-Protestant premises on modern Luther-research has not been sufficiently taken into account in the interpretation of Luther's Reformation theology and therefore might need reassessment.

A reliable Luther-research situates Luther's theology in its historical context and focuses especially on the theological and philosophical discussions of the fifteenth and sixteenth centuries. Therefore, Finnish scholars have paid special attention to the medieval philosophical and theological background of Luther's theology and noticed relevant similarities between Luther and preceding scholastic theologies, overlooked in many Luther studies.[24] Tuomo Mannermaa, for example, claims that Luther's criticism of metaphysics does not justify the conclusion of "mainstream" German Luther-research that Luther is proposing a modern relational ontology. According to Mannermaa Luther's expressions on the real presence of Christ and real participation can be understood from a point of view that is not necessarily Aristotelian substance-ontology but linked with the traditional Christian idea of *theosis* (divinization).[25]

HEIDELBERG DISPUTATION: THE SUMMARY OF LUTHER'S THEOLOGY OF THE CROSS

Biblical Basis for the Theology of the Cross

When Luther is using the Bible, he has in mind that Christology and especially the doctrine of justification is the center of Christian theology. In his lectures and commentaries he is interpreting the Bible in the light of Christian core doctrines and also in other texts he is frequently using the Bible as the basis for his teaching. This style he is using also in the Heidelberg Disputation and in other texts connected to the theology of the cross. Three biblical texts recurring frequently can be seen as the biblical basis for his theology of the cross: Exod 33:12—34:9, especially 33:18–23 (Moses' demand to see God's glory); John 14:8–14 (the Apostle

---

24. See, e.g., Työrinoja, "Proprietas Verbi," 141–78; "Nova vocabula et nova linqua," 221–36; "Opus theologicum," 117–60; Kirjavainen, "Luther und Aristoteles," 111–29; "Uskonkohteiden spesifiointi Lutherilla," 101–15. See also White, *Luther as Nominalist*.

25. Mannermaa, "Hat Luther eine trinitarische Ontologie?" 9–27; "Theologische Ontologie bei Luther?," 37–53; "Hat Luther eine trinitarische Ontologie?," 43–60. See also *Union with Christ*.

Philip's conversation with Jesus on seeing the Father) and 1 Cor 1:18–31 (the wisdom of the world and the folly of the cross).[26]

On the basis of Exod 33:12—34:9, Luther conceives the fundamental difference between God and the human beings.[27] God is God and a human being is a human being. As mortal beings we cannot see God directly. God's glory is hidden from us and we cannot grasp it in itself. Luther often uses this text to describe how Moses wanted to see God's glory, but the only thing he got to see was God's back (*posteriora Dei*). According to Luther this story elucidates how God hides himself into the humanity and the suffering of Christ. Because it is impossible to see God directly all theology which "looks upon invisible things of God" is vain. This idea becomes a fundamental cornerstone of the theology of the cross.[28]

In the Heidelberg Disputation Luther presents John 14:8–14 as an example of the theology of glory.[29] Luther stresses that with his request "show us the Father" Philip represents a theologian of glory, not content to see Christ but trying to see God directly. Luther describes how "Christ forthwith set aside his flighty thought about seeing God elsewhere and led him to himself, saying 'Philip, he who has seen me has seen the Father.'" The task of the theology of the cross is to reject the ideas of the theologian of glory and to show that the only way to God and to real knowledge of God is in Jesus Christ and therefore all other methods and

---

26. *StA* 1, 208, 1–18.

27. Exod 33:12—34:9, esp. 18–23: "Then Moses said, 'Now show me your glory.' And the LORD said, 'I will cause all my goodness to pass in front of you, and I will proclaim my name, the LORD, in your presence. I will have mercy on whom I will have mercy, and I will have compassion on whom I will have compassion. But,' he said, 'You cannot see my face, for no one may see me and live.' Then the LORD said, 'There is a place near me where you may stand on a rock. When my glory passes by, I will put you in a cleft in the rock and cover you with my hand until I have passed by. Then I will remove my hand and you will see my back; but my face must not be seen.'"

28. See also *WA* 3, 596, 23–597, 11; 604, 33–39.

29. John 14: [1] 8–14: "Philip said, 'Lord, show us the Father and that will be enough for us.' Jesus answered: 'Don't you know me, Philip, even after I have been among you such a long time? Anyone who has seen me has seen the Father. How can you say, "Show us the Father"? Don't you believe that I am in the Father, and that the Father is in me? The words I say to you are not just my own. Rather, it is the Father, living in me, who is doing his work. Believe me when I say that I am in the Father and the Father is in me; or at least believe on the evidence of the miracles themselves.'"

ways to approach God are wrong and will lead to a false understanding of God.[30]

The central text for the theology of the cross is 1 Cor 1:18–31.[31] In this text Paul emphasizes that God does not accept human wisdom, but God's wisdom manifests itself in foolishness and especially in the crucified Christ. From this idea derives the main concept of Luther's theology of the cross: God remains unattainable with human wisdom or with good works. The crucified Christ is the only means to true knowledge of God, even if this appears to be the essence of foolishness to human wisdom. Luther stresses: "Now it is not sufficient for anyone, and it does him no good to recognize God in his glory and majesty, unless he recognizes him in the humility and shame of the cross."[32]

Theology of the Cross and Theology of Glory

Luther was aware that the main idea of his theology of the cross might look excessively critical and controversial; therefore he characterized the theses of his Heidelberg disputation as "*theologia paradoxa*," the theology of paradoxes.

---

30. *StA* 1, 208, 14–18.

31. 1 Cor 1:8–31: "For the message of the cross is foolishness to those who are perishing, but to us who are being saved it is the power of God. For it is written: 'I will destroy the wisdom of the wise; the intelligence of the intelligent I will frustrate.' Where is the wise man? Where is the scholar? Where is the philosopher of this age? Has not God made foolish the wisdom of the world? For since in the wisdom of God the world through its wisdom did not know him, God was pleased through the foolishness of what was preached to save those who believe. Jews demand miraculous signs and Greeks look for wisdom, but we preach Christ crucified: a stumbling block to Jews and foolishness to Gentiles, but to those whom God has called, both Jews and Greeks, Christ the power of God and the wisdom of God. For the foolishness of God is wiser than man's wisdom, and the weakness of God is stronger than man's strength. Brothers, think of what you were when you were called. Not many of you were wise by human standards; not many were influential; not many were of noble birth. But God chose the foolish things of the world to shame the wise; God chose the weak things of the world to shame the strong. He chose the lowly things of this world and the despised things and the things that are not to nullify the things that are, so that no one may boast before him. It is because of him that you are in Christ Jesus, who has become for us wisdom from God that is, our righteousness, holiness and redemption. Therefore, as it is written: 'Let him who boasts boast in the Lord.'" Similar ideas can be found also in 1 Cor 2 and in Rom 1.

32. *StA* 1, 208, 5–13. See also *WA* 1, 101, 19–102, 32; 139, 24–140, 7; 171, 25–172, 8; 270, 36–271, 8.

In the Heidelberg Disputation Luther has one main target; he criticizes the love of man (*amor hominis*), which takes two problematic forms in human reality: one is the problem of human works, the other that of human wisdom.

According to Luther, a human way of thinking and acting is to trust in God's law, good works, merits and the liberty of the will. These things are in themselves good and belong to God's creation, but humans abuse them. As human beings we are and remain sinners, and for this reason we are always searching our own merits and our own good, thus neglecting our neighbor and abusing of God's good gifts, although we believe that we are doing good and living according to God's law.

Human wisdom is often connected to philosophy. By human wisdom Luther intends all kind of human speculations which try to comprehend God's essence by intellectual means and inspection of the created world. According to Luther, the use of intellect is not bad in itself, but because human beings are thoroughly affected by sin, they tend to ignore God's revelation, especially his revelation in Christ and his cross, and this leads them to a false image of God, forged by their human will and needs.

Luther calls this form of thinking the theology of glory. He seems to intend the speculative theology, but when we are considering the whole disputation, it becomes obvious that for Luther human works are an essential part of the theology of glory.

The theology of the cross is an opposite way of thinking. Its starting point is not human wisdom or goodness, but genuine self-knowledge. Humans should understand and see themselves as sinners before God. In thesis 18 Luther asserts: "It is certain that man must utterly despair of his own ability before he is prepared to receive the grace of Christ."[33] It is essential that the human being does not trust in his works or his wisdom before God (*coram Deo*). Tragically, this is humanly impossible and therefore God needs to take the first step, depriving the human being of his self-confidence. Luther even states that God makes man into nothing (*nihil*).

This depriving work of God is called his alien work or the work of his left hand (*opus alienum Dei*). By this alien work God makes evident to the human being his true position in the world, showing him that he is nothing before God. Luther describes this in thesis 24: "He, however,

---

33. *StA* 1, 207, 18–19.

who has been emptied [Cf. Phil 2:7] through suffering no longer does works but knows that God works and does all things in him. For this reason, whether man does works or not, it is all the same to him. He neither boasts if he does good works, nor is he disturbed if God does not do good works through him. He knows that it is sufficient if he suffers and is brought low by the cross in order to be annihilated all the more."[34]

For Luther, the alien work of God is the only possible preparation for grace; this is why the theology of the cross is not the end of the process, but its beginning. After having done his alien work, God begins his proper work, the work of his right hand (*opus proprium Dei*). This means that God justifies, gives his grace and makes the sinner righteous.

Luther says: "He is not righteous who does much, but he who, without work, believes much in Christ.... For this reason he does not seek to become justified or glorified through them [works], but seeks God. His justification by faith in Christ is sufficient to him. Christ is his wisdom, righteousness, etc.... The law says, 'do this,' and it is never done. Grace says, 'believe in this', and everything is already done.... For through faith Christ is in us, indeed, one with us. Christ is just and has fulfilled all the commands of God, wherefore we also fulfill everything through him since he was made ours through faith."[35] Luther even says that this means to be born anew: "one must consequently first die and then be raised up with the Son of Man".[36]

Theology of Love

I will now shift my focus to the theology of love, which is the essential key to Martin Luther's theology of the cross. The core of the Heidelberg Disputation is Luther's theological question about true wisdom before God (*coram Deo*). In other words: how can the human being obtain true knowledge of God (*cognitio Dei*), and how does true love towards God and to one's neighbor arise? Luther's answer to these fundamental questions is his theology of love. The last theological thesis (28) is structured by the paradox distinction between love of man (*amor hominis*) and

---

34. *StA* 1, 210, 13–17.
35. *StA* 1, 210, 20–211, 14.
36. *StA* 1, 210, 16–17. Luther's idea of the relationship between Christ and a Christian presupposes a notion of Christ's real presence in the Christian. This theme is explicit and essential in the theses 25–27, but, unfortunately, it has usually been ignored in studies on the Heidelberg Disputation.

love of God (*amor Dei*): "The love of God does not find, but creates, that which is pleasing to it. The love of man comes into being through that which is pleasing to it."[37]

Thesis 28 is not only the summary of the theological part of the disputation but also prepares the ground for the Aristotle-criticism in the philosophical part. According to Luther, it is characteristic for *amor hominis* that love arises by the value of its object; a loving person loves, because he/she finds the object valuable, desirable and pleasing. God's love does not arise from the value of its object and it does not try to benefit from its object. Luther asserts that God loves sinners, evil persons, fools and weaklings in order to make them righteous, good, wise and strong.

Luther's theological theses are focused against a form of scholastic theology that understands the relation between God and man in accordance with the principles of self-love. Luther's criticism is directed especially against the theological tradition following Gabriel Biel. According to this tradition true love for God initiates as a form of self-love (*amor concupiscentiae*), which gradually develops into a real love of friendship (*amor amicitiae*).[38]

In his theological theses Luther judges severely people's habit to trust in their works imagining to merit their salvation by this means. He criticizes especially the doctrine of *facere quod in se est* (to do everything that is in one's power) and the doctrine of *liberum arbitrium* (free will). According to Luther, human beings are so completely overcome by corrupted love and sin that they necessarily abuse God's gifts. Luther emphasizes that they are unable to choose good works according to God's will. Therefore, the only possible preparation for grace is "preaching concerning sin".[39]

Accordingly Luther criticizes the use of human wisdom in theology. He concludes that human wisdom, as revealed in philosophy, led the scholastics to derive their theology from the principles of *amor hominis*. The theologians of glory imagine that they can reach true knowledge or recognition of God by their own human wisdom. Luther comes to the conclusion that "the true theology and recognition of God are in cruci-

---

37. StA 1, 212, 4.

38. See Biel, *Coll.* III d. 26 q. I art. 3 dub. 2 and IV. D. 14 1. I art. 3 dub 7. Cf. Oberman, *Harvest of Medieval Theology*, 133–4, 153–4; Grane, *Contra Gabrielem*, 103–5.

39. StA 1, 207, 3–16.

fied Christ."⁴⁰ Luther's criticism of the scholastic theology, theological and philosophical speculations, the theology of glory and Aristotelian philosophy are focused on the same unacceptable principle of the *amor hominis*.

THEOLOGY AND PHILOSOPHY IN THE HEIDELBERG DISPUTATION

If we compare the philosophical part of the Heidelberg Disputation with the theological theses, it looks like an entirely independent text that has not very much in common with the core issues of its theological counterpart. If, however, we are looking at Luther's philosophical theses from the perspective given by the distinction of *amor hominis* and *amor Dei*, the connection becomes understandable. The analysis demonstrates that Luther's intention in the philosophical theses is also theological. Luther tries to reveal that the Aristotelian philosophy cannot be used in the service of Christian theology.

The purpose of these philosophical theses can be explained by the content of the last theological thesis (28), where Luther summarizes his central theological ideas and, at the same time, criticizes the Aristotelian philosophy. Luther probably feels that the basis of his Aristotle-criticism should be more explicit. Therefore he tries to explain his intense criticism in the philosophical part, which is an excursion specifying his idea of the usefulness of human wisdom and philosophy and gives a detailed analysis of the controversial issues in the Aristotelian philosophy.[41]

The theological motivation of the philosophical part and Luther's conception of the distinction between theology and philosophy are obvious in the first two philosophical theses.[42] According to Luther, perverted love ignores God's word and revelation and leads to a worldview based solely on sense perception and rational reasoning. Luther considers philosophy to be good in itself, but it is easily perverted into a corrupt form of theological speculation. When Luther criticizes the theology of glory, he emphasizes that it is impossible to know God by rational speculations

---

40. StA 1, 208, 17-18.

41. Luther makes a similar excursion in his *Disputation against Scholastic Theology* (*Disputatio contra scholasticam theologiam*, 1517), StA 1, 165-72 (=LW 31, 9-16).

42. WA 59, 409, 1-410, 12.

or human wisdom (philosophy). True knowledge of God is possible only through God's revelation in the crucified Christ (theology).

The criticism in the Heidelberg Disputation does not imply a total rejection of philosophy or rational reasoning. Luther admits that rationally reflecting on theological and doctrinal questions is possible and wise, and in this perspective, even the use of philosophy can be helpful, the true task of philosophy being the observation and the study of the created world. A philosopher though must recognize and accept his limited capacities in rational reasoning, so that philosophy fulfills its original function and is no longer a corrupt form of man's self-realization.[43]

Luther maintains that philosophy makes human beings believe that they can achieve and know more than they actually do. He emphasizes that the only possibility to break free from the corrupt love of knowledge (*amor sciendi*) is stultification and annihilation through the theology of the cross. In reality human wisdom is foolishness before God and the true wisdom lies in the wisdom of the cross (*sapientia crucis*).

The analysis of the philosophical theses demonstrates that Luther considers Aristotelian philosophy to be secular and immanent by its nature. It can be applied to the phenomena of nature, but it is in contradiction with many Christian doctrines. When applied to Christian theology Aristotelian philosophy turns the scholastic theology into an unacceptable theology of glory. The main reason for this problem is sin and the corrupted love of man. Luther also thinks that there are condemnable teachings in Aristotelian philosophy as such and mentions the Aristotelian ideas of mortality of the soul and the eternity of the world as examples.[44]

The opposition of Aristotle and Plato in the philosophical theses 8–10 of the Heidelberg Disputation has been a puzzling issue in Luther-research.[45] Luther's criticism of Aristotle is an essential theme in his rejection of scholasticism, emphasizing the immanent character

---

43. Kopperi, *Paradoksien teologia*, 233–39.

44. These two Aristotelian ideas were intensively discussed throughout Middle Ages. See, e.g., Pluta, *Kritiker der Unsterblichkeitsdoktrin* and Dales, *Medieval Discussions of the Eternity of the World*.

45. WA 59, 424, 5–426, 20. See the introduction in WA 59, 406–8 and Bauer, "Die Heidelberger Disputation Luthers," 265–68, Clemen, "Beiträge zur Lutherforschung," 109; Junghans, "Die Probationes zu den Philosophischen Thesen der Heidelberger Disputation im Jahre 1518"; zur Mühlen, "Die Heidelberger Disputation Martin Luthers."

of Aristotelian philosophy and its unacceptability for Christian theology. Luther's attitude to Plato is more positive, but this does not make him a philosophical Platonist. With his positive statements on Plato, Pythagoras, and Anaxagoras, Luther tries to demonstrate that other philosophical systems can be more suitable for Christian theology than Aristotelianism.

The analysis of the Heidelberg Disputation proves inappropriate the conclusion that Luther's theology of the cross is especially focused on Aristotelian ontology. The analysis shows clearly that Luther's rejection of the theology of glory is not based on its concept of being, but is focused on *amor hominis*, an attempt to attain knowledge of God and salvation by rational reasoning, through good works and the created world. Therefore the problem of the theology of glory is not the concept of being but human reasoning, which, after the fall, abuses God's creation and seeks human glory in one's own works.

While Luther criticizes the Aristotelian philosophy, he uses Aristotle's classical ontological concepts. It is not because of these concepts that Aristotle is refuted, but because his philosophy leads Christian theology into false theological conclusions. At the same time Luther appreciates Plato's view on the participation of ideas. Luther seems to think that Plato's philosophy is better and more suitable for describing the Christian teaching of participation which includes traditional ontological concepts and metaphysical statements. With Platonic notions, the transcendence and the immanence of God can be illustrated in an appropriate and understandable way without limiting the theological content of God's revelation. This does not prevent Luther from taking an opposite position in some of his other writings where he criticizes Plato while accepting an Aristotelian position.[46]

Luther's theory of the relationship between theology and philosophy can be seen as a revised version of the classical concept of philosophy as a handmaid of theology. Essentially philosophy has, according to Luther, its own independent and beneficial function, but it is always in danger of degenerating into a form of perverted human wisdom driven by the principles of *amor hominis*. In theological questions philosophy loses its relevance because it cannot adequately explain paradoxical theological doctrines. In theological questions and doctrines, God's revelation in Christ defines the boundaries of the philosophical concepts.

46. WA 15, 630–31.

CONCLUSIONS

With his paradoxical theses Luther rejects all patterns of thinking or acting which follow the principle of *amor hominis* (the doctrine of *facere quod in se est*, merits, the idea of free will [*liberum arbitrium*], the theology of glory, Pelagianism and Aristotelian philosophy) and emphasizes God's love and deeds in accordance with the principle of *amor Dei*. From a human point of view *amor Dei* seems to be folly, because it bestows good and concentrates on the poor, the weak and the sinners. According to Luther God's love manifests itself in the cross of Christ that changes the values and hierarchies of human wisdom. Luther emphasizes that the true purpose of God's love and the cross of Christ is to reveal the true knowledge of God, the world, good works and human wisdom.

The essence of the theology of the cross can be summarized in four aspects:

1. God in his glory and majesty remains unattainable for the human being. God can only be apprehended through the crucified Christ and his passion.

2. Salvation is possible only through the cross. God first does his alien work and annihilates the human being, so that the human being perceives to be a sinner and therefore nothing before God. Then God starts his proper work by saving and making sinners just, wise and Christians.

3. God's alien work is not a singular episode in the salvation process, but it is a continuous experience in Christian life. A Christian always remains a sinner and therefore he is confronted with God's alien and proper work every day.

4. God is hidden—not only from this world, but he remains hidden also in his revelation. Therefore the human being cannot comprehend all aspects of God. Something always remains hidden.

9

The Virgin Mary

Anja Ghiselli

Usually, Luther's attitude toward Mary has been seen—by both scholars and laypeople alike—as ambiguous or even negative. I argue, however, that Luther's criticism is not aimed at Mary and it does not imply suspicion of her essential place in the context of Christian faith and theological deliberation. Instead, Luther delivers a heavy blow to certain mediaeval and contemporary interpretations of Mary's place in popular piety. In Luther's theology, Mariology does not appear as a *locus* of its own, rather it is connected to the *loci* of Christology and soteriology. In this chapter, I will concentrate on the essential perspective of Luther on Mary, namely how the she appears as a paradigm of the theology of the cross.[1] First, I will examine Luther's ideas about Mary as an example for Christians. Then, I will turn to Luther's own formulation of Mariological doctrines.

THE VIRGIN MARY AS AN EXAMPLE FOR CHRISTIANS

There are two sides to Luther's Mariological coin: Mary is both archetype (*das Urbild*) and example (*das Vorbild*) for all Christians. As an archetype, based on her nature as a created being, Mary is fully human and only human; she lives under the same universal laws as everyone else. Yet she becomes an example through God's gracious selection of her. In her, God's grace and love are shown in a visible way.

---

1. A similar claim has been made by Eric W. Gritsch, "Embodiment," 136.

Luther calls Mary the best example of God's mercy. God gazes down on Mary and addresses her through the voice of an angel. According to Luke (1:38), Mary responds: "Be it unto me according to thy word." At that moment God's mercy and love encounters Mary's humility and she is made pregnant through the Holy Spirit.[2] Luther appropriates this event through his theology of the cross. According to him, Mary's intention in her *Magnificat* is to express the idea that God has looked on her, a poor, despised, unworthy girl, although he could have chosen someone from the families of the rich and the famous; yet God chose her, someone of no value. The reason is that *coram Deo*, no one can boast of his or her significance. Everything results from God's mercy and grace, not from Mary's own worthiness.[3]

Luther's words emphasize both God's gracious acts and Mary's humility and unworthiness. In the medieval Mariology, Mary's humility was a central theme. It was the virtue of Mary that made her worthy in the eyes of God and consequently the choice for the mother of his Son. It must be borne in mind that in this interpretation, it is Mary's attribute (as a contingent property) that sets her above everyone else. This interpretation of humility has caused many scholars to conclude that humility, as a theological and spiritual theme, must be part of Luther's pre-Reformatory phase, which eventually fades away after the Reformatory breakthrough. While it is true that the aforementioned account of humility appears only in Luther's early writings (in the Commentaries on the Psalms 1513–1515), the idea of humility does not fade but remains central to Luther's theology and Mariology. Nevertheless, Mary's humility must be set in the context of the theology of the cross: there, humility is a space created by God's alien work (*opus alienum*) to bring forth his kingdom.

In his commentary on the Magnificat Luther states that humility takes rather coarse forms in the lives of human beings, including in Mary's life. Externally, we may perceive God's alien works, which hide within them his proper works (*opus proprium*). These works become visible in hunger and poverty; we have to endure suffering personally in order to understand that we cannot help ourselves. True help comes from God alone, and what is impossible for everybody else is possible for

---

2. *WA* 27, 230, 27–31; *WA* 41, 354, 7–14.
3. *StA* 1, 329, 36–43.

him. Thus, we should not try to avoid lowliness and suffering, as God is doing his work for us.[4]

Mary's humility is made manifest in her voluntary "lowliness." Mary does not ask for honor, even though she knows that she has been called to be the Mother of God. She takes care of all household duties as before; she washes the dishes and mops the floor. Other women and neighbors do not consider her to be any better than before. Luther claims that she does not even ask for the respect but wants to remain in the company of ordinary people. Luther expresses his admiration thus: "O how simple and pure is this heart, how magnificent a person!" In Mary great things are hidden in simple form.[5]

Yet this is not to be taken as a reduction of Mary's importance or denigration of her dignity and honor, even such interpretations exist. Indeed, Luther praises Mary as a "magnificent person." The heart of the matter lies in Luther's emphasis on the secret nature of humility. "True humility never knows that is it humble."[6] Simultaneously, he wants to point out that true humility attaches itself to ordinary life and is manifested in love of one's neighbor and in devoting one's life to the service of others.

Humility, as Luther understands it, does not take us closer to God. A humble person begins to understand the true nature of herself more deeply. She understands that she has been living a lie: she has sought idols instead of the Living God. Truly, one cannot separate self-knowledge from the knowledge of God. Only when one recognizes and confesses her sins and neediness may she experience God's grace and love. Luther examines this lesson in his commentary on Psalm 51 (1538). God loves wretched and broken beings. He is the God of the humble. God cannot be approached through power and wealth, but only through suffering. God asks from us only sighs and calls for help: "Help us, O Lord."[7]

This is the paradox of the theology of the cross. Suffering reveals the true nature of God and of the self. Natural reason (*ratio*) does not perceive these things, but the heart knows and feels them. This wisdom it is not opened to speculation, but is learned through poverty and need. This experience brings the certainty that God's grace is present, even in

---

4. StA 1, 356, 25–34.
5. StA 1, 341, 34–342, 1.
6. StA 1, 331, 5.
7. WA 40 II, 458, 7–459, 10.

the face of contrary evidence. Thus, human beings can trust in God even in the midst of the severe trials, while one should be afraid in moments of the greatest confidence.[8]

According to Luther, Mary is such a person. Hence, he sets up Mary as an example and as an archetype of correctly understood humility. Humility (*humilitas*) and pride (*superbia*) are set against each other. God can help those who are humble, meaning those who understand they are in need. Those who are proud trust in their own powers; they have nothing to learn and are fully satisfied. The person made humble by God needs to suffer when finding the way back from the depths of trouble, such a person remains silent and waits for God's help, without which one cannot proceed. God encounters the humble in human needs and raises us up. This is exactly how God acts with regard to the abandoned Mary and takes her as his own Mother, as the Mother of God.[9]

Luther depicts Mary's life through his theology of the cross. Mary is the *Mater Dolorosa*. Being the Mother of the Son of God meant lifelong suffering. Before her pregnancy, Mary was a poor orphan of lesser descent. Yet it was after the angelic visitation that her sufferings began in earnest. In public she was considered a whore. Even Joseph wanted to abandon her, which would have meant that Mary would have been stoned to death. Mary suffered the jealousy, wrath, and scorn resulting from Jesus's public activity. Eventually she had to witness the crucifixion of her Son. All of this she suffered and endured. It is for these reasons that Luther presents Mary as an example of suffering: if Mary, the Mother of God, suffered such difficulties, then suffering cannot be bad. Therefore no one who undergoes tribulations, should be afraid.[10]

Luther describes Mary's trials and sufferings in his exegesis on Luke 2:42–52, where the twelve-year-old Jesus encounters the Pharisees in the temple. Even though Mary is a saint and the highly venerated Mother of God, her own son neglects her. When Jesus disappears into the temple, Mary faces the pain prophesied by old Simeon, which was preceded by giving birth in the stable of Bethlehem and the flight to Egypt.[11] Luther states that the disappearance of Jesus caused Mary enormous pain. Although at one moment she was above everything else, as if in heaven,

8. WA 40 II, 463, 8–12.
9. WA 37, 92, 15–29.
10. WA 41, 363, 5–20; 629, 27–35.
11. WA 17/II, 17, 28–18, 16; WA 10 I, 1, 63, 5–10; 63, 15–21.

she was suddenly cast down into hell. The guilt of losing Jesus makes her tremble in horror and suffer acute pain. She becomes desperate and, according to Luther, wills her own death.[12]

The severity and realities of human life are emphasized in the sufferings of Mary. The anguish she feels for her Son are comparable to the torments of hell. The pain she goes through is the deepest and severest trial that God uses to test humans, even the holiest of saints. Luther calls this *desertio gratiae*. The heart thus tormented feels that God's mercy has abandoned her once and for all. Mary feels that God does not want to have anything do with her; wherever she turns, she sees only anger and terror.[13]

Luther's vivid depiction demonstrates that when it comes to God's alien work, Mary does not stand above other people; she is fully human, the archetype for all humans. Luther makes it clear that even though Mary is a saint, God's alien work has a purpose in Mary's life as well as in the lives of other saints. Yet while saints, Mary included, have received special grace they are not perfect, and hence, God's alien work is needed. Its purpose is the same for everyone. Saints should not grow complacent, but need to maintain self-knowledge: everything comes from God and is dependent on his grace. Thus, God makes their faith weak and causes their hearts to doubt. Pride must be crushed again and again in order to make room for humility.[14]

Luther compares Mary to other saints and underlines the severity of her sufferings. Saints and martyrs usually go through external pain and torture. Mary's agony is something different because it is purely internal. Luther believes that the greatest pain is caused by the torture of the heart. He refers to ascetic exercises and points out how many martyrs, such as St Agnes, looked down on bodily pain. This implies only "half-pain" because torture touches only the body, while the heart and soul can still rejoice. But there is no relief for the pain in Mary's heart. To endure it, one needs special strength of the spirit and grace. And these strengths were bestowed on Mary.[15]

Luther takes a critical stance toward martyrdom and asceticism, which according to him, can even be pleasurable experiences. He seems

12. *WA* 17/II, 19, 34–37.
13. *WA* 17/II, 20, 31–38.
14. *WA* 17/II, 22, 16–28.
15. *WA* 17/II, 21, 39–22, 10.

to think that martyrs may deliberately expose themselves to external sufferings and thus try to earn their way to God. Luther thinks this is not right. The sufferings of Mary are caused by God's alien work, but simultaneously God comes down to meet Mary *in* this suffering. The true humility of Mary appears in her perfect surrender to God's will. Mary responds to the angel's address with words, "Behold, I am the servant of God; be it unto me according to thy word."[16] Luther sees this as an expression of Mary's humility and faith in God, and her sincere love towards all human beings. Mary surrenders in humility and obedience to God and announces her willingness to follow his will.[17]

Luther argues that Mary's suffering is meant for every Christian so that everyone may learn from it, namely that Mary is able to endure through everything. Hence, she shows us an example of how we should endure in our sufferings. We should not despair, but learn to find consolation and help in our tribulations, Luther advises.[18] Mary's role as an example is set in a paradoxical context. The exemplary nature of a saint has two opposite effects: a saint causes fear in those who are complacent and consoles those who are frightened. For those who are undergoing trial the example of the saints works as remembrance and consolation.[19]

Luther emphasizes that God seeks to lead people to repentance through the example of Mary. The "thick-skinned" and unrepentant should compare themselves to Mary and other saints so that they could change their ways and learn to avoid sinning when they perceive the terror and fear of God's wrath in the saint. Even Mary needs to wrestle with her conscience for three days and experience feelings of guilt when Jesus is lost in the temple.[20] But the fearful receive consolation through Mary's example and God's proper works penetrate through his alien work. The acts, which brought fear upon the complacent, are now the comfort of the anxious who perceive how even the holiest of saints need to bear the same pain and agony. Not even the Mother of God is spared. So people learn that they are not alone and despair cannot get hold of them; they learn to stay calm and wait for God's intervention, which has helped all

16. *WA* 52, 633, 1–2.
17. *WA* 52, 633, 2–5.
18. *WA* 17/II, 20, 39–21, 4.
19. *WA* 17/II, 23, 8–9.
20. *WA* 17/II, 23, 9–17.

the other beloved saints.[21] For the weak, saints appear as mirrors and objects of imitation. They share the same pain and receive the same help and remedy. This way God's alien work paradoxically stirs up hope so that one's faith is strengthened and trust is made stronger.

Mary is also an example of faith. The angel's message to Mary went beyond everything comprehensible: Mary will bear a child and yet remain a virgin. This paradox insults natural reason and experience. There is nothing in the whole of creation that Mary could use to back up this message and strengthen her in a natural way. Reason or elaborate justifications in the mind and thoughts are of no avail. Also the content of the faith—a young unworthy girl from Nazareth shall give birth to the Son of the Most High—puts faith to the test; the only way to endure is to trust in the words of God delivered by the angel.[22] Luther summarizes the content of faith as follows: "The true nature of faith is that it in all of its heart and in the simplest way hangs onto the word, which rings in one's ears."[23]

In his commentary on the Magnificat, Luther explains the concept of the "darkness of the faith." He emphasizes that God lives in the darkness of faith where there is no light, and human beings are now called on to believe that , which cannot be seen, felt, or understood.[24] Luther sets this darkness of faith against the light of reason, which depends on speculation according to the sentiment expressed in Hebrews (11:1). The works of God are not revealed by speculative reason, which holds onto what can be seen. From the point of view of the theology of cross, this is the basis and the foundation of faith.[25]

In this state Mary confronts the angel. She does not see anything except the words of the messenger. She does not feel like the Mother of God; she is after all a virgin, untouched by men. Yet she hears the word and holds onto it, and at that moment she becomes pregnant. This is surely a miracle and blessing from God. God's word is not without power, even if we perceive it only fragmentarily. The word breaks forth in its own power and creates what it promises. Even when we cannot believe or even comprehend the word of God, it still remains faithful and

21. WA 17/II, 23, 25–36; 27, 6–9.
22. WA 17/II, 399, 24–400, 4; 400, 21–27.
23. WA 27, 74, 25–28.
24. StA 1, 321, 12–14.
25. StA 1, 353, 3–14.

true. The word is not dependent on faith, yet faith is dependent on the word.[26] In the darkness of faith, the word of God is the efficient power (*verbum efficax*).

These reflections demonstrate how Luther approaches faith within the context of the theology of the Cross. The darkness of faith asks for complete trust in God's grace against the evidence of the senses and reason. In the moment of the actual event, God's works are hidden and beyond recognition, but the believer will not be led astray through momentary impressions. She trusts in the promise of the word and the strength of the Holy Spirit. According to Luther, "faith is benevolent trust in the invisible grace promised to us."[27]

Nevertheless, Mary is made of flesh and bones just as everyone else is. Therefore, reason and faith clash even in her mind. Reason does not comprehend the angel's message, and all that remains is the witness of the word of God; this is what Mary grasps. Luther explains how Mary's faith is "glued" to the word and she "hangs in it." The nature of faith is of a kind that it cannot be based on anything but the word alone.[28]

In Luther's interpretation, the angel says to a dazzled Mary: "Let your reason go." She needs to choose "unreason" or "non-reason" (*unvorstandt*), so that she does not know how the angel's promise will be fulfilled. It is not a matter of Mary's inability to comprehend, but of the incomprehensible nature of angel's message, which is not within the realm of logical knowledge. Mary hears the words of the angel and responds spontaneously: "Be it unto me according to thy word." This is the mystery of faith.[29]

According to Mary's example, reason should remain silent in matters of piety and salvation. The light of reason must fade, and we should follow the path of Mary. Then we become pregnant with the Spirit, and Christ is born in us in spiritual way.[30] Although Mary is no exception with regard to her humanity, she is braver than most of us. She does hesitate, but eventually faith prevails, and she takes a step without the warrant of reason and surrenders to God in faith. This should be our way as well, says Luther.

26. *WA* 34 I, 565, 12–28.
27. *StA* 1, 322, 15–16.
28. *WA* 17/II, 399, 11–15; 404, 13–16.
29. *WA* 9, 625, 14–18.
30. *WA* 9, 625, 18–23.

Trust in God, and the experience of God's love is born in the moments of distress. Trust enables the believer to experience God's works in life, and through this experience to attain deeper understanding and knowledge of God.[31] Experience makes faith alive and leads to love. It enables the experience God's gracious works, and the possibility to love God and neighbor.[32] Experience is the power that sets the wheels in motion. Through it Mary hastens to Elizabeth to offer her help.[33] Mary's heart is oriented toward Elizabeth, because she remembers the words of the angel about Elizabeth's pregnancy. Mary cannot rest before she is with Elizabeth. Other reasons for Mary's journey are joy, love, humility, and care. All these are born in the experience of the living faith.[34]

Luther's Mariology joins together faith and love. Love is the fruit of faith; where there is true faith, there is also love and all other virtues such as humility.[35] The relationship of faith and love is defined so that when the Holy Spirit vivifies the experience of faith, it is always united with love and care for one's neighbor. With regard to neighbors, this is manifested in Mary's works of love and charity. The vivid experience of God's love for her enables Mary to love God.

For Luther, Mary represent the purest of all loves, which is standard picture of Mary in the history of theology. Her pure love is focused on God for his own sake. She does not look for anything to benefit herself. "This is a high, pure, and sensitive way to love and give praise, which fits perfectly the high and beautiful spirit, which this Virgin is."[36] The pure love of God is love of the cross, for there one is willing to give up her belongings. Mary does not cling to the goods she has received from God and does not take advantage of them, but rather submits to God's will.[37] Luther uses the concept *gelassen* (tranquility, certainty)—well-known in mystical theology—to depict Mary.[38] Luther praises Mary as follows: "This must be such an example that no human being will ever reach. For

---

31. StA 320, 2–9.
32. StA 1, 318, 12–16; 323, 35–37.
33. WA 29, 445, 1–2; 5–9.
34. WA 29, 446, 11–16.
35. WA 20, 452, 8–9.
36. StA 1, 326, 4–10.
37. StA 1, 327, 24–30.
38. StA 1, 346, 42.

rare is such a soul that which does not become contemptuous because of God's gifts and who is untouched by poverty."[39]

Mary's love for God is manifested in her *Magnificat* as thankful praise; she gives thanks for a God who is merciful and does such great things for her.[40] Mary's life demonstrates how God's love is a unifying power (*vis unitiva*). God shares his love with Mary in his gaze and chooses her to become the Mother of his Son. Mary's love is manifested in words of praise and unquestionable surrender to God's will and in serving and consoling her neighbors.

LUTHER AND MARIOLOGICAL DOCTRINES

Luther's writings on Mary demonstrate that he accepts the doctrine of Mary as God-bearer (*Theotokos*) in the specific form in which the doctrine was approved in the Council of Ephesus in 431. The person of Jesus Christ is one without division or confusion, and Christians must confess that the two natures of Christ are hypostatically united, as was formulated in Chalcedon in 451.[41] Luther subscribes to the doctrine of *communicatio idiomatum*: the Son of God and the Son of Mary are one and the same, and what we say of the divine nature and its properties relates to human nature as well.[42] Luther criticizes Nestorius who separates the human and the divine natures.[43] Against Manichean Docetism, Luther underscores the true humanity of Christ.[44]

In Luther's interpretation of the *theotokos* doctrine, there is a paradoxical twist. Incarnation takes place *sub contraria specie*, hidden in opposites; it is a miracle incomprehensible to reason, being *articulus fidei*.[45] Luther binds Mary to Christ, and Mariology to Christology. Mary is the Mother of God, yet she remains a virgin. Christians must believe in this sign and word of God in order to understand that Christ has been born without sin. The Virgin Mary is chosen by God to become the God-

---

39. WA 15, 644, 1–3.

40. StA 1, 319, 34–320, 9; WA 41, 365, 12–18.

41. WA 40/III, 703, 4–9; WA 50, 587, 10–28.

42. WA 40/III, 703, 26–704, 4; WA 47, 632, 7–13; 15–18; 21–24; WA 47, 705, 6–14; WA 50, 589, 21–28.

43. WA 50, 591, 22–592, 5; 592, 10–15; WA 47, 633, 36–634, 4; WA 47, 633, 25–28; 30–33; WA 47, 702, 12–18.

44. WA 36, 60, 7–10; 14–18; WA 46, 137, 5–22.

45. StA 1, 360, 33–361, 4.

bearer so that the Son may rescue the human race from the captivity of sin.[46] Thus, Luther's Mariology directly serves soteriology.

The connection of Mariology and soteriology inevitably raises the question of the sinlessness of Mary. Pope Pius IX implemented the formulation of the doctrine *conceptio immaculata Mariae* as late as the year 1854. In Luther's times this doctrine was still under debate, and Luther scholarship has attributed differing views to Luther regarding the issue. Sometimes Luther has been considered a defender of Immaculate Conception, meaning that Mary was free from original sin. However, this view is based on an uncritical use of the sources. The passage that has been used to argue this point of view (WA 17 II, 288, 17–289, 1) is not Luther's text but originates from the hand of his editor, Thomas Roth. A critical reading of the sources implies that Luther does not argue either for Immaculate Conception or Mary's sinlessness. Indeed, Mary remains burdened with original sin, since she is completely human.[47] The only person without sin is Jesus Christ, but he was the God-man.[48] Luther's view of Mary's humanity grows stronger over time, and in 1524 he speaks explicitly about Mary's sin in the context of Jesus's disappearance into the temple.[49]

Holding onto liberty from original sin would create a conflict with Luther's basic theological principles, especially with his understanding of sin. If Mary is without sin at the moment of conception, then there is no need for alien righteousness because she has been perfect from the start. Consequently, there is no need for God's grace at the moment of Christ's conception if Mary is already filled with grace. Nevertheless, Mary needs to be without sin at the moment of Christ's conception if we want hold on to the full motherhood of Mary as Luther does.[50] Luther solves this problem in a sermon from the year 1538 by posing a rhetorical question: is not the One who has created everything from nothing able to cleanse the Mother of his Son? Luther answers: even if this mother is descendant of Adam, the Holy Spirit purifies her and does not choose a corrupt but a purified substance (*ex ea sumpsit non*

---

46. WA 45, 48, 26–49; WA 46, 136, 1–13; 231, 8–232, 2.

47. WA 36, 143, 13–144, 1; WA 47, 860, 35–38.

48. WA 9, 492, 1–7; WA 39/II, 107, 7–13.

49. WA 15, 415, 4–14; WA 17/II, 19, 1–11, 17–22, 24–28; 23, 8–19; 25, 11–18; 26, 20–27, 9.

50. WA 41, 629, 18–26.

corruptam, sed mundatam substantiam). This interpretation has some blind spots; Luther goes on to claim that this was a matter of faith even for Mary and for everybody else as well. Nevertheless, it is of such great importance that believing in Mary's virginity becomes a prerequisite for salvation: *Haec nostra fides. Si das verlieren, amittimus salutatem*.[51] Here too Mariology is transformed into soteriology. Luther concludes that Mary is made sinless through God's special grace and the work of the Holy Spirit at moment of Jesus's conception, and this state lasts until the birth of Jesus. In all other respects, Mary is like any other human being and bears the burden of original sin.

Regarding the perpetual virginity of Mary, Luther takes a rock-solid stand. He argues for perpetual virginity *ante, in et post partum*: *virgo conceptit, virgo peperit, virgo permansit*. This was declared to be the official teaching of the Catholic Church in 649.[52] Mary gave birth without pain and without injury.[53] As for the scriptural reference to Jesus's brothers, Luther interprets this as referring to Jesus's other relatives. Perpetual virginity is a sign of God's miracle, and this sets Mary apart from all other people. Luther never doubts Mary's virginity. This doctrine works as the foundation for his theological deliberations on Mary.

Luther departs from medieval tradition in regarding virginity as not meritorious for Mary; instead, it was a cross to bear, *magna crux*. Virginity is set within the context of the theology of the cross. Mary becomes pregnant while a virgin and while engaged to Joseph who was about to abandon her. Therefore, she was stripped of her virginity and made a whore. Luther claims that the Holy Virgin cannot achieve glory if she is not disgraced.[54] Virginity is not a value in itself but becomes one in the context of Christology and soteriology.[55] It is a gracious choice of God. Virginity ensures the sinlessness of Jesus and enables Him to become the innocent victim for the world: a sinless one who is made Sin. Simultaneously, Jesus' true humanity and divinity are guaranteed in being conceived by the Holy Spirit and born of the Virgin Mary.[56] For Christians, this means a miracle beyond comprehension, even an absur-

---

51. WA 46, 230, 3–26; 136, 4–13, 24–30.
52. WA 11, 319, 32–320, 7; 324, 10–18; WA 49, 174, 4–8; 182, 30–32; 183, 31–37.
53. WA 5, 624, 30–37; 625, 1–3; WA 32, 254, 10–12.
54. WA 27, 481, 9–483, 9; 484, 1–4.
55. WA 11, 319, 8–16.
56. WA 49, 60, 40–61, 8; 174, 24–37; WA 47, 704, 5–18.

dity. Yet God is all-powerful, and nothing is impossible for him. He may even act against his own created order and make a virgin give birth to a child if he so desires. In keeping with this, Luther makes clear that Mary's virginity remains a matter of faith; it is a theological truth.[57] Nevertheless, Luther does not repudiate the physical reality, but defends the concrete untouchability of Mary's body.[58] Early on, Luther expressed doubts about the doctrine of the assumption of Mary (*Assumptio Mariae*, which was doctrinally fixed in 1950), and in 1523 Luther rejects it completely.[59] The reason for this rejection is that this doctrine overshadows and distorts the doctrine of Christ's assumption in popular piety and causes confusion in lay people, leading them to idolatry and superstition.[60]

To sum up, Luther's Mariology—both the exemplary nature of Mary and his relation the Mariological doctrines—is set in the context of his Theology of the Cross. His own doctrinal points of emphasis on Christology and soteriology control his reading of contemporary Mariological doctrines (*Theotokos* and *Semper Virgo*) and especially those that received their official form much later (*Conceptio immaculata Mariae* and *Assumptio Mariae*).

---

57. WA 36, 130, 15–141, 14; 138, 2–139, 18.
58. WA 5, 549, 1–9.
59. WA 10/III 268, 14–20; WA 11, 159, 13–14.
60. WA 52, 681, 1–31.

10

Sex

SAMMELI JUNTUNEN

LUTHER BEGAN TO WRITE and preach about sex and marriage quite early in his career as a reformer. The reason was that in his view the prevailing Catholic teaching and the popular ideas of the late-medieval European society about sex and marriage were severely distorted.[1] Four of these distortions may be mentioned here.

First, marriage was seen as a spiritually lower state than celibacy. A priest, a monk, or a nun, who had to give vows of celibacy, was considered more pleasing to God than a husband or a wife who led a sexual life and had children. According to Luther, people felt spiritually inferior because of their sexuality. Young people were often ashamed to tell their parents about their love and their desire to marry. Some were forced by their parents into monasteries in order to improve their spiritual rank before God. For Luther such a move was spiritually lethal. The consequences of such thinking could also be seen in society as a whole. The backbone of any society, namely family life with its responsibilities, such as raising children and earning a living, was considered almost sinful in itself. There were writings by popular authors, who despised women and advised people not to marry, in order to avoid the miseries of family life.[2] However, the official teaching of the church was never this gloomy,

---

1. See, e.g., WA 6, 558, 2–7. Lähteenmäki (*Sexus*, 176–81) and Suppan (*Die Ehelehre*, 20–21) list the most important passages in which Luther writes about sex and marriage.

2. See, e.g., WA 2, 169, 20–26; WA 8, 607, 18–24; WA 10/I, 1, 708, 10–15; WA 10/II, 292, 22–293, 2; WA 10/II, 302:6–9; WA 12, 93:6–10, 94:3–8; WA Tr 3, no 3523. See also Lähteenmäki, *Sexus*, 21–22.

because marriage was one of the holy sacraments. Yet according to Luther, the idea of sacramental matrimony did not relieve family life of the stigma of spiritual inferiority. In the minds of the people the ascetic ideal of celibacy was strong.

Second, the ideal of celibacy had led to widespread prostitution, openly practiced and tolerated not only by society but also by the church. If a priest could not adhere to the celibacy required of him, it was (at least in some parts of Europe) quite normal to use the services of a prostitute if the priest paid a fine to his bishop. This was a lesser sin than to give up the priesthood altogether and marry. There were professional prostitutes even in post-reformation Wittenberg. Some of the students at the University of Wittenberg used prostitutes, who operated somewhere in the vicinity of the town's pig-market. Luther opposed this practice with an essay called "Gegen die hurn und speckstudenten" (Against the Whores and Fat-Students). He also demanded that public brothels be closed.[3]

Third, Medieval Europe was permeated by the idea of courtly love, *ars amandi*, which was sexual through and through. Noble knight sang *Minnelieder*, songs of praise of the lady of knight's heart in which he dreamed of "picking her rose." It was a part of the game that often the object of affections was already married to someone else and the knight had to perform inhuman and wonderful deeds before his love was pure enough to receive the lady's favor. This mixture of suppressed and purified, yet deeply sexual longings had created an atmosphere of secrecy around sexual matters.[4]

Luther confronted this atmosphere in the form of "secret engagements" and "secret marriages." The Catholic Church considered an engagement to be binding, when ever a man and a woman promised each other "I will take you as mine" (*ego te recipiam in meam / meum*). This engagement could also be made in secret, without any witnesses. Because there was little or no difference in the binding character of an engagement and marriage, even marriage could be secret (*matrimonia clandestina*) and the Catholic Church considered secret marriages valid. People who were bound by such secret promises could not divorce or

---

3. WA Tr 4, 552, 20—554, 26; WA 48, 278, 19–22; WA 27, 554-55; WA 10/II, 150, 15–23; WA 6, 262, 14–34, 467, 17–23.

4. A standard work on courtly love is C. S. Lewis, *Allegory of Love*.

remarry.⁵ In Luther's time secret marriages were not rare, because often parents did not give their children permission to marry at all. It is understandable then that in an atmosphere of *ars amandi*, secret marriage was an exciting and romantic venture for young lovers. But it is also understandable, that the practice brought problems. Luther was very much opposed to secret marriages.⁶

Fourth, there were, of course, many other kinds of problems that people had with sex and marriages. Luther felt that the Catholic Church had not been able help people sufficiently with its teachings. Rather it had confused people with the complex commandments of Canon Law. Therefore, Luther felt that he had to construct a new view of sexual ethics. This he did in private correspondence to those who asked his advice, in private conversations, in public sermons and in writings about "*eheliche Leben*" (married life). In doing this Luther spoke in a way that was unusually open for his time and perhaps even for us today. In a sense, Luther was the man for "All You Ever Wanted to Know About Sex, but Didn't Dare to Ask" of his time. Or rather "All that has Troubled your Conscience about Sex and How to Overcome Those Troubles."⁷

LUTHER'S THEOLOGY AS THE FRAMEWORK FOR HIS IDEAS ABOUT SEX

Luther's teachings about sex were a part of his theology. In sexual matters, as elsewhere, the main theme for Luther was how could a Christian believe in God with a clear conscience and love his neighbor by performing concrete deeds. Before proceeding a few general comments are in order about Luther's theology.

Creation: All reality is created by God. God works everything, including sexual life. For Luther, there is no secular world or secular reason in the modern sense. It is true that human reason, can according to

---

5. See Suppan, *Ehelehre*, 60–62, 67, and Lähteenmäki, *Sexus*, 100.

6. At that time, the legal foundation of marriage was the mutual will of a man and woman (*consensus facit nuptias*) and their carnal copulation. This was taken from Roman law into canonical Church law. Secret marriages were therefore binding before God, even though they could be in doubt before others. Because there were no marriage registers, it was not clear who was married and who was not. See Kretschmar, "Luthers Konzeption von der Ehe," 181–91.

7. The reason the text of "*Vom ehelichen Leben*" (1522) was published was "to give advice to a confessor who is visited by a man or a wife who wants learn what they are supposed to do" (*WA* 10/II, 278).

Luther, know many things about the created order without God's specific revelation. But even those things are parts of creation, totally dependent on the Creator's constant work.[8]

Sin: Adam's sin distorted everything in the world, including sex. For Luther, sin is not "natural" in the sense that God created it or that it is God's will. Sin is a distortion of God's good creation. But it is such a deep distortion that, according to Luther, the "natural human being" (*homo naturalis*) commits sinful deeds from the depth of his or her being and will. Luther thus differs sharply from such modern thinking whereby that which is empirically common, and in this sense "normal", for us humans, cannot be a sin or a distortion.

The Bible and essentialism: Luther's anthropology is essentialist. He believed that there is an essential human nature, which is created and willed by God. For Luther, human nature includes things like two genders, man and woman. Normally, essential human nature requires that one man and one woman marry and have children. Thus, the family forms the basis of a society. Furthermore, it is part of human nature for people to know through their natural reasoning that there is a God, whom they should love and obey. They also know naturally that they should love others and prevent evil. This knowledge leads to the formation of political rule (*Obrigkeit*).[9]

Luther believed in this way, because it is written thus in the Bible, which tells who God is and what human being is. The basic elements of Luther's teachings about sex, therefore, are taken from the Bible.[10] This theory is very different from the sexual ethics of modern western civilization, which is more psychological, medical, and naturalistic than Luther's. For Luther, sex outside marriage was a sin, because God says so in the Bible.

---

8. See Kretschmar, "Luthers Konzeption," 178; WA 43, 294–300.

9. WA 43, 294.

10. The most important biblical passages for Luther in matters of sex and marriage were Gen 1: 27, Gen 2:18-24 and 1 Cor 7:1-40. These passages were also used in the tradition before him, e.g., in Lombard's Sentences. The also tradition used often Matt 19:3-12, but Luther seldom used these verses. Kretschmar, "Luthers Konzeption," 182, 203. The following texts are good examples of how Luther takes his ideas of sex and marriage from the Bible: WA 2, 166, 27–29: "Das alls seynd gottis wort, yn welchen beschrieben ist, wo man und weyb herkummen, wye sie zussammen geben seynd, und wo zu eyn weyb geschaffen, und was vor liebe seyn soll ym eelichen leben." WA 43, 299, 26–27: "Haec vero non docentur in iure nec canonico, nec civili, nec in medicorum arte, sed in scriptura sancta." See also WA 10/II, 299, 6–4.

Luther's essentialist anthropology means that in the natural order of things, there are two genders: men, who naturally feel sexual lust for women, and women, who naturally feel sexual lust for men. However, Luther knows, from the Bible and from experience, that there are exceptions to this order: "... some are eunuchs (*verschnytten*) because they were born that way; others were made that way by men; and others have made themselves eunuchs because of the kingdom of heaven" (Matt 19:12)." To the first group belong the so-called impotents, who can be either men or (more seldom) women who are sexually incapable. God has created them, with a lack in their human nature, just as God is also the Creator of the blind and the lame people.[11] The second group consists of castrated men, the eunuchs. According to Luther, eunuchs are especially unhappy people. Even though they are not capable of consummation of marriage, they still have a constant lust for women, which is even stronger than before the castration. Eunuchs therefore become "womanly" (*weybish*).[12] To the third group (less than one out of a thousand persons) belong those with the supernatural and divine gift of chastity. It is likely that still in early 1520s, Luther believed he was in this group.[13]

However, Luther was not in all respects a biblicist. This can be seen, for example, in his attitude to divorce. Even though Christ (Matt 19:8) forbids divorce, Luther teaches that in certain difficult situations divorce is allowed for a Christian. On the other hand, Luther wants to take the reasons for an acceptable divorce from the New Testament.[14] However, it is clear that he develops his arguments much further than the New Testament, with the help of two principles: *agape* love and the human need for sex.

Natural law and natural reason: Luther also criticizes the Bible and its sexual ethics, especially Mosaic Law. He does this by referring to the natural law written in the hearts of all people. Its content is the Golden Rule: "Do unto others as you would have them to do unto you." The commandments of the Old Testament are in force insofar as they

11. WA 10/II, 278, 1–31.

12. WA 10/II, 279, 7–14. I have not found any references to gays or lesbians as special groups of people in Luther's writings.

13. WA 10/II, 279, 15–23. According to Lähteenmäki (*Sexus*) Luther does not speak of himself as having had a "constant burning" for women. It seems that his sexual temptations in the monastery were temporary in character, which, according to him, was normal also for people having the *donum castitatis*.

14. Suppan, *Die Ehelehre*, 108–9, 119; Oberman, *Luther,* 236–37; WA 10/II, 289.

are in accordance with the Golden Rule. In some cases Luther even uses the Golden Rule against sexual ethics in the New Testament, literally understood.[15]

However, we have to keep in mind that for Luther the "natural reason" is quite different from what we understand by this idea. Luther lived in a culture that was permeated by Christianity and its ways of thinking. In Luther's time it was clear for almost all rational people that there was a God, a God who had created the world and its people; therefore, it follows that there is an objective human essence, God speaks in the Bible, and marriage is an institution given by God. In our secular civilization there is no longer such general rationale. We have a plurality of rationales, plurality of anthropologies, and plurality of ideas about what is a sexually good life for human beings.

This difference between Luther's understanding of "natural reason" and ours makes it difficult to use Luther's reasoning in modern sexual ethics. At least in Finland, Luther's emphasis on natural reason and natural law has led to "Lutheran" ideas that are clearly against Luther's thinking. A good example is the following citation from a recent high-school textbook on religion:

> It is not a part of the Lutheran ethical tradition to define detailed moral norms. In sexual ethics this means that the sexual act as a physical or biological act is not the most important matter. Most important is that love is fulfilled. The basis of ethics is the so-

---

15. See Luther's argument in cases, in which a husband was impotent, but had refrained from telling his wife before the marriage. *WA* 6, 559, 1–9. However, we should not overemphasize this point. In recent discussion in the Finnish church media about sexual ethics, "Lutheran" ethics often seems to be something based on the formal principle of *agape* alone. This thinking is set against "reformed" ethics, which takes its principles from the Bible. However, this contrast is not Luther's point, when he speaks of *lex naturalis*. See, e.g., *AWA* 2, 28, 1–29, 3; 178, 19–25; 203, 3–204, 5. See also Hütter, *Bound to be Free*, 134–44. I also think that it is anachronistic to use these advices privately given as a "Lutheran" basis for an ecclesiastical blessing of a homosexual relationship. It is possible to do this, if one picks certain elements of Luther's thinking and ignores others that are at least as important for Luther's ethical thinking. For instance, *lex naturae*, *agape* love, and the power of the sexual drive interpreted in a certain way would result in something similar if isolated from Luther's essentialist anthropology, the doctrine of the created orders and the Bible as the source of knowledge about God's will. Such anachronisms are no longer based on research. If Luther had blessed a homosexual relationship—which I very much doubt—he would have done it privately in a situation of pastoral counseling. But he would never have accepted a same-sex relationship as a social institution that is willed by God or that has his blessing.

called Golden Rule: All that you want people to do unto you, you do unto them (Matt 7:12).... The basis of Lutheran sexual ethics is the principle of love toward one's neighbor.

For this reason, according to Lutheran understanding, it is not sensible to answer such questions very definitely, as in which stage of life sexual relations can be started, or whether it is wrong to watch porn, to legalize prostitution, or what attitude to take toward one-night-stands. Everyone must take responsibility for his or her sexual morals. To see that love is fulfilled, to put oneself in another's place, and to protect those weaker than oneself are the also principles for sexual morality. The other person and humanity must always be considered as an end in themselves, never as means to something.[16]

It is obvious that the, idea that "everyone must take responsibility for his or her sexual morals" is more Kantian than Lutheran. For Luther, there are natural orders created by God, and sexuality should be expressed according to God's commandments.[17] Personal responsibility has to be exercised within the boundaries of these natural orders. We know what these orders are from the word of God.

Law and the Gospel: The idea of dialectic between Law and the Gospel is a persistent theme. Luther was opposed to the prevailing teaching about sexuality, because it led to "righteousness of the law," to attempts to please God with celibacy. This kind of thinking had to be replaced by teachings in which neither marriage nor sexual abstinence offered way to salvation.

"*Worldly regiment*" *and* "*spiritual regiment*": According to Luther, sexual life belongs to the "worldly regiment," wherein God rules through his law, not through his word, sacraments or faith (the spiritual regiment). His law commands people to marry, to stay faithful in their marriage, to raise and love their children, and to work for a living. These commandments of God are "external" in the sense that they force people "from the outside", through the institution of family and political rule, which are matters of society and not spiritual matters of the church. These laws of the "worldly regiment" are still God's laws. God pours out his love to people through these laws, because they force people to do good for others, at least externally. The "worldly orders" are family (*oeco-*

---

16. Heinimäki & Järveläinen, *Tosi paha hyvä: Etiikka*, 41–42. Translation mine.
17. WA 12, 94, 28–31. WA 12, 98, 1–5. WA 10/II, 298, 9–21.

nomia) and political rule (*politia*).[18] However, sex and marriage are matters in which the "spiritual regiment" (the church and faith) is absolutely needed. Luther emphasizes that "faith makes all things good, unbelief makes all things bad."[19] A marriage is such a difficult calling that without faith in Christ, without his love, and without forgiveness, it is spoiled through quarrelling and all kinds of sins.

The struggle between God and Satan: For Luther the world was an arena of constant struggle between God and Satan. Sex, marriage, and family life were areas in which much of the struggle was carried out. By attacking marriage, Satan could harm people deeply. Here too the battle, according to Luther, is fought between faith and unbelief. It is a matter of whether people believe in God's words about sex and marriage.[20]

THE POWER OF THE SEX DRIVE AND THE VOW OF CHASTITY

The most important sexual issue that concerned Luther's reformation movement in its early years was the doctrine of celibacy. The Roman Catholic Church demanded a vow of celibacy from all monks and all nuns. Priests did not always give a personal vow, but lifelong celibacy was required of them. Luther found this very problematic. In the monastery he had himself seen that the sexual drive was something that humans could not resist.[21] At the beginning of the 1520s, Luther began to criticize the vows of chastity, in such writings as *An der Christlichen Adel* (1520) and in *De votis monasticis* (1521). In these writings Luther's approach was quite practical. His point was that only those vows of celibacy are permitted that are freely given then only "insofar as human weakness allows." If an absolute vow is required from candidate for the priesthood, it should not be given, because such a vow is not man's to keep. It requires "angelical power and heavenly virtue."[22]

---

18. Suppan, *Ehelehre*, 22–23, 27, 83–88; See WA 54, 437. WA 30/III, 205, WA 30/II, 555. The worldly character of marriage can also be seen in that the ecclesiastical wedding ceremony was, according to Luther, not an act that instituted marriage. It was an act of blessing a marriage that was already valid on the basis of the public consent of the couple to begin living together as husband and wife.

19. WA 12, 108, 3–5.

20. WA 42, 110, 25–27; WA Tr 2, 98, 15–99; WA Tr 6, 262–64; WA 47, 320–21.

21. WA 10/I, 708–9.

22. WA 6, 441, 35–442, 9; WA 7, 37, 1–15. All translations from WA are mine.

Soon Luther's opinion became more severe. Even freely given vows of celibacy were not permitted. They were against "nature" and freedom of conscience, and for that reason no one should take a vow of celibacy. It would be as impossible to promise as if someone promised to destroy the Turkish empire or to live as long as Methuselah. Such things are not within our power.[23] To attempt such a thing leads to a "burning . . . in every limb"[24]; such ways of trying to quench a lust, about which Luther does not even want to speak. In the end a "Martyr of the Devil" is created.[25] To take a vow of chastity is to sin against healthy human life, against the grace of Christ and the Holy Spirit. It is a blasphemy toward God and his orders of creation.[26] No one should give such a vow. If somebody has done so, then, according to Luther, he or she is freed from the vow and is free to marry because such a promise is given to the Devil, not to God.[27] The reason for this total condemnation is that the vow of chastity becomes a means of pleasing God, an expression of "self-righteousness." It takes place in the hearts of people where only grace and forgiveness should reign:

> . . . in their opinion, they vow in order to prepare righteousness and salvation with their vows. This is an opinion they should have only about the merciful God, but they give it to works of their own. So with their vows they serve and adore their own works, instead of God. Faith is namely the opinion of the heart, that only the real and the one God should be served. Therefore, unbelief is both a perversity of the heart and the highest impiety. This unbelief is to be avoided in these times in which hardly one in a thousand takes a pious vow. It is probable that people would not

23. WA Br 2, 382-86, 405; WA 8, 324-25, 658-59. When Melanchthon and Bugenhagen received this text (*Themata de Votis*, October 1521) from their friend hiding in Wartburg castle, they thought it was groundbreaking. Luther's earlier writings about the issue would not have changed the official status of monks and nuns. See the editors' notes in WA 8, 317.

24. WA 12, 117: "To put it briefly, 'burning' is the heat of the flesh that rages and won't stop. It is the daily longing for a woman or a man. . . . Such burning is in every limb. . . . most of them cannot stand such burning and in fact they do not. They do what they can to get rid of it; I don't want to speak about it now. But when they get rid of it, outside marriage, then soon a [bad] conscience is present and that is the most unbearable misery and situation in life." Priests who followed Luther's advice and married often gave as an important reason the need to "save their conscience."

25. WA 10/I, 1, 692-93.

26. WA Br 2, 383, 31-53; WA 24, 54, 13-15; WA 8, 583, 20-28.

27. WA 8, 332-34; WA 10/I, 1, 699-700.

have taken the vow, if they knew that they would not receive the righteousness or salvation with these vows. They confess this by saying, "What else would I do in the monastery [other than earn salvation]?" All such people profess a religion that is against the Lord and Christ. Therefore, such vows are to be strictly punished, even destroyed. And such monasteries should be considered offerings given to Satan and as his brothels.[28]

According to Luther, it is God himself who is manifest in human sexuality. It is the effect of God's word that causes the "basic instinct," even when the sinfulness of humankind makes the result anything but pious. Therefore,

> If one is not within these three groups [impotent, castrated, or having a special gift of chastity], then he or she should marry. There is no other way; you will not stay pious for it is impossible. It is God's Word that has created you and said: "Grow and multiply." It stays in you and rules in you; you cannot consider it as meaningless, or you must continuously commit terrible sins.[29]

According to Luther sex is not a religiously "neutral" matter in which the individual could decide how to express his or her sexuality. The basic instinct has to be fulfilled in "correct use," i.e., in marriage. In normal cases the question of whether to marry or not to marry at all is not for an individual to decide:

> Nature wants to get out. It wants to cast its seed and multiply. And God does not want this outside of marriage. So, because of this necessity, everyone has to get married, that is, those who otherwise cannot live in good conscience and with God.[30]

However, Luther does not say that celibacy is not allowed. There exists a special gift of God called *donum castitatis*. According to Luther,

---

28. WA 8, 325, 3–18. Luther's emphasis on the inhuman character of promising chastity seems contradictory to the ideas of the recent movement called "True Love Waits." In this movement young Christians publicly promise not to have sex before marriage. The principle itself is in accordance with Luther's sexual ethics, but the act of promising chastity publicly seems different from Luther's emphasis on the power of the sexual drive, which is stronger an individual's will. On the other hand the promises given in the "True Love Waits" movement are not made for life, and they are not intended to raise the person to a spiritually higher level.

29. WA 8, 317.

30. WA 12, 114, 30–32; 10/II, 276, 14–31. See also Kretschmar, "Luthers Konzeption," 187, and Oberman, *Luther*, 288.

only about one in a thousand people have such a gift.[31] It is a gift of special freedom, a grace that is above the natural state of things. It is a precious gift, because it frees a person from the troubles of family life and allows more time to be spent with the word of God.[32] Such a gift needs no vows of celibacy.

Luther's freedom fight for priest, monks and nuns was indeed victorious. Many left their religious institutions and married. Around 1522, papal supporters launched a campaign against the Lutherans.[33] In response, Luther had to explain his ideas, in numerous times.[34] Luther himself broke his vow on June 13, 1525 and married a runaway nun, Katherina (Käthe) von Bora.[35] However, his original idea was not that the breaking of the vow of celibacy would necessarily lead to an emptying of the monasteries. He believed that monks and nuns could marry and live in monasteries as in ordinary homes. Monasteries would become a kind of Christian school for boys and girls.[36] Luther himself fulfilled much of this idea. His former monastery, the Black Cloister of Wittenberg, became

31. WA 15, 667, 27-29; WA 30/1, 162, 12-19.

32. WA 10/II, 302, 10-13; WA 12, 99-100; WA 10/III, 108, 6-7; WA 24, 54, 25-34; WA 47, 322, 34-40.

33. The editor's introduction to Luther's *Begleitbrief* to Johann Apell's *Defensio pro suo coniugio* from the year 1523 (WA 12, 68-70) shows quite convincingly that breaking celibacy was a major issue. Johann Apell was a *Canonicus* of the Würztburg diocese and therefore obliged to live in celibacy. At the beginning of the year 1523 he and his friend Friedrich Fischer both married secretly. Johann married a nun from a convent in Würtzburg in order to "save his conscience." Both couples kept their marriages secret for a while, but in the spring of 1523, the bishop of Würtzburg was informed of these marriages by enemies of the couples. The bishop demanded that Apell send the nun back to her convent. Apell refused to obey, because he claimed that she was his wife. He asked for a chance to defend his decision publicly. He wrote a *Defensio pro suo coniugio* in support of which Luther published his *Begleitbreif* (WA 12, 71-72). Luther was falsely informed that both Apell and Fischer had been burned at the stake. Yet things did not become quite that bad. Both men were "thrown in the deep bottom of a tower" and kept there for several months. Investigations were made, and books containing "the damned Lutheran doctrine" were found. There was the real threat of churchly jurisdiction, which could have led to capital punishment or a lengthy imprisonment. Still, the prisoners would not accept the annulment of their marriages; they "could not renounce the Word of God." In the end, the *Reichsregiment* came to their aid and demanded that the bishop free both Apell and Fischer.

34. E.g., WA 26, 528-54.

35. Around 1521, Luther no longer considered himself bound by his vow of celibacy. See, e.g., WA 8, 576, 14-21.

36. WA 10, I, 1, 700, 8-20.

his and Käthe's home, where they raised many children, six of their own and four orphans. In addition, Käthe provided lodging for students.

MARRIAGE AS "REMEDY AND MEDICINE FOR WHORING"

According to Luther, the true definition of marriage is this:

> Marriage is a divine and legitimate joining (*coniunctio*) of a husband and a wife in the hope of having children, and in order to avoid fornication and sin, to the glory of God. The ultimate goal is to obey God, to avoid sin, to call upon God for help, to ask for children, to love and raise them to God's glory, to live with one's wife in fear of God, and to carry the cross.[37]

The institution of marriage exists "in order to avoid fornication;" it is protection against and medicine (*erzney*) for sin.[38] The sexual drive is insuperable, but marriage comes to man's aid: between a married wife and her husband, sex is not a sin. Luther takes this argument (which was also common in the tradition before him) from 1 Cor 7:2: "to avoid fornication every man should have his own wife and every woman should have her own husband." When a husband and wife have sufficient physical relations with each other, the sexual "burning" is quenched, and they are not in danger of committing sins by lusting other women or men. The unquenchable power of the sexual drive means for Luther that people normally should marry at a relatively young age—and not just anyone, who can quench sexual desire, but they should pray for the right spouse.[39]

Luther follows the Apostle Paul when he teaches that spouses have sexual duties responsibilities to one another. The right of spouses to have enough sex is in a certain sense in Luther's thinking, comparable to material possessions. He writes that, for example, if a wife does not want to fulfill her duties to her husband, the husband should think of his wife as having been stolen from him by robbers.[40] Similarly, Luther writes about a case, in which man had not told his fiancée about his impotence. His wife discovered the condition only after the wedding. Luther viewed the fraud committed by the man as outrageous. Because the man was inca-

---

37. WA 43, 310, 24–28, 558–59.
38. WA 42, 89, 35–36; WA 12, 104, 1–2, 115, 7; WA 30 I, 162, 18–19; WA 43, 299, 13–15.
39. WA 43, 378, 9–17.
40. WA 10/I, 290, 13–20; 10/II, 290–91.

pable of fulfilling the duties of a husband, he was not a real husband, but just a roommate. Luther advised the woman to start a sexual relationship with someone else—albeit with the permission of her husband. If the husband would not permit the relationship , then the wife should run away and start a new life somewhere else with another husband.[41]

Luther writes that each couple should decide how much sex they need.[42] Later, in a source that I have not been able to identify, there is according to the literature the "well-known Luther-advice" (*wohl bekannter Luther-Regel*) to have sex: two or three times a week in marriage.[43] More important is the general idea: there should be enough sex in a marriage that immoral lusts or impure thoughts do not arise in the spouses. In this context Luther writes lines that may sound offensive: If a wife is totally cold to the idea of sex with her husband, "... then it is time to say: 'If you don't want, then another one will. If the wife does not want sex, then let the maid come.' However, this should only be said when the husband has warned her wife two or three times, and thereafter he has informed other about her stubbornness ... if even then the wife is unwilling, then let her go and let an Esther be given to you, and let the Vasthi go, just as King Ahasuerus did [Esther 1]."[44]

As shown in the earlier example, a husband's unwillingness or inability to have sex with his wife is a reason for divorce. However, Luther makes it very clear that a disease that makes a spouse sexually incapable is not a reason for a divorce or unfaithfulness:

> How is it then, if someone has a sick spouse who is of no help in the fulfilling marital duties, is he allowed to take another? No way! Serve God in your sick spouse! Think that God has given a holy thing (*heyllthum*) into your house, through which you can attain heaven [sic]. You are blessed and blessed again, if you realize such a gift and grace in your spouse and serve him or her in God's will. But if you say: Oh, I cannot hold myself back, you lie. If you serve your sick spouse earnestly and realize that God has sent him or her to you and if you thank Him for that, so let Him take care. Certainly He will give you grace, so that you do not have to carry more than you are able.[45]

41. WA 6, 558–59.
42. WA 6, 559.
43. Lähteenmäki, *Sexus*, 59 n. 3.
44. WA 10/II, 290, 8–14.
45. WA 10/II, 291, 25–292, 3.

What is it that enables sex within marriage not to be a sin? According to the Catholic Church, it was the sacramental character of marriage itself. Sex is sinful in itself, yet because of this sacrament, sex is acceptable in the eyes of God when it takes place between the spouses under this sacrament. In his earliest sermon about marriage (1519) Luther explains the acceptability of sex in marriage in the traditional way.[46] However, in 1520, Luther changes his mind: marriage is not a sacrament. Only the Eucharist and baptism are sacraments, because only they have the two things required of a sacrament: Christ's explicit words of institution and a material sign that is connected with Christ's words.[47] Marriage is a "worldly institution" in the sense that even pagans and non-believing Christians have totally valid and legal marriages in the eyes of God.

However, change in Luther's thinking about the sacramental character of marriage does not change his argument about the sinfulness of sex outside marriage and its acceptability inside marriage. Even though after 1520 marriage is no longer a sacrament for Luther, it is still a godly institution, one that God has blessed with his word. These words of God that institute marriage can be read in the Bible (e.g., Genesis 2), but at the same time they are present in all creation and in all cultures, even among pagans. Also in pagan cultures men and women marry publicly, promise fidelity to each other and live together as a family, raising their children together. This unit is instituted by the word of God, by which all is created. This word of God, this divine institution of marriage, means that carnal copulation of a married husband with his wife is not fornication, but the will of God.[48] Outside marriage, that is, outside the institution made by God's word, all sex is sin.

In some sense Luther's new explanation for the acceptability of marital sex becomes even more "spiritual" than the Catholic view in which the mutual consent of will and the carnal copulation were the *materia sacramenti*, and the marriage was based on "natural law" (*ius naturale*). Luther criticizes the Catholic experts of Canon law for this attitude. For them copulation is the essential thing that makes a marriage a marriage. However, they should pay more attention to God's words. Marriage is not simply a matter of *ius naturale*. God's will and God's words present in the creation cause that the marriage is a "divine and legitimate uniting of

---

46. WA 2, 168, 10–13, 30–37.
47. WA 6, 550–53; Suppan, *Die Ehelehre*, 28–32.
48. See, e.g., WA 43, 294:40–295, 4; 294, 19–26.

a husband and wife ... in order to avoid fornication." This is not simply a matter of mutual assent and copulation of the two persons involved.[49]

WAS LUTHER MORE POSITIVE TOWARD SEXUALITY THAN HIS PREDECESSORS?

It has been a matter of dispute whether Luther's ideas about sexuality were an improvement or setback, when compared with medieval Catholic theology. For many Catholic scholars Luther's sexual thinking was brutally carnal, if not perverted.[50] On the Protestant side Luther is seen as a great reformer, who liberated Christianity from its age-old condemnation of sexuality and who considered sex a positive aspect of God's creation.[51]

Obviously, the traditional Catholic view of Luther is wrong. We have already seen that even when Luther denies the sacramental character of marriage, marriage is still for him a divine institution. But the traditional Protestant interpretation is also mistaken. Luther was in a sense just as opposed to human sexuality as Catholic theologians were. Also for Luther, sex in itself is something dirty and shameful (*turpis*), even in marriage. God tolerates the sex act of a married couple because of his word and his institution, which purify sex and forgive its sinful lust. But in the sex drive, in the libido itself, there is nothing pure or beautiful for Luther.[52]

> If you judge according to reason and outward appearance, marital coitus is in no way different from adultery. Still, the former is chaste and honest under the forgiveness of sins, under blessing, and pleasing to God; the latter is shameful and damned by God. The reason is that in matrimony God protects his institution and order in the midst of libido and shame.[53]

Luther seems to think that the sinful corruption that was caused by the fall of Adam and Eve shows in the ecstatic drive of the sexual act. Adam and Eve had sex even before their fall, but then the act was still

49. WA 43, 294-95.
50. See, e.g., H. Denifle, *Luther und Luthertum*.
51. See, e.g., Oberman, *Luther*, 288-90, and Lähteenmäki, *Sexus*, 61, 66.
52. WA 2, 167, 16-21, 169, 1-7; WA 8, 94, 25-37; WA 10/II, 304, 6-12; WA 43, 297, 302.
53. WA 43, 302, 24-28.

seen as good. After the fall, the human sexual act became an animal-like, a gross and shameful thing.[54]

Behind these thoughts loom St Augustine and his thinking and the influence of Stoicism, because of which, Augustine's concept of *concupiscentia* is ambiguous. On the one hand, Augustine follows the New Testament and teaches that concupiscence is sinful egoism, perverted self-love. Concupiscence causes humans to use other people and God as a means to gratify self-love. On the other hand, Augustine explained concupiscence by means of Stoic anthropology. According to the Stoics, a human being should always be ruled by reason. All such emotions or lusts that are stronger than reason are bad. The evil of concupiscence is in the theory that concupiscence is irrational. It is evil, because it is not led by human reason.

This has strange consequences for Augustine's teaching about the human state *ante peccatum*. According to Augustine, when Adam and Eve had sex in paradise before the fall there was no irrational *concupiscentia* or libido in the act. Therefore, their genital organs obeyed their rational will and "the seed of offspring, therefore, would have been sown by the man and received by the woman at the time and in the quantity needed, their genital organs being moved by the will and not excited by lust."[55]

The fall meant that sexual drive was no longer rational. It had become full of irrational libido and therefore sinful.[56] Luther seems to have inherited some of Augustine's Stoicism in his thinking about sexuality. After the fall the sex act is no longer a beautiful creation by God. One reason, according to Luther, is that sex does not obey human reason. Sexual libido is ecstatic. People today tend to think that it is just this ecstatic, irrational character that makes sex so beautiful. For medieval Christians, for Luther as well, this irrational libido (*wueten, brennen, böser lust, misera libido*) had nothing positive about itself.[57] It made people

54. WA 40/II, 381, 33–39. See WA 2, 168, 35–36, 169, 5–7. In this early sermon (1519) Luther seems to think that a Christian couple should temper their sex drive so that the sex act does not happen "in carnal lust, like the animals do it."

55. *De civitate Dei*, 14, 23–24.

56. I thank Lic. Theol. Timo Nisula for the ideas about Augustine. See Lamberigts, "Critical Evaluation of the Critiques of Augustine's View of Sexuality," 176–97, and Rist, *Augustine*, 321–27.

57. WA 2, 168, 30–37; WA 40/II, 381, 32–39; WA 12, 114, 10–12; WA 43, 301, 33–39.

no better than animals. After the fall, sexual passion became unavoidable; it is tolerated and forgiven by God if it happens in marriage. In some places Luther even say that God's blessing is hidden in the libido of marriage. However, in such passages the context shows that this thought is an example of the "theology of the cross." Just as life is hidden in death, heaven in hell, and righteousness in sin, so blessing is hidden under the libido of the sexual act of a married couple. In itself sexual libido is negative, just as death, sin, and hell are negative.[58]

However, in certain sense Luther's theological thinking allows a much more positive attitude toward sex than the theology of Augustine or Thomas Aquinas. The reason is that Luther left behind the Augustinian basic scheme of the *ordo caritatis*, the order of love, which dominated much of medieval theology.

Ordo caritatis thinking is based on a hierarchical understanding of reality. At the top of the *ordo* is God, the Highest Good. Next come the angels, who are rational spirits without *materia*. Below them are humans, rational yet physical beings. Then come the animals, material beings of a lower order, incapable of intellectual thinking. Beneath the animals are the plants, whose life is even lower than that of the animals. The lowest stage of existence is that of material things. The idea in the *ordo caritatis* is that each being should love those things that lead to a good end for its existence. What is good for a pig is to eat, wallow in the mud, and make little pigs. Therefore, a pig loves those things and fulfills the good of a pig by doing them. A human being, on the other hand, stands higher on the scale of things. As an intellectual and spiritual being, the good of a human person is more than the good of material things. The good of a human being is nothing less than the highest good, God himself. Therefore, a human being should love God as his or her final good, which fulfills the longing for the human essence (*frui*). A human person may also love material things and other persons, but only insofar as they serve the attainment of the final goal, the love of God (*uti*). Things that are higher on the scale of being, should be loved more than those that are lower. In medieval theology this scheme was used to interpret the relationship of a Christian to God.

After the fall of Adam and Eve, human beings love wrong things in their natural state. People love the goods of the material world and love

---

58. WA 43, 302, 9–17. On the other hand, it is the egoism of the natural affects that make these sinful for Luther. See e.g. WA Br 3, no 3529.

themselves as the final end. The whole idea of the Christian life is that with the help of sacramental grace, prayer, faith, and works of charity, such perverted love is redirected to the true Good End of humankind, God. This idea was often expressed with the slogan *fides caritate formata*, faith formed by love. Faith in itself is simply cold, intellectual knowledge about true dogmatic statements. Faith needs to be brought to life by correct love, which follows the *ordo caritatis* and seeks God in everything as its final end.

It is understandable that in such thinking, sex is considered something spiritually low. Sex is an act of the physical body and therefore low on the scale of being. If there is anything good in sex, it is this basic longing for the good of an individual. But in order to make something truly good from this drive, sexual longing should be harnessed in the service of seeking the immaterial Highest Good. This thought seems to be behind all sexual abstinence in the name of religion. Spiritually directed sexual love loses its bodily character and becomes the means for a right relationship with God.

Luther abandoned this basic scheme of theology quite early in his career, before the year 1515.[59] According to Luther, *ordo caritatis* is a subtle form of pagan egoism. It defines love in a way that is unacceptable to theologians. In *ordo caritatis* thinking, to love something is to seek that which is good for the lover. This is also Aristotelian thinking and, according to Luther, contrary to the biblical understanding of love. In the Bible to love is to give good things to those who are in need; not to seek good for oneself, but to give good away. When God loves us in Christ, he does not love us because that we are good and loveable, but because we are sinful and need his love to save us.

This change in the doctrine of love means that Luther's understanding of the relationship to God changes from the scholastic way of thinking. The love striving after good (*eros*) loses its function as the organ of relationship with God. According to Luther, to live in God is not to strive toward a higher Good and abandon the lower and the material. It is to receive God's love. And God is love (*agape*), which comes down to us. God is love, which does not love that which is high and good and worthy, but loves that which is sinful, unworthy, and even nothing. The means to receive this creative and saving love of God is

---

59. See Raunio, *Summe des Christlichen Lebens*, 124, 155–56, 354–55.

not to direct one's love correctly but to have faith in the promise of the Gospel's words about Christ.

However, Luther did not foresee the consequences that abandoning the *ordo caritatis* as the framework for his theology would have had for his sexual ethics. The Stoic understanding of concupiscence, which Luther inherited from Augustine, was so strong in this area of Luther's thinking that the irrational character of the sex act made it something dirty in itself, even within marriage.

CHILDREN AS THE OBJECTIVE OF SEX

As we saw earlier, children are an essential part of Luther's definition of marriage. A marriage is "... a divine and legitimate joining of a husband and a wife in the hope of having children ... The ultimate goal is to obey God, to avoid sin, to call on God for help, to ask for children, to love and to raise them to God's glory."[60] That the result of sexual life is normally the birth of a child is something that makes the sexual act of a married couple acceptable and even blessed in the eyes of God, just as the divine word and institution of marriage are blessed.[61]

In Luther's time there were no real methods of contraception, not even the periodic continence accepted by the Catholic church of today. However, there were some more or less superstitious beliefs about birth control. Luther was against all such methods.[62] Children were God's blessing. To try to prevent them from coming into the world was to act against God. This does not mean that a married couple should have sex only in order to have children. Sex is also needed as a remedy for fornication. If the spouses stay faithful to each other, God tolerates more sex than is needed for procreation.

> If both spouses bind themselves to each other ... so that all other ways of the flesh are closed and one is satisfied with just one bedmate, then God considers that the flesh is tempered enough ... and he accepts that in such fidelity this same lust is consented to, even more than what is necessary for the fruits of the union—

---

60. WA 43, 310, 24–28. See also WA 43, 558, 18–21, 559, 1–11.

61. WA 40/II, 383, 15–24. See also WA Tr 3, no 3529; WA 12, 114, 12–16. See also WA 43, 302,14–15.

62. Lähteenmäki, *Sexus*, 166 n. 3.

however so that you truly moderate yourself and do not make a dung-pile or hog-house out of it.[63]

For Luther, a wife's health is not a good reason for not bearing children. If a wife is afraid of the pain of child's birth, then the husband should comfort her in the following way:

> Think, my beloved Greta, that you are a woman, and that God is pleased with this work in you. Comfort yourself with his will and let him have his right in you. Deliver the baby and do that with all your might; if you die in it, so let it be good for you. You die in a noble work and in obedience to God. Yes, if you were not a woman, then you should hope to be one, because only doing the work of the woman could you suffer and die in such a precious way in God's work. It is God's Word, the same that has created you that has also put such a distress on you.[64]

Luther emphasizes that it is not enough to give birth to children. Husband and wife also have to love their children and raise them. In making this point, Luther uses figures of speech that seem to go directly against the core of his theology if taken literally. This shows how important the matter was for him.

> It is nothing to build churches, finance masses, or to do any other works compared with this matrimonial work of raising children. This is the most direct way to heaven, and there is no better means to attain heaven than this . . . And contrariwise, there is no better way to earn a place in hell than through your own children. And no one can commit a more harmful deed than to neglect children . . .[65]

LUTHER AND ROMANTIC LOVE

If we look again at Luther's definition of marriage, what stands out is that love between the spouses has no part in it. Children must be loved, but about the relationship of the spouses the definition says only that the

---

63. *WA* 2, 169, 1–7.

64. *WA* 10/II, 296, 17–24. To complain made by one woman that giving birth very often is so strenuous that it can kill, Luther replied: "Better to lead a short and a healthy life than a long and unhealthy one." *WA* 10/II, 301, 14–15, *WA* Tr 2, no 2764.

65. *WA* 2, 170, 2–9. See also *WA* 2, 169, 30–35.

goal of marriage is "to live with the wife and carry the cross." Was Luther hopelessly unromantic?

There are some passages that give the impression that Luther was not unromantic. In his earliest sermon on marriage (1519) Luther describes the love of spouses quite beautifully:

> ... love of a man and a wife is or should be the biggest and purest of all loves ... There are three kinds of love: False love seeks that which is for its own [benefit], just as you love money and property, honor, and women outside of marriage against God's command. Natural love is the love between father and son, brother and sister, between friends, or between son-in-law and father-in-law-and the like. But above them all is marital love, i.e., the bridal love (*Brawtliebe*). It burns like fire and it does not seek anything other than the spouse, and it says: "I do not want that which is yours; I do not want gold or silver, not this or that; I want to have just you yourself, or I want nothing." All other kinds of love look for something else, and love only them; this love alone wants to have the beloved as its own.[66]

This sounds romantic and beautiful. However, the *Brawtliebe* is neither the *Minne* of the medieval troubadour poetry nor the modern romantic love of a dating couple. The concept of *Brawtliebe* is taken from medieval mysticism (*Brautmystik*). It is *agape* love that Christ and the church have for each other. Luther could have found the same idea in the formula of marriage used in Wittenberg. There the pastor said to the bridegroom: "From now on she is your wife. My son, love her as Christ has loved the church," and to the bride: "From now on he is your husband and love him as the church has loved Christ."[67]

But isn't it unromantic to urge a couple to love each other? The noble knight and the lady of his heart did not need any special urging. Their love sprang from their whole being towards each other with a power that could not be resisted. Luther is unromantic but realistic. He believes that after the fall, the "bridal love" of a man and his beloved is not as pure and beautiful as it was meant to be. Therefore, a marriage cannot be based on bridal love alone. It needs other things as well, such as mutual fidelity, and above all, the "cross." With the cross Luther means all the troubles of normal life that force a person to seek Christ as the ba-

---

66. *WA* 2, 167, 22–34.

67. Kretschmar, "Luthers Konzeption," 184. See also *WA* 12, 101, 14–19. *WA* 30/I, 163, 17.

sis for life, over and over again. Such a life "under the cross" and in faith causes that Christ and his *agape* love permeate the life of a Christian more and more. Marriage becomes one example of *agape* love, the love that a Christian must have toward his or her neighbor. Of course, marriage is a special kind of *agape* love. But the reason for the uniqueness of love in marriage is not so much its romantic or erotic character, but the fact that marriage is a special order (*oeconomia*) instituted by God.[68] This *agape* love Luther describes in very literal terms:

> Now tell me: If a husband goes and washes diapers or does some other kind of despised work, and everyone makes fun of him and says that he is a stupid weakling (*maulaffen*) and a womanly man, and this man does it in Christian faith, then my love, tell me, who is making fun of whom? God rejoices with all his angels and with all the creation, not for the reason that he washes diapers, but for the reason that he does it in faith. Those who make fun of him and see only the work and not the faith; those people God makes fun of, with all the creation, as the biggest fools on earth; yes, they make fun of themselves, and they are the devil's stupid weaklings in their wisdom.[69]

The life of a married couple with children is especially a "bearing of the cross," and is such a difficult calling (*Beruf*) that it forces people to build their faith. In Luther's case this has to be understood in literal sense. A priest who married lost all protection of the law and had no economic security for his family.[70] Nevertheless, Luther decided to marry openly. There were other options, such as secret marriage, which Zwingli chose, for example. For some people, Luther's public marriage was an act of obedience toward God, but for many, it was a lethal sin. Even in the circle of Luther's friends, Katharina's and Martin's marriage was somewhat embarrassing, even banal.[71] When Katharina and Martin were expecting their first child, it was not without *angst*. According to a popular belief, the only result that could be born of the copulation of a

---

68. *WA* 2, 168, 38–169, 7. *WA* 43, 450, 34–36.
69. *WA* 10/II, 296, 26–297, 4.
70. See *WA* 18, 275–78. *WA* 12, 107, 21–27.
71. Kretschmar, "Luthers Konzeption," 188–89. Luther's colleague Hieronymus Schurff wrote: "If this monk marries, then the whole world and the devil will laugh and he will himself destroy all that he has created." See also Melanchthon's secret letter, *MW* VII, 1, 238.

monk and a nun would be a two-headed monster.[72] All this shows that Luther was really far from the well-off security of Protestant pastors' homes of later generations. We also have to bear in mind that he started a family in a situation in which he had no economic security. For Martin and Katherina to marry was really an act of faith.[73]

So far we have not found much real romantic love in Luther. And it is true, Luther was no great lover. He did not marry because of his romantic love for Katherina or his erotic feelings toward her. This can be seen from a letter written to his friend Nicolaus Amsdorff.

> The rumor is true, that I have just been united with (*copulatum sum*) Katherina . . . I did not want to take away from my father the hope of offspring. I also wanted with this deed to confirm what I have taught. So many seem to be timid in the light of the Gospel. But I am not in love with my wife (*ego enim nec amo*); neither am I hot for her (*nec aestuo*), but I love and respect her (*sed diligo uxorem*).[74]

However, five months later Luther wrote the following to his friend Spalatin, who was also newly married:

> Sweet greetings to your wife! . . . When you take her, your Katherina, with sweet kisses and embrace her, you should think: "This human being, this wonderful work of God, has my Christ given to me. Glory and honor to him!" In the evening of the same day, when you receive this letter, I will love my wife in the same way and remember you.[75]

72. Oberman, *Luther*, 292.

73. In Luther's "*Wagnis des Glaubens*" (Oberman, *Luther*, 299; *WA* Br 3, 533, 8) to marry, there is much to be learned about marriage. A life long promise of fidelity seems today too much for any person to give. We do not have such an essentialist worldview or such a static society as pre-modern or even modern people had. Our culture is more existentialist. We are supposed to make our lives ourselves. In this situation a person considering marriage is almost forced to think constantly: How do I know that just this person is the right one for me? How do I know that tomorrow I won't meet a better one? And even if this one feels so utterly wonderful now, how do I know that she or he will be that way after two or forty years? When a young person asks such questions, he or she is almost compelled to think in theological terms.

74. *WA* Br 3, 541, 2–8 (June 21, 1525). When Luther writes in his letter *copulatum sum Catharina*, he means that he and she have publicly expressed their will to marry and have had sex (June 13; even this had to have a public witness). This made their marriage binding. Later the Luthers had a wedding celebration with a festive meal for their friends. The wedding ceremony in the church probably took place on the same day.

75. *WA* Br 3, 635, 23–28.

Later in Table Talks, Luther speaks:

> It is a most high grace of God, if love flourishes continuously in a marriage. In the beginning love is glowing, like drunken love, so that we get mixed with each other (*damit wir geblendet werden*) and go into marriage. But when we sleep away the drunkenness, then for the pious, there is sincere marital love, but the impious have only regret.[76]

At first, Luther's marriage was a *Vernunftehe* (a marriage of reason), but it became a happy one. The spouses developed a true and enduring love for each other, a love that matured and endured till the end of their lives.[77] One indication are the letters that Luther wrote to his wife during the last year of his life, when he was away from home in political negotiations.[78] They contain words that reveal true affection and friendship in a way that is very different from what one would expect from the technical and impersonal descriptions of marriage as "medicine for whoring" that the reformer also wrote.

---

76. *WA* Tr 3, no 3530.

77. *WA* Tr 1, no 49: "Ich wolt mein Ketha nicht umb Frankreich noch umb Venedig dazu geben." *WA* Tr 1, no 1110: "Ketha, du hast einen fromen Mann, der dich lieb hat; du bist ein keysirin."

78. See, e.g., *WA* Br 11, 269, 275, 284, 291, 300.

11

Music

Miikka E. Anttila

Luther's ideas about music are not difficult to determine. In his view music was "the greatest gift of God" and "next to theology."[1] It is a startling comment about a thoroughly cultural phenomenon in an era when the idea of the composer as a creative genius had yet to emerge. There is no doubt that Luther was a great admirer of music. He was given a thorough musical training and he was active as a lute and flute player and eventually as a composer.[2] How seriously his view of music should be taken and how theologically relevant it is, are other questions entirely. Opinions vary. For some, Luther's sayings about music are merely enthusiasms of a music-lover. For others, they tell about a source of divine revelation, a Lutheran version of natural theology.[3]

---

1. WA 31 II, 43: "Music is a Gift of God"; WA Tr no 3815: "Music is an outstanding gift of God and next to theology"; WA Tr no 4441: "Music is God's greatest gift"; WA Tr no 7034: "Music is an endowment and gift of God, not a gift of men."

2. The most recent and most searching account of Luther's musicianship is found in Leaver, *Luther's Liturgical Music*, 21–64.

3. "Enthusiasm of a music-lover" (*Schwemerei eines Musikliebhabers*) and "the natural form of the gospel" (*Naturform des Evangeliums*) are expressions coined in Alfred Dedo Müller's study *Musik als Problem lutherischer Gottesdienstgestaltung* and thereafter widely discussed, especially in German studies. Most of the studies and articles have found that there is deep theological insight in Luther's ideas about music. On the other hand, to consider music as a natural form of the Gospel, puts us at odds with Lutheran theology in general. It is hard to imagine a source of divine revelation beside the Bible and to claim it as Luther's view. Christoph Wetzel tries to solve this dilemma by holding on both to Müller's idea of music as *Naturform des Evangeliums* and Lutheran *sola scriptura* principle. Wetzel states that music is the natural form of the Gospel *a posteriori*, as

"Luther and music" is a topic often written about. Most of those who have dedicated themselves to this theme have been first and foremost musicians, musicologists, or hymnologists.[4] Scholars working in the field of systematic theology have had remarkably little to say on the subject. No doubt they have a good excuse: intimidated by the danger of being swallowed by musical or aesthetic issues they have avoided the topic altogether. This state of affairs has meant that, in spite of all interesting details of Lutheran chorale and of music as a part of Lutheran propaganda, the theological profundity of Luther's view of music has largely been dismissed.

If we take Luther's statements about music seriously, then we must ask what it that is so special in music that justifies the expression *optimum Dei donum*, "the best gift of God"? Two answers immediately come to mind. The first involves the Pythagorean *music of the spheres*. In the philosophy of ancient Greece, all universe was believed to move in harmony with which it was created, making sounds that humans are incapable of hearing, either because they are so used to them or because they are themselves out of tune. This idea has been highly influential one, coming through Plato's *Timaeus* and transmitted through Augustine, Boethius, and Neoplatonic mysticism. It was also a part Luther's musical education. It is therefore tempting to think that music is the best gift of God for Luther precisely because it reflects the eternal laws of the universe, the beautiful order of creation. There are passages in Luther's works that can be read this way. For instance, the most extensive text about music written by Luther himself, the *Encomion musices*[5], begins with a notion that "there is nothing without a sound or a sounding number (*numero sonoro*)." Luther would presumably not have denied the harmony of the spheres. On the other hand, the Pythagorean view of music

---

a consciousness dependent on faith. There is one God acting in creation and salvation. Music and the Gospel should not be separated, although a distinction must be made between them. Wetzel, *Träger des liturgischen Amtes*, 302.

4. The most outstanding studies on the topic are: Söhngen, *Theologie der Musik*; Krummacher, *Musik als praxis pietatis*; Guicharrousse, *Les Musiques de Luther*; Block, *Verstehen durch Musik*; and Leaver, *Luther's Liturgical Music*. In addition, the dictionary entries on Luther by Walter Blankenburg in *Die Musik in Geschichte und Gegenwart* and Leaver in *Grove Music Online* are instructive.

5. For the sake of convenience I refer to *Praefatio zu den Symphoniae iucundae* (1538) by the name *Encomion musices*, the preface to a polyphonic collection of motets by the Wittenberg musician and printer Georg Rhau.

was contested in the musical theory of Luther's day. Johannes Tinctoris, the French-Flemish music theoretician of the fifteenth century, was of the opinion that the heavens make neither actual nor potential sounds. If one wants to find out what music is, then one should play a musical instrument rather than look at the stars. Regardless of whether or not Luther believed in the harmony of the spheres, it is clear that this idea is not the reason why music is so special in his beliefs. He never develops the thought further, and it seems not to be that important to him.

It is also possible to view Luther's musical ideas in educational terms. Music is a useful tool for teaching the Gospel. When people sing hymns, they learn the Christian doctrine more easily and more readily than by reading the Bible or listening to sermons. As St Ambrose wrote: "A psalm is learned without effort and retained with delight." No doubt Luther thought this way, too. Creating vernacular songs for liturgical use was a crucial part of Luther's reform of worship. The educational use of music was not restricted to the hymnals. The Wittenberg Reformation made use of liturgical chant as well. In *The German Mass* Luther created a liturgical order that could be sung throughout with the exception of the sermon and the Lord's Prayer. Yet we still have not answered *why* music is so important to Luther.

"Music is the mistress and governess of human affects," says Luther in the *Encomion musices*. Luther is interested in the power music has over the human soul. It can govern the human *affectus*, the hidden inner will, the innermost directedness of human personhood. In a letter to the composer Ludwig Senfl Luther boldly states: "Indeed I plainly judge, and do not hesitate to affirm, that except for theology there is no art that could be put on the same level with music, since except for theology, music alone produces what otherwise only theology can do, namely, a calm and joyful soul."[6] Thus, it is the power of music for the human soul, that is the special thing in music. Music can have various effects on a human mind: it can "encourage the despairing, humble the proud, calm the passionate, or appease those full of hate," as Luther writes in the *Encomion*. Some of the effects may be unwelcome, such as arousing lustful desire. Luther is aware of this, but his emphasis is on the positive effects of music. In a short but celebrated draft from the year 1530, Luther summarizes his view of the power of music as follows:

---

6. *WA* Br 5, 639; *LW* 49, 428.

1. Music is a gift of God and not of man
2. It creates joyful hearts
3. It drives away the devil
4. It creates innocent delight.[7]

It becomes clear at this point that Luther sees the power of music as essentially good. Not only does he say almost the same thing twice when he states that music creates "joyful hearts"(*facit letos animos*) and "innocent delight" (*innocens gaudium facit*) but he also states that music drives away the enemy of joy, the spirit of sadness or, in other words, the devil. The relationship between the devil and music is principally that music vanquishes the devil. Since Satan is the spirit of sadness, he cannot stand music. The Biblical grounds for music were in the Pythagorean tradition, as seen in *Wis.* 11:20: "You have ordered everything according to measure, weight, and number," but for Luther, it was 1 Sam 16:23 that was of the utmost importance: "And so it was, whenever the spirit from God was upon Saul, that David would take a harp and play it with his hand. Then Saul would become refreshed and well, and the distressing spirit would depart from him."[8] That it is possible for the devil to use music is not excluded. That humans can be led to sinful desires with the help of music is proof of the devil's cunning and his ability to spoil even God's greatest gifts. Yet in music itself there is absolutely nothing devilish. For Luther, it is not correct to say that music is neutral either. It is divine. The nature of music is to praise its Creator. Luther emphatically calls the devil "the enemy of nature and of this lovely art."[9] It is obvious that here nature is a completely positive thing, meaning creation as gift of God. To scorn music is an attitude of *Schwermerii*, "fanatics." What does music do when it is used properly? The answer has been in front of us for a long time, but somehow it has escaped our attention: it creates innocent delight!

---

7. *WA* 30/II, 696. Robin Leaver has suggested that this draft with a Greek title "Peri tēs mousikēs" was intended for a larger treatise on music, which remained an unfulfilled project for Luther. Leaver, *Luther's Liturgical Music*, 85–97.

8. Luther refers to this incidence throughout his career, from *Operationes in Psalmos* (*WA* 5, 98, 40) to *The Last Words of David* (WA 54, 34, 6–10) and in various sections in *Table Talk* (*WA* Tr 1, 968; 2, 2545a).

9. *WA* 50, 374, 4–5: "aduersarium naturae et artis huius iucundissimae"

If a thing that causes delight and pleasure in us is a thing that can be called "the best gift of God," then what does this state of affairs tell about the theological significance of pleasure? This is exactly the new door music opens for Luther scholarship. With the help of music, pleasure can be seen as a central aspect of Luther's theology. Surprising as it may sound, it is quite logical and easy to substantiate. Pleasure is connected to joy, and as for joy, no one would deny that it is central to Luther. Music, for its part, is the logical consequence of joy. "*Euangelion*, the Gospel, is a Greek word," Luther writes in his preface to the New Testament (1524), "that means good news, that one sings, speaks and is happy about." The word order, *singen, sagen und fröhlich ist*, is hardly arbitrary. In the same text Luther uses the verb *singen* three times to convey the joy brought by the Gospel. And every time, *singen* is first. As an example of how to react to good news, Luther tells about the Israelites who were "singing and jumping and happy" when David defeated Goliath. In a similar manner he relates Christians' response to the salvation God has given through Christ in "singing, thanking, praising God and being happy forever."[10] Thus, in a short passage of text, where Luther wants to depict the quintessence of the Gospel, music is mentioned three times in connection with joy. Joy as a fruit of the Spirit (Gal 5:22) is, for Luther, musical by nature. In his great *Commentary on Galatians* (1531) Luther defines joy as follows: "Sweet cogitations of Christ, wholesome exhortations, *pleasant songs of praise and thanksgiving*, whereby the pious do instruct, stir up and refresh themselves. God loves not heaviness and doubtfulness of spirit. He hates unsound doctrines and sorrowful cogitations; and he loves cheerful hearts. He has not come to oppress us but to cherish our hearts."[11] Joy is a sign of certainty. Every uncertain teaching about God is *tristis doctrina*, a sorrowful doctrine. This makes understandable Luther's statement printed in the 1545 hymnal preface: "He who believes this earnestly cannot be quiet about it. But he must gladly and willingly sing and speak about it so that others also may come and hear it. And whoever does not want to sing and speak of it shows that he does not believe and that he does not belong under the new and joyful testament, but under the old, lazy, and tedious testament."[12] Christian joy is something different from earthly pleasures and carnal delights. According to Luther, the

10. *WA* DB 6, 3, 23–24, 11.
11. *WA* 40/II, 117, 24–28. Emphasis mine.
12. *WA* 35, 477, 5–12; *LW* 53, 333.

latter are not really joys at all. Passing, earthly pleasures cannot move the human heart nor fill its depths. The real source of joy is God. To rejoice in God is not possible if there is sin and fear of God's punishment on one's conscience. To hear the Gospel makes us trust that God is merciful toward us in Christ, and that we are reconciled with God through Christ. When this Gospel reigns in the human heart, God is recognized as favorable and pleasing (*suss und lieblich*). It is not easy, though, always to remain state of joy. It is a constant "spiritual exercise" to rejoice in the Lord. It is not a question of a psychological disposition one has to force oneself into, but simply of letting Christ be greater than our sins.

Joy in Christ is something that concerns the innermost part of the human soul. Nevertheless, it is obvious that joy does not remain inside. Rather, it bursts out in every possible way: in song and laughter, in jumping and shouting.[13] Music is so closely involved in the expression of Christian joy that it can be ranked among the signs of the true church (*notae ecclesiae*). In *On Councils and the Church* (1539) Luther gives seven signs that characterize the true church: the word of God, baptism, the Eucharist, the confession of sins, the office of preaching, prayer, and the cross. It is true that music is none of these. However, the sixth sign, prayer, is presented in very musical terms: ". . . the holy Christian people are externally recognized by prayer, public praise, and thanksgiving to God. Where you see and hear the Lord's Prayer prayed and taught, or psalms or other spiritual songs sung, in accordance with the word of God and the true faith, there is God's holy, Christian people."[14]

Joy and pleasure or joy and willingness (*freude und lust*) are common combinations in Luther's works. To do something with joy means to do it willingly and with pleasure. This is the attitude that arises from faith and the Gospel. The notion of pleasure leads us into one of the most difficult dilemmas of Luther's theology: the question of *The Bondage of the Will*. Perhaps a better title for the work Luther wrote against Erasmus in 1525 could be *The Bondage of Delight*, since it seems that it is the heart's delight that remains unchanged in a person, regardless how much he or she wants to change. On the surface it seems senseless to say that a per-

---

13. Birgit Stolt has examined Luther's use of the German word *fröhlichkeit*. She observes that for Luther, *fröhlich* is a far stronger feeling than the same word conveys today. For Luther, *fröhlich* includes, in addition to a mental attitude, physical expressions such as jumping around and clapping hands. Its Latin equivalent is *exultare*, while the inner feeling of joy is better translated as *laetari*. See Stolt, *Martin Luthers Rhetorik*, 105.

14. *WA* 50, 641, 20-34; *LW* 41, 164.

son cannot decide to obey God. As Erasmus pointed out, the Bible is full of passages in which God expressly calls us to choose to obey and follow him. To put Luther's argument briefly, one can say that a human being is free to choose things that are below him or her, but not things that are above. Moreover, if faith is understood in terms of love, then freedom of choice becomes problematic. One cannot decide to love something one does not love. This view of love could be contested, as marriage counsellors often do: Is not love sometimes just a stern decision to act lovingly, although one does not have any feelings of love at all? Doubtless, this is true between human beings. In relation to God, it is not the same. "Love the Lord your God with all your heart and with all your soul and with all your mind" (Matt 24:39). Love is about pleasure. One can be forced to do something one does not like to do. But one cannot be forced to like something one does not like. Our will remains unchanged even when we do things that seem to prove otherwise. "A man void of Spirit of God does not evil against his will as by violence . . . but he does it spontaneously, and with desiring willingness (*sponte et libenti voluntate*)," Luther writes to Erasmus. The same holds for the justified. After our will is changed by God, it remains immutable: "When God works in us, the will, being changed and sweetly breathed on by the Spirit of God, desires and acts, not from compulsion, but responsively, from pure willingness, inclination, and accord (*mera lubentia et pronitate ac sponte*)."[15]

In the history of theology pleasure has been treated mainly in two ways: either as a temptation or as a reward. Carnal, earthly pleasures tempt Christians here below, and spiritual, eternal pleasures await them in the state of blessedness. It is possible to make music fit into the model of spiritual, non-corporeal blessings. After all, is it not the most non-corporeal and non-representative of all the arts? The leading music theologian of our time, Jeremy Begbie, rejects this kind of view of music as "a cluster of overplayed half-truths."[16] On the contrary, the pleasures of music are wholly temporal, physical, and sensual. What distinguished Luther both from his monastic tradition and from his spiritualist contemporaries and later puritan followers was that he fully recognized the value of earthly pleasures. "Who loves not women, wine, and song, he lives a fool his whole life long" is a saying that one does not find in critical editions of Luther's works, yet it is one of the most famous, if

15. *WA* 18, 634, 21–635, 7.
16. Begbie, *Theology, Music and Time*, 34.

inauthentic Luther quotations. Nevertheless, it conveys Luther's point well. Ecclesiastes 3:12–13 says: "There is nothing better for men than to be happy and do good while they live. That everyone may eat and drink, and find satisfaction in all his toil—this is the Gift of God." Commenting on this, Luther says that not only are these things gifts of God, but also the ability to enjoy them is a gift of God.[17] On the other hand, Luther is by no means a straightforward hedonist. His attitude to sensuous pleasure has some reservations. Sexual pleasure is a case in point. Granted that sexuality is created by God and that sexual intercourse in Paradise was without the taint of sin, our sexuality since the fall has become somewhat bestial. There is something sinful in sexual desire, even in Christian marriage, an estate instituted and blessed by God. Sexual pleasure in marriage is a good thing when it is used to conceive a child, to fulfill a natural need, or to restrain inchastity.[18] Sexual pleasure is thus a pleasure with a purpose, not an end in itself. Music, however, is a sensuous pleasure that has nothing sinful in it. The delight in music is, to use an aesthetic term, disinterested pleasure, something to be entertained for the sake of itself. Luther does warn against the abuse of music, but his more vehement judgments are addressed to those who do not appreciate the beauty of music: "... whoever is only mildly moved and heeds not the inexpressible marvel of the Lord [i.e., music] should not be considered human and should not hear anything other than the bray of the donkey and the grunt of the sow."[19]

Only humans take pleasure in sensible objects for its own sake, said Thomas Aquinas.[20] Thus, music opens a new window for understanding Luther: the significance of aesthetic perception. Aesthetics has been a difficult field of investigation for theologians, few of whom have ventured to write about theological aesthetics. In the few such attempts Luther has played virtually no part at all. Perhaps the greatest achievement in theological aesthetics in the twentieth century, Hans Urs von Balthasar's *The Glory of the Lord*, serves as a good example. Balthasar says that Luther's theology allows no opportunity for aesthetic contemplation. Balthasar depicts Luther in strictly actualistic terms. The faith is a "lightning-flash" event, in which a human being finds himself or herself as righteous and

17. WA 20, 64, 22–25. *LW* 15, 54.
18. For a fuller treatment, see Sammeli Juntunen's article in this book.
19. WA 373, 14–17.
20. *ST* I, 91q, a.3, ad 3.

sinner at the same time (*simul iustus et peccator*). Actualism means that faith cannot have breadth or permanence in the world. The contemplative element of faith disappears, because seeing the beauty of God would lead to a "theology of glory."[21] It is useless to blame Balthasar for interpreting Luther in a way that afterward appears one-sided and, indeed, misleading. Protestant Luther studies have greatly contributed to this misreading of Luther and have neglected his aesthetics as well. For the most part this is due to the inability to read Luther superficially enough. Isn't beauty, after all, a superficial thing—something belonging to the surface of things? When scholars tend to ask profound doctrinal questions of Luther's texts, his aesthetics usually escapes their notice.

Luther has a peculiar view of beauty. It consists of two parts, of which the first is typical of the young Luther and the latter of the old Luther. The first idea of beauty could be called the "beauty of the cross." It is paradoxical by nature. In the cross of Christ there is supreme beauty concealed beneath the most abominable ugliness. Yet there is no ugliness in God. The ugliness of the cross belongs to us, whereas the beauty is God's. God is most beautiful not only when compared to us. He proves to be most beautiful when he makes us beautiful, that is, gives his beauty to us. This is an aesthetic variation on the doctrine of justification. This idea of beauty is present in Luther's earliest sermons and psalm lectures. It does not disappear, but makes room for another view: an appreciation of outward beauty. This does not mean that as an old man Luther becomes somehow more permissive or that his aesthetic judgments soften as he ages. Beauty is not a matter of *adiafora* at all. To see the beauty of the world is an act of faith. This view contains a paradox too, albeit a different one. No one can truly perceive the essential beauty of the world save a Christian. "The better someone knows God, the more he appreciates the creatures," says Luther in his commentary on Genesis.[22] Moreover,

---

21. Accordingly, Balthasar sees Kierkegaard as a consistent Protestant theologian and true heir of Luther when he makes "the aesthetic" as the lowest stage of existence. Bultmann leads the Protestant program to its consummation when he makes of Christianity nothing other than the absolute inwardness of the decision of faith without any imagery or outward facts to rely on. Balthasar, *Seeing the Form,* 45–70. It is noteworthy that even the more recent theological aesthetics, such as David Bentley Hart's *Beauty of the Infinite,* written from an Eastern Orthodox standpoint, find no use for Luther.

22. WA 43, 276, 18–20: "Quo enim sanctior quis est, et quo propius Deum cognoscit, hoc magis intelligit et adficitur creaturis."

seeing the beauty of the world is an act of faith because the world does not look beautiful in many respects. Praising God and believing in him means that one delights in the fact that there is *anything beautiful at all*, however small. *The Beautiful Confitemini*, a commentary on Psalm 118 from the year 1530, is a call to praise God that there is not merely bloodshed and war in the world, but also at least some moments of peace. Likewise, it is a source of great praise that there are not only heretics and sects in the Church, but the word of God and the sacraments are there. The greatest gifts of God are so obvious that we often forget to give thanks for them. What would happen if the light of the sun would fail us for a moment?[23] Faith opens the human mind to see and appreciate the goodness of God in everything. Thus, faith is a deeply aesthetic way to look at the world.

Beauty and pleasure appear to be important for understanding Luther's view of music. The basic idea is not difficult at all. Most of us do not listen to music in order to become better persons, to do something right, or to look smart. We listen to music because *it is good*: it affords joy, pleasure, and relaxation. Luther was of the same opinion. To experience such a superficial thing as beauty or delight is not superficial at all. It belongs to the innermost of human personhood. Luther's view of music could be summarized as follows: to recognize the pleasure of music as a gift of God is a sign of faith in a loving and generous Father. To be superficial enough means to admit one's creatureliness. It means to know that God is the source of all beauty and to know him is the highest pleasure. The idea of beauty has traditionally been seen as divine condescendence, whereby God uses pleasing, temporary things to draw humans into deeper, spiritual understanding.[24] The notion of condescendence does not convey Luther's thoughts about music. If I see (or hear) the beauty of music as a gift of a loving God who wants to delight me with it, what is the deeper understanding I should aspire to? God does not hide himself

---

23. WA 31/I, 78–84.

24 This is a typical approach to the sensuous and erotic language of the *Song of Songs*. Gregory the Great begins his commentary on it by saying: "Since humanity has been closed to the delights of Paradise and has entered into the exile of the present life, its heart is blind to spiritual reality. If God's voice were to say to this blind heart: 'Follow God' or 'Love God'—as God says to it in the Law—the heart would not understand that because of its exile, frigidity, and insensibility. Therefore, the word of God speaks in parables to this cold and insensible soul, and, speaking about things that the latter knows, secretly inspires in it the love it does not know" *Grégoire le Grand*, 314, 68.

in pleasure. Undoubtedly, Luther speaks often about how God conceals himself, but he conceals himself on cross, in death and in suffering, not in pleasure. In pleasure God is present in an immediate, not to say superficial, way. However, we are not used to reading Luther this superficially, and certain questions arise immediately. Is the theology of pleasure a kind of natural theology? No it isn't, at least not in the sense that the experience of beauty is independent of the word of God. The Gospel of Jesus Christ tells us about the glory of God in his creation. The word of God leads us to discern our Creator in his gifts.

Another critical question could be addressed to the "theology of pleasure": Is it not just a form of the "theology of glory" in contrast to the "theology of the cross"? In the *Heidelberg Disputation* (1518) Luther precisely denies the possibility of gaining true knowledge of the invisible essence of God through his works (*per ea quae facta sunt*). The cross of Christ seems to make nonsense of the theology of pleasure. On closer examination it is important to observe, however, that the antithesis in the *Heidelberg disputation* is not between the cross and the creation, but between the visible and invisible features of God. The theologians of glory approach God through his invisible features, such as virtue, justice, divinity, wisdom, and goodness. A theologian of the cross wants to meet God instead in his visible features, which are seemingly contradictory to the invisible: God's humanity, weakness and foolishness.[25] In this regard it is exactly the theology of glory that is inward and spiritual, detached from any sensuous passion or pleasure. The theology of the cross by contrast, is sensuous, this-worldly perception. The cross opens up the appreciation of created beauty and the sensitivity to God-given delight, of which music is the foremost messenger. Music is the messenger in both directions: from God to us and from us to God. Its beauty makes us feel the generosity of our Lord, and in making music we express our gratitude to him in an optimal manner. To read the explanation of the first article of faith in *The Large Catechism* with an eye to music is instructive:

> For this reason we ought daily to practice this article, impress it upon our minds, and remember it in everything we see and in every blessing that comes our way. Whenever we escape distress or danger, we should recognize how God gives and does all of this so that we may sense and see in them his fatherly heart and his boundless love toward us. Thus our hearts will be warmed

---

25. StA 1, 207, 26–208, 5.

and kindled with gratitude to God and a desire to use all these blessings to his glory and praise.[26]

In conclusion, it is possible to see music deeply embedded in the most essentially Lutheran tenets of theological thought. The true significance of music is in the fact that it is a completely outward, physical phenomenon. This feature has a bearing on the sacramental theology. In confrontation with spiritualist reformers Luther wanted to emphasize the importance of outward reality as the bearer of spiritual reality. There is no inner word without the outer word. There is no inner meaning of baptism without the outward sign of baptizing. Moreover, music is an aural and auditive phenomenon. This connects music to the theology of the word. The word of God is for Luther in the first place the word that is proclaimed and heard. He mentions many times that Christ himself wrote nothing; even the apostles did not write very much. The word proceeds through hearing.[27] As stated above, the greatest blessing of music is its ability to touch human emotions. This is related to Luther's view of faith. When the word of God is sung, it moves both human intellect and affect. Faith grasps the whole personhood. The depths of human will are inaccessible but for music and the word of God. Music is instituted in the Bible, as all the means of grace are. Its words of institution are for Luther the story of David driving the devil away by playing the harp (1 Samuel 16). Thus, music is a tool against the devil. The devil wants people to lose faith and become insecure and sad. Music is one of the most powerful tools against "the spirit of sadness," among other earthly pleasures and the word of God. Music also helps us to discern the cooperation between God and humans. As a distinctively human phenomenon and a work of humans music is a gift of God. The realm of culture is thus neither heteronomous nor autonomous, but something genuinely human only when understood as a gift of God.[28] Finally, music is a way to

---

26. *BC*, The Large Catechism, The Creed, 23.

27. On the external and spoken character of the word see Bayer, *Martin Luther's Theology*, 88–90.

28. At this point I employ terms borrowed from Paul Tillich's theology of culture. Tillich advocates the idea of *theonomous* culture. He tries to overcome the distrust between Christianity and culture as follows: culture, and art as a part of human culture, is not in its proper sense autonomous. Here autonomy means that man himself is the source and measure of culture. This humanist standpoint is not supportable, according to Tillich. On the other hand, neither should culture be considered heteronomous. Heteronomy asserts that man as a cultural being is unable to act correctly, and thus

experience beauty. Despite the fact that the Christian life is a ceaseless struggle against sin, death, and the devil, God wants us to see the beauty of his creation. At its best, music anticipates the bliss of heaven, where the original beauty of the world is restored. Music tells us that there is the possibility of experiencing pleasure that is completely physical, time-embedded, and sensuous, without sin. Music is a realm of disinterested pleasure. It reveals the importance of the aesthetic dimension of reality.

---

man needs a law, superior and strange to him. Against both autonomy and heteronomy, theonomy asserts "that the superior law is, at the same time, the innermost law of man himself, rooted in the divine ground which is man's own ground: the law of life transcends man, although it is, at the same time, his own." Tillich, *Protestant Era*, 56–57.

12

Luther as a Reader of the Holy Scripture

Tuomo Mannermaa

Seldom, if ever, do students in theological faculties receive instruction on the spiritual reading of the Holy Scripture. By spiritual reading I mean an approach in which the texts of the Holy Scripture are read with trust that God will personally reveal his face so that the reader truly encounters God in the act of reading. In this encounter God's word, which is the Spirit, is joined together with the reader's heart, the center of the personality. The word enlightens the understanding and the intellect illuminating the will to enact in divine Gift-love. In this kind of reading the real participation takes place where the reader is made one with God the Father, in the Holy Spirit, through Christ.

At least in the Nordic countries, academic biblical scholarship is quite often sharply separated from spiritual reading, which is classified as something the church does, and consequently it is the church's business, not academy's, to instruct in this way of reading. Academic scholarship and teaching do not necessarily even pose the question of whether the Scripture is revelatory or how it could be understood as revelatory.

It is natural that when there is a clear tension between the academic and the church's way of reading, an uncertainty prevails regarding the correct interpretation of the Scripture. One way forward through this situation is to clarify what the spiritual reading is in its own context. In this article, I will concentrate on Luther's spiritual understanding of the Scripture. I believe that the Reformer's thought and practice will open spiritually fruitful perspectives on the Scripture, which to a large extent have been forgotten. However, it must be taken into account that Luther's understanding of where in the Christian life this reading is located from later Lutheranism. The difference results from how the doctrine of justification is understood. I shall return to this question below.

Yet before I address how Luther read the Scripture, I will briefly examine his notions of the Holy Scripture and its relationship to tradition, for this helps us to grasp Luther's assumptions about biblical hermeneutics. In other words, Luther did not separate the Scripture from church's subsequent interpretation of or the doctrinal formulations as if they were two separate entities. The Reformer did not hold the widespread view that we do not need to observe tradition when reading the Scripture. Instead, he believed that if a church father or the church doctrine is clearly in accordance with the Scripture, then the doctrine is true and therefore shares the authority of the Scripture.

This point is important for my overall theme since Luther's way of interpreting the Scripture is based on the concept of the Trinitarian *Logos*, which sometimes appears openly, although sometimes it is only implied in the texts. Second, Luther's view of the relationship between authentic biblical tradition and the Scripture itself enables him to raise the meditation on catechism to equal status with the meditation on the Scripture, since the catechism contains the Decalogue, the Creed, the Lord's Prayer, and the sacraments of Baptism and the Eucharist. I will return to this point below.

Although we may easily think otherwise, Luther's basic view of the Scripture as the norm and measure of all doctrinal teaching was shared both by him and by his Catholic adversaries. No scholastic or Lutheran theologian has ever denied that the Scripture is the norm and the measure of the church's dogma. The reason for the conflict lay instead in the Catholic claim that Luther suffered hubris when he dreamed that he alone understood the Scripture properly and that he measured all teachings of the church fathers against his subjective understanding: one theologian places himself grandiosely "above all the holy Fathers, St. Augustine, St. Ambrose, St. Gregory, St. Leo, St. Cyprian, St. Chrysostome and St. Bernard, claiming to understand the Scriptures in a better way than all the Fathers combined."[1]

Hence, Luther was described as a hubristic individualist, who made all authorities suspicious, his own subjective reason and opinions notwithstanding. Luther's answer to this criticism was as follows.

---

1. The words of Johann Eck, in *WA* Br 460, 22.

He [Eck] says: No one should interpret the Scripture based on their own reason, but rather they must follow the teaching of the Fathers. Against them I have said: when I have a clear and lucid Scriptural text, I would stay with its meaning, even if the interpretation of the Fathers contradicts this meaning, as St. Augustine has often done and advised to do as well.[2]

We should thus let the texts of the Scripture speak its own meaning to the readers. It is specifically this meaning, which is the norm and measure, not all the differing interpretations of the text presented in the course of the history of the church. The difficult passages must be interpreted within the overall context of the Scripture, and not through such things as the philosophical framework of the interpreter.

Luther's famous retrospective description of his reformatory breakthrough offers insight into what he meant by the clarity of the Scriptures and the striving to understand its text. Luther's primary intention is not to share biographical information when he tells how he reads the Scriptures and how he learned to understand it. In fact, he represents here the concise core of biblical hermeneutics.[3]

Famously Luther's breakthrough took place while he was meditating, over a period of time, on passage in Romans (1:17): "For therein [i.e., in the Gospel] is the righteousness of God revealed from faith to faith; as it is written: 'The just shall live by faith.'" Luther tells us how he yearned to know better Paul's letter to Romans. He had not been hindered by "the slowness of the heart" but "by a single word in the first chapter": God's righteousness is revealed in the Gospel. Luther hated the words "God's righteousness." The doctors of the church had taught him that God's righteousness means God's "active" righteousness, "whereby God is righteous and punishes sinners and the unrighteous." Luther could not consider himself righteous for he did not love God, but hated God who only punished sinners—as if there were not enough suffering when poor sinners and those forever damned for original sin were tormented by all kinds of tribulations; yet God added still more pain by threatening humans even in the Gospel with his righteous anger. Luther writes about wrestling with Paul's text in the following way:

---

2. *WA* Br 1, 468, 10. Translation mine.
3. *WA* 54, 176. See also Slenczka, "Die Schrift," 66.

> Thus, I raged with a fierce and troubled conscience. Nevertheless, I beat importunately upon Paul at that place, most ardently desiring to know what St. Paul wanted.[4]

Then he tells us about his reformatory breakthrough as follows.

> At last, by the mercy of God, meditating day and night, I gave heed to the context of the words, namely, "In it [the Gospel] the righteousness of God is revealed, as it is written, 'He who through faith is righteous shall live.'" There I began to understand (*coepi intelligere*) that the righteousness of God (*iustitia Dei*) is that by which the righteous lives by the gift of God, namely, by faith. And this is the meaning: the righteousness of God is revealed by the Gospel, namely, the passive righteousness with which a merciful God justifies us by faith, as it is written, "He who through faith is righteous shall live." Here I felt that I was altogether born again and had entered paradise itself through open gates. There a totally different face of the entire Scripture showed itself to me. Thereupon I ran through the Scripture from memory. I also found in other terms an analogy, such as the work of God, that is, what God does in us (*in nobis*), the power of God, with which he makes us wise, the strength of God, the salvation of God, the glory of God. And I extolled my sweetest word with a love as great as the hatred with which I had before hated the words "righteousness of God." Thus, that place in Paul was for me truly the gate to paradise.

Luther's central reformatory idea was that God's righteousness is not the requiring and punishing righteousness (*iustitia activa*) that he had learned from tradition. Instead it is the gift (*donum*) of righteousness by which God makes a person righteous (*iustitia activa*). This hermeneutical insight brought other ideas as well. First, *faith is reception* and God is the *God who gives*. These notions also include *the distinction between the Law and the Gospel*. Luther claims that by virtue of understanding Paul's concept of God's righteousness, he came to understand not only one chapter, but also the whole central content of the Scripture. The Scripture was now opened to him through this center, through the idea of the God who gives to others. The Scripture showed a totally new face to him. He felt that he was being born again and stepping through open doors to paradise.

Finding the "new face" implied that the other central concepts that depict God in the Scripture follow a similar structure and analogy as

---

4. *WA* 54, 186. Translation from *LW* 34, 336–37.

"God's righteousness." Because God's righteousness is the righteousness by which (*qua*) God makes us righteous, so is "God's deed" (*opus Dei*), a deed that he accomplishes in us (*quod operatur in nobis Deus*); God's power is the power by which he makes us powerful (*qua nobis potentes facit*); God's wisdom is the wisdom by which he makes us wise (*qua nos sapientes facit*); and so forth. Thus, Luther found everywhere in the Scripture the idea of a God who gives, which was indicated in Paul's terminology.

Luther's discovery and the new understanding of the Scripture did not entail purely mental, cognitive events. The depth of his idea can only be fathomed through the passage in Romans (1:17), which caused a great deal of trouble for young Luther: "For in it [the Gospel] the righteousness of God is revealed from faith to faith." The word "Gospel" is of great importance here. God not only donates information, but he personally approaches us and donates himself to us. When we receive the Gospel, we receive the triune God, for the second person of the Trinity, the *Logos*, Christ, is present in the Gospel through the Holy Spirit, the Spirit of Christ.

Luther's frequent expression "the faith of the Christ" (*fides Christi*) takes this idea of presence to extreme: our faith is the faith of Christ, that is, Christ himself believes in us. Christ himself loves in us. The Christian participates in Christ in God's self-donating love, and receives the new light of understanding, the new skill of judgment. The Christian also shares eternal life, for God is personally the Eternal Life. In these ideas the grounding for the spiritual reading of the Scripture is manifested.

Luther's account of his reformatory breakthrough may create the perplexing impression that his doctrine of justification would be purely effective; the Reformer does not explicitly mention atonement or the forgiveness of sins. Instead, he speaks at length about *making* sinners righteous, powerful, wise, and brave. In other words, Luther does not clearly speak of God's favor, but rather of God's gift. Yet Luther's account reflects the same doctrine of justification that appears in his other writings.

Typically, Luther represents the content of the Gospel with the help of two basic concepts, a favor and a gift. Favor means the beneficial attitude of God's heart toward people that results from the acts of atonement and the forgiveness of sins. The gift means that God donates himself in the Gospel, that is, his essence and all his attributes (although inchoately and awaiting eschatological fulfillment). Favor deals with God's merciful relationship with people as a forensic concept. Gift, on the other hand, is an effective concept that expresses God's donation of himself and consequent presence.

The impression of the purely effective doctrine of justification results from Luther's retrospective use of words in which he uses "grace" synonymously with favor: "merciful God" justifies/makes someone righteous. Second, the Formula of Concord describes justification, at least at the terminological level, as a purely declaratory action and not in terms of effective change. This indicates that justification is somehow separated from the presence of the triune God and his gifts to believers, which are a matter of sub-sequent sanctification and regeneration, the logical consequences of justification. However, the exact nature of the relationship between justification and sanctification remains unaddressed in the Formula of Concord.

In Luther's theology justification is both declaratory and effective. Both aspects are joined in the present person of Christ, in his forgiveness and other gifts. From the viewpoint of later Lutheranism, it is hard to understand the following passage from Luther's *Preface to Romans*: "the grace is so effective that we are imputed totally and fully righteous before of God. For His grace cannot be divided or chopped up like ordinary presents but grace takes us wholly in favor because of Christ, our intercessor and mediator, *and because these gifts have started to dwell in us and have an effect in us.*"[5]

This passage is not a peripheral part of Luther's theology but integral to his thinking. It has to be borne in mind that the gifts of new understanding, love, power, joy, hope, participation in God's eternal life, and the like, are Christ's *own* reality. Even if they are *in us*, they are not *ours*. Therefore, the gifts as Christ's life are imputed to us, as Luther states above.

The well-known scholar on Luther and Lutheranism Bengt Hägglund claims that the effects of the description of justification in the Formula of Concord have been "enormous."[6] The doctrine of justification has been significantly impoverished. If faith is merely trust in God's mercy and the instrument of acceptance of forgiveness, then is there any role for faith in sanctification? In other words, is there any use for

---

5. *WA* DB 7, 9, 18–22: ". . . und umb das in uns die Gaben angefangen sind." Translation and emphasis mine.

6. Hägglund, "Rezeption Luthers," 118.

Luther's central doctrine, namely that the triune God is truly present in faith, who is both the justification and the sanctification of the sinner? The idea of *communio*—the doctrine of our participation by the Holy Spirit through Christ in the Father that takes place in the Word—and the Sacraments start to lose their organic and natural place that they enjoyed in Luther's theology. Simultaneously, the place of meditation on God's word in prayer becomes indeterminate in the overall context of spiritual life. I wonder whether therein lies one of the reasons why secularization has advanced so well, especially in Lutheran countries.

In Luther's theology faith is a vivid presence of Christ in the deepest, hidden places of the human being; yet this is expressed more succinctly in the Formula of Concord. For Luther, faith is like the holy of holies in the Temple of Jerusalem, where darkness abounds, yet God himself is present in that darkness. In similar fashion, faith is the "darkness and cloud," wherein reason loses its bearings, but where Christ truly dwells through the Spirit. *Christus praesens* is "without division and confusion," the favor and mercy of God as well as God's regenerative presence, sanctification. This interpretation of faith crystallizes Luther's reformatory insight of a giving Deity, who is not merely a cognitive idea but a God who truly gives himself to us—although in a hidden way. These ideas have significant bearing on how the nature of the Scripture is understood.

Somewhat surprisingly, Luther's writing on the catechesis sheds important light on how to read the Scripture. The Reformer asserts that the catechism is a copy or a duplicate of the entire Holy Book: it includes everything the Scripture contains and that Christian churches preach. Luther keeps repeating that the whole meaning of the Scripture will be opened through this duplicate. The content of the catechism is thus equal to the Scripture. Luther explains the heart of the catechism, the Scripture and the entirety of Christian faith as follows. The Law—Decalogue—expresses what God requires from us, but what we are unable bring forth with our natural powers, namely joyful and spontaneous love of God and of our neighbors. In fact, the demand of the Law refers to the Spirit of God outside of itself, for only in the Spirit the love demanded by the Law is given to us.

The Creed expresses what God gives us so that we can begin to fulfill the demands of the Law, that is, selfless love. The triune God donates all the goods of Creation, Atonement, and Sanctification. The first article of the Creed expresses how God the Creator gives himself as a gift in all created goods. Consequently, these good gifts must be received in faith and with praise for the Creator for these gifts. According to the second article, God gives himself in Christ through incarnation, and bears the load and punishment of hell on behalf of the entire human race. Simultaneously, the human being is made to share in everlasting life. The third article explains how the Holy Spirit makes both Christ and all his works and gifts present in the believer.

Finally, the Lord's Prayer (and other prayers as well) expresses how *we* are the objects of God's giving. True, God gives his gifts objectively all the time, but they can be received personally only in prayer and in the state of prayer.

The idea of a God who gives is therefore basic to the overall concept of the catechesis as it is also in the Scripture as well. The idea is already visible in the Decalogue, wherein the most important commandment is the first. It commands us to keep God as the God who gives, the deliverer of everything that is good. This commandment is like one of a string of pearls; it keeps all the other commandments together within the framework of the Christian faith as whole. The relationship between commandments, the Creed, and prayer forms the simple and understandable outline, a sort of key that opens the contents of the Scripture. The purpose of spiritual reading is that this idea of a giving God more and more penetrates the reading and understanding of the Scriptures. Thus catechism is the way that leads into the Scriptures. Yet the catechism is not only at the beginning of the road but also at the end. It functions as a small treasure chest; it can be used to store the understanding gained through meditation on the Bible, and its nature as the synopsis of faith helps to keep the basic structure of faith more easily in mind.

The meaning of God's word is not only to deliver accurate information about faith. Instead, the reader's right attitude is one of meditative prayer. The catechism is also a book of meditation. God's word must be approached in prayer. Luther recommends that we pray aloud, concentrating on one passage or one theme at a time and bringing it to God, praying for the illumination of God's spirit so that we open up its meaning through the general framework of faith and simultaneously locate it in the context and practice of everyday life in prayer.

> Meditating in prayer on the central texts of Christian faith joins our inner being with the dynamics of the Spirit of God. These

texts and the light of faith illuminating from them pull us away from malignant thoughts, vague restlessness of the heart, and form a strong fortification against demonic angst.[7]

Luther advises us to meditate God's word in prayer in the morning, in the middle of the day, and in the evening. Luther tells how he himself prays, not only in these moments, but also when owing to hurry or carelessness his meditation was only done fleetingly, the mind is restless, or he feels incompetent. We are told that the Reformer spent from two to three hours in a day in prayer and meditation.

In the midst of meditating on God's word in prayer, the reader may experience the Holy Spirit "preaching." Suddenly new thoughts begin to flow swiftly, like a brook. Then Luther advises us to grasp a pen, forget everything else, and write this "sermon" down. The passage that was the object of meditation is made one with human heart, which is now taken over by inner force and energized to perceive and to act.

---

7. Peters, *Kommentar zu Luther's Catechismen I*, 31. Translation mine.

Bibliography

Althaus, Paul. "Luthers Abendmahlslehre." *Jahrbuch der Luthergeschellschaft* (1929) 2-42.
Aquinas, St. Thomas. *Summa Theologiae*. Biblioteca de Autores Cristianos: Matriti, 1955.
Aristotle. *De anima*. Clarendon: Oxford, 1956.
Augustine. *De civitate Dei. The City of God Against Pagans*. Edited and translated by R. W. Dyson. Cambridge: Cambridge University Press, 1988.
———. *De trinitate. The Trinity*. New York: New City, 1991.
Aulen, Gustav. *Den kristna försöningstanken. Huvudtyper och brytningar*. Stockholm: Svenska kyrkans diakonistyrelse, 1930.
Balthasar, Hans Urs von. *The Glory of the Lord*. Vol 1: *Seeing the Form*. Edinburgh: T. & T. Clark, 1982.
Bauer, Karl. "Die Heidelberger Disputation Luthers." *Zeitschrift für Kirchengeschichte* 21 (1901) 233-68, 299-329.
Bayer, Oswald. *Martin Luthers Theologie: Eine Gegenwärtigung*. Tübingen: Mohr, 2003.
———. *Martin Luther's Theology: A Contemporary Interpretation*. Grand Rapids: Eerdmans, 2008.
Bayer, Oswald, et al. *Caritas Dei: Beiträge zum Verständnis Luthers und der gegenwärtigen Ökumene*. Helsinki: Luther-Agricola Gesellschaft, 1997.
Begbie, Jeremy. *Theology, Music, and Time*. Cambridge: Cambridge University Press, 2000.
Bell, Daniel M., Jr. *Liberation Theology after the End of History: The Refusal to Cease Suffering*. London: Routledge, 2001.
Benedict XVI. *General audience on Wednesday November 19 2009*. Vatican, 2009.
———. *Spe salvi. Encyclical letter*. Vatican, 2007.
Beutel, Albrecht. "Antwort und Wort." In *Luther und Ontologie: Das Sein Christi im Glauben als strukturierendes Prinzip der Theologie Luthers*, edited by Anja Ghiselli et al., 70-93. Helsinki: Luther-Agricola-Gesellschaft, 1993.
Biel, Gabriel. *Collectorium circa quattuor libros Sententiarum*. Edited by Wilfrid Werbeck & Udo Hofmann. Tübingen: Mohr/Siebeck, 1973-1992.
Bielfeldt, Dennis. "Luther's Late Trinitarian Disputations: Semantic Realism and the Trinity." In *The Substance of the Faith: Luther's Doctrinal Theology for Today*, edited by Paul R. Hinlicky et al., 59-130. Minneapolis: Fortress, 2008.
Billings, J. Todd. "John Calvin: United to God through Christ." In *Partakers of the Divine Nature: The History and Development of Deification in the Christian Traditions*, edited by Michael J. Christensen and Jeffrey A. Wittung, 200-218. Grand Rapids: Baker, 2007.
———. "John Milbank's Theology of the Gift and Calvin's Theology of Grace: A Critical Comparison." *Modern Theology* 21 (2005) 87-105.
Blankenburg, Walter. "Luther, Martin." In *Musik in Geschichte und Gegenwart* 8:1334-46.

Blaumeiser, Hubertus. *Martin Luthers Kreuzestheologie: Schlüssel zu seiner Deutung von Mensch und Wirklichkeit. Eine Untersuchung anhand der Operationes in Psalmos* (1519–21). Konfessionskundliche und kontroverstheologische Studien 60. Paderborn: Bonifatius, 1995.

Block, Johannes. *Verstehen durch Musik: Das gesungene Wort der Theologie: ein hermeneutischer Beitrag zur Hymnologie am Beispiel Martin Luthers.* Tübingen: Francke, 2002.

Boehme, Armand J. "Sing a New Song: The Doctrine of Justification and the Lutheran Book of Worship Sacramental Liurgies." *Concordia Theological Quarterly* 43 (1979) 96–119.

Bornkamm, Heinrich. *Das bleibende Recht der Reformation: Grundregeln und Grundfragen evangelischen Glaubens.* Stundenbuch 17. Hamburg: Furche, 1963.

———. *Luther im Spiegel der deutschen Geistesgeschichte.* Göttingen: Vandenhoeck & Ruprecht, 1970.

———. "Die theologischen Thesen Luthers bei der Heidelberger Disputation 1518 und seine theologia crucis." In Heinrich Bornkamm, *Luther, Gestalt und Wirkungen: Gesammelte Aufsätze*, 130–46. Gütersloh: Mohn, 1975.

Boyer, Louis. *Eucharist: Theology and Spirituality of the Eucharistic Prayer.* London: University of Notre Dame Press, 1968.

Braaten, Carl E., and Robert W. Jenson. *Christian Dogmatics.* Vol. 2. Philadelphia: Fortress, 1986.

———. *Union with Christ: The New Finnish Interpretation of Luther.* Grand Rapids: Eerdmans, 1998.

Brand, Eugene L. "Luther's Liturgical Surgery: 20th Century Diagnosis of the Patient." In *Interpretating Luther's Legacy: Essays in Honor of Edward C. Fendt*, edited by Fred W. Mauser and Stanley D. Schneider, 108–19. Minneapolis: Augsburg, 1969.

Brecht, Martin. *Martin Luther: Sein Weg zur Reformation* 1483–1521. Stuttgart: Calver, 1981.

———. *Martin Luther: Die Erhaltung der Kirche* 1532–1546. Stuttgart: Calwer, 1987.

Brightman, F. E. *Liturgies Eastern and Western: Principal Liturgies of the Church. Vol. I. Eastern Liturgies.* Oxford, 1896.

Brilioth, Yngve. *Eucharistic Faith and Practice: Evangelical and Catholic.* London, 1930.

———. *Nattvarden i evangeliskt gudtjänstliv.* 2. upplagan. Stockholm: Svenska Kyrkans Diakonistyrelses, 1951.

Bring, Ragnar. *Dualismen hos Luther.* Lund: Håkan Ohlssons, 1929.

Briskina, Anna. "An Orthodox View of Finnish Luther Research." *Lutheran Quarterly* 22 (2008) 16–39.

Cabié, Robert. *The Church at Prayer: Introduction to the Liturgy.* Volume 2, *The Eucharist.* Translated by Matthew J. O'Connell. Collegeville, MN: Liturgical, 1986.

Christensen, Michael J., and Jeffrey A. Wittung. *Partakers of the Divine Nature: The History and Development of Deification in the Christian Traditions.* Grand Rapids: Baker, 2007.

Clemen, Otto. "Beiträge zur Lutherforschung." *ZKG* 27 (1906) 100–11.

Cleve, Fredric. *Luthers nattvardslära mot bakgrunden av Gabriel Biels uppfattning av nattvard och sakrament.* Åbo: Åbo Akademi, 1968.

Dales, Richard C. *Medieval Discussions of the Eternity of the World.* Brill's Studies in Intellectual History 18. Leiden: Brill, 1990.

Delius, Walter. "Der Augustiner Eremitenorden im Prozeß Luthers." *Archiv für Reformationgeschichte* 63 (1972) 22–42.

Denifle, H. *Luther und Luthertum in der ersten Entwicklung.* Mainz, 1904.

Devasahayam, V. *Frontiers of Dalit Theology.* Gurukul, Madras: Indian Society for Promoting Christian Knowledge, 1997.

Dieter, Theodor. "Amor hominis—amor crucis. Zu Aristoteleskritik in der Probatio zur 28. These der Heidelberger Disputation." *Neue Zeitschrift für Systematische Theologie und Religionsphilosophie* 29 (1987) 241–58.

———. *Der junge Luther und Aristoteles. Eine historisch-systematische Untersuchung zum Verhältnis von Theologie und Philosophie.* Theologische Bibliothek Töpelmann 105. Berlin: Walter de Gruyter, 2001.

———. *Die Philosophischen Thesen der "Heidelberger Disputation" Luthers und ihre Probationen. Ein kritischer Kommentar.* Inaugural-Dissertation zur Erlangung der Doktorwürde der Evangelisch-theologischen Fakultät der Eberhard-Karls-Universität zu Tübingen. 2., durchgesehene Auflage, 1992.

Ebeling, Gerhard. *Luther. Einführung in sein Denken.* Tübingen: Mohr (Siebeck), 1981.

———. *Lutherstudien (=LuSt).* Band I (1971); Band II, Disputatio de homine. Teil 1. Text und Traditionshintergrund (1977); Teil 2. Die philosophische Definition des Menschen. Kommentar zu Theses 1–19 (1982); Teil 3. Die theologische Definition des Menschen. Kommentar zu Theses 20–40 (1989); Band III Begriffsuntersuchungen—Textinterpretationen—Wirkungsgeschichtliches (1985). Tübingen: Mohr/Siebeck, 1971–89.

———. "Zu Luthers Wirklichkeitsverständnis." *Zeitschrift für Theologie und Kirche* 90 (1993) 409–24.

———. *Das Wesen des christlichen Glaubens.* Tübingen: Mohr, 1959.

Ellwein, Eduard. "Die Entfaltung der theologia crucis in Luthers Hebräerbriefvorlesung." In *Theologische Aufsätze. Karl Barth zum 50. Geburtstag,* edited by E. Wolf, 382–404. München: Chr. Kaiser, 1936.

Finlan, Stephen, and Vladimir Kharimov. *Theosis: Deification in Christian Theology.* Princeton Theological Monograph Series 52. Eugene, OR: Pickwick, 2006.

Flogaus, Reinhard. *Theosis bei Palamas und Luther: Ein Beitrag zum ökumenischen Gespräch.* Göttingen: Vandenhoeck & Ruprecht, 1997.

Forde, Gerhard O. *On Being a Theologian of the Cross: Reflections on Luther's Heidelberg Disputation, 1518.* Grand Rapids: Eerdmans, 1997.

Forsberg, Juhani. "Die finnische Lutherforschung seit 1979." *Lutherjahrbuch* 72 (2005) 147–82.

———. "Rukous tekona, uhrina ja jumalanpalveluksena." In *Rukous ja jumalanpalveluselämä: Suomalaisen Teologisen Kirjallisuusseuran vuosikirja 1988,* edited by Tapio Lampinen, 29–42. Helsinki: Suomalainen Teologinen Kirjallisuusseura, 1988.

Ghiselli, Anja, et al. *Luther und Ontologie: Das Sein Christi im Glauben als strukturierendes Prinzip der Theologie Luthers.* Helsinki: Luther-Agricola-Gesellschaft, 1993.

Grane, Leif. *Contra Gabrielem. Luthers Auseinandersetzung mit Gabriel Biel in der Disputatio Contra Scholasticam Theologiam 1517.* København: Acta theologica Danica, 1962.

———. "Erwägungen zur Ontologie Luthers." *Neue Zeitschrift für systematische Theologie und Religionsphilosophie* 13 (1971) 188–98.

Gregory, Eric. *Politics and the Order of Love*. Chicago: University of Chicago Press, 2008.

Gregory the Great. *Grégoire le Grand: Commentaire sur le Cantique. Introduction, traduction, notes et index par Rodrigue Bélanger*. Sources Chrétiennes 314. Paris: Cerf, 1984.

Gritsch, Eric W. "Embodiment of Unmerited Grace. The Virgin Mary according to Martin Luther and Lutheranism." In *Mary's Place in Christian Dialogue*, edited by Alberic Stacpoole. Wilton: Morehouse-Barlow, 1988.

Guicharrousse, Hubert. *Les Musiques de Luther*. Gèneve: Labor et Fides, 1995.

Hacker, Paul. *Das Ich im Glauben bei Martin Luther*. Graz: Styria, 1966.

Hallonsten, Gösta. "Theosis in Recent Research: A Renewal in Interest and a Need for Clarity." In *Partakers of the Divine Nature: The History and Development of Deification in the Christian Traditions*, edited by Michael J. Christensen and Jeffrey A. Wittung, 281–93. Grand Rapids: Baker, 2007.

Hardt, Tom. *G. A. Venerabilis & adorabilis eucharistia: en studie i den lutherska nattvardsläran under 1500-talet*. Uppsala: Studia doctrinae Christianae Upsaliensia, 1971.

Hart, David Bentley. *The Beauty of the Infinite: The Aesthetics of Christian Truth*. Grand Rapids. Eerdmans, 2003.

Hays, Richard B. *Faith of Jesus Christ: The Narrative Substructure of Galatians 3:1—4:11*. Grand Rapids: Eerdmans, 2001.

Hägglund, Bengt. *De homine. Människouppfattningen i äldre luthersk tradition*. Lund: Gleerup, 1959.

———. "Luthers Anthropologie." In *Leben und Werk Martin Luthers. Festgabe zu seinem 500. Geburtstag*, edited by Helmar Junghans, 63–76, 747–8. Göttingen: Vandenhoek & Ruprecht, 1983.

———. "Die Rezeption Luthers in der Konkordienformel." In *Luther und die Bekenntnisschriften*, 107–120. Erlangen: Luther-Akademie Ratzeburg, 1981.

Hänggi, Anton, and Irmgard Pahl. *Prex eucharistica: Textus e variis liturgiis antiquioribus selecti*. Spicilegium Friburgense 12. Freiburg: Editions universitaires, 1968.

Heinimäki, Jaakko, and Petri Järveläinen. *Tosi paha hyvä: Etiikka*. Helsinki: Otava, 1996.

Helmer, Christine, editor. *The Global Luther: A Theologian for Modern Times*. Minneapolis: Fortress, 2009.

———. *The Trinity and Martin Luther*. Mainz: von Zabern, 1999.

Herms, Eilert. *Luthers Auslegung des Dritten Artikels*. Tübingen: Mohr/Siebeck, 1987.

Hilgenfeld, Hartmut. *Mittelalterlich-traditionelle Elemente in Luthers Abendmahlschriften*. Zürich: Theologischer Verlag, 1971.

Holm, Bo. *Gabe und Geben bei Luther*. Berlin: de Gruyter, 2006.

———. "Nordic Luther Research in Motion." *Dialog* 47 (2008) 93–104.

Huovinen, Eero. "An der Unsterblichkeit teilhaftig: Das ökumenische Grundproblem in der Todestheologie Luthers." In Eero Huovinen, *Baptism, Church, and Ecumenism. Collected Essays—Gesammelte Aufsätze*, edited by Antti Mustakallio. Helsinki: Luther-Agricola-Society, forthcoming.

———. *Fides infantium: Martin Luthers Lehre vom Kinderglauben*. Mainz: Zabern, 1997.

———. *Kuolemattomuudesta osallinen: Martti Lutherin kuolemanteologinen perusongelma*. Helsinki: Suomalainen Teologinen Kirjallisuusseura, 1981.

Hütter, Reinhard. *Bound to Be Free: Evangelical Catholic Engagements in Ecclesiology, Ethics, and Ecumenism*. Grand Rapids: Eerdmans, 2004.

———. *Suffering Divine Things: Theology as Church Practice*. Grand Rapids: Eerdmans, 2000.
Iserloh, Erwin. "Abendmahl," III/2 (Mittelalter). In *Theologische Realenzyklopädie* 1:89-106.
———. "Existentiale Interpretation in Luthers erster Psalmenvorlesung." *Theologische Revue* 59 (1963) 73-84.
Jansen, Reiner. *Studien zu Luthers Trinitätslehre*. Bern: Herbert Lang, 1976.
Jasper, R. C. D., and G. J. Cuming. *Prayers of the Eucharist: Early and Reformed*. 3rd ed. Collegeville, MN: Liturgical, 1987.
Jenson, Robert W. "Response to Seifried, Trueman, and Metzger on Finnish Luther Research." *Westminster Theological Journal* 65 (2003) 245-50.
Joest, Wilfried. *Ontologie der Person bei Luther*. Göttingen: Vandenhoeck & Ruprecht, 1967.
Jorgenson, Allen G. "Luther on Ubiquity and a Theology of the Public." *International Journal of Systematic Theology* 6 (2004) 351-68.
Junghans, Helmar. "Luther on the Reform of Worship." *Lutheran Quarterly* 12 (1998) 315-36.
———. "Die Probationes zu den Philosophischen Thesen der Heidelberger Disputation im Jahre 1518." *Lutherjahrbuch* (1979) 10-59.
———. *Wittenberg als Lutherstadt*. Berlin: Union, 1982.
Jungmann, Josef A. *Missarum sollemnia: eine genetische Erklärung der römischen Messe*. Wien, 1952.
Juntunen, Sammeli. *Der Begriff des Nichts bei Luther in den Jahren von 1510 bis 1523*. Helsinki: Luther-Agricola Gesellschaft, 1996.
Kass, Amy A. *Giving Well, Doing Good: Readings for Thoughtful Philanthropists*. Bloomington: Indiana University Press, 2008.
Kärkkäinen, Pekka. "Interpretations of the Psychological Analogy from Aquinas to Biel." In *Trinitarian Theology in Medieval West*, edited by Pekka Kärkkäinen, 256-79. Helsinki: Luther-Agricola-Society, 2007.
———. *Luthers trinitarische Theologie des Heiligen Geistes*. Mainz: Zabern, 2005.
———. "Nominalist Psychology and the Limits of Canon Law in Late Medieval Erfurt." In *Lutheran Reformation and the Law*, edited by Virpi Mäkinen, 93-110. Boston: Brill, 2006.
———. "Martin Luther." In *Mediaeval Commentaries on the Sentences of Peter Lombard: Current Research*, Vol. 2, edited by Philipp W. Rosemann, 471-94. Leiden: Brill, 2010.
———. "Objects of Sense Perception in Late Medieval Erfurtian Nominalism." In *Theories of Perception in Medieval and Early Modern Philosophy*, edited by Simo Knuuttila and Pekka Kärkkäinen, 187-202. Dordrecht: Springer, 2008.
———. "On the Semantics of 'Human Being' and 'Animal' in Early 16th Century Erfurt." *Vivarium* 42 (2004) 237-56.
———. "Theology, Philososphy, and Immortality of the Soul in the Late *Via Moderna* of Erfurt." *Vivarium* 43 (2005) 337-60.
———. *Trinitarian Theology in the Medieval West*. Helsinki: Luther-Agricola Gesellschaft, 2007.
Kärkkäinen, Veli-Matti. *One with God: Salvation as Deification and Justification*. Collegeville, MN: Liturgical, 2004.

———. "Salvation as Justification and Theosis: The Contribution of the New Finnish Luther Interpretation to Our Ecumenical Future." *Dialog* 45 (2006) 74–82.

Kitamori, Kazoh. *Theology of the Pain of God*. Richmond, VA: John Knox, 1965.

Kitanov, Severin. *Beatific Enjoyment in Scholastic Theology and Philosophy, 1240–1335*. ThD diss., University of Helsinki, 2006.

Kittilä, Seppo. "A Typology of Tritransitives: Alignment Types and Motivations." *Linguistics* (2007) 453–508.

Kirjavainen, Heikki. "Luther und Aristoteles, Die Frage der zweifachen Gerechtigkeit im Lichte der transitiven vs. intransitiven Willenstheorie." In *Luther in Finnland*, edited by Miikka Ruokanen, 111–29 Helsinki: Luther-Agricola Gesellschaft, 1986.

———. "Uskonkohteiden spesifiointi Lutherilla myöhäisskolastisen semantiikan valossa." In *Tutkimuksia Lutherin ajattelumuodosta*, edited by Anja Ghiselli and Simo Peura, 101–15. Helsinki: Suomalainen Teologinen Kirjallisuusseura, 1987.

Kolb, Robert, and Charles P. Arand. *The Genius of Luther's Theology*. Grand Rapids: Baker, 2008.

Kopperi, Kari. "Luthers theologische Zielsetzung in den philosophischen Thesen der Heidelberger Disputation." In *Nordiskt Forum för studiet av Luther och luthersk teologi*, edited by Tuomo Mannermaa et al., 67–103. Helsinki: Luther-Agricola Gesellschaft, 1993.

———. *Paradoksien teologia. Lutherin disputaatio Heidelbergissä 1518*. Helsinki: Suomalainen Teologinen Kirjallisuusseura, 1997.

Kotila, Heikki. *Liturgian lähteillä: Johdatus jumalanpalveluksen historiaan ja teologiaan*. Helsinki: University of Helsinki, 2000.

Knuuttila, Simo. "Luther's View of Logic and the Revelation." *Medioevo* 24 (1998) 219–34.

Knuuttila, Simo, and Risto Saarinen. "Innertrinitarische Theologie in der Scholastik und bei Luther." In *Caritas Dei: Beiträge zum Verständnis Luthers und der gegenwärtige Ökumene*, edited by Oswald Bayer et al., 243–64. Helsinki: Luther-Agricola-Society, 1997.

Kretschmar, Georg. "Luthers Konzeption von der Ehe." In *Martin Luther 'Reformator und Vater im Glauben'*, edited by Peter Manns, 178–207. Stuttgart: Franz Steiner Verlag, 1987.

Krodel, Gottfried G. "The Great Thanksgiving of the Inter-Lutheran Commission on Worship: It is the Christians' Supper and Not the Lord's Supper." In *The Cresset: Occasional Paper* 1 (1976) 19–20.

Krummacher, Christoph. *Musik als praxis pietatis. Zum Selbstverständis evangelischer Kirchenmusik*. Göttingen: Vanderhoeck & Ruprecht, 1994.

Lähteenmäki, Olavi. *Sexus und Ehe bei Luther*. Helsinki: Schriften der Luther-Agricola Gesellschaft, 1955.

Lamberigts, M. "A Critical Evaluation of Critique of Augustine's view of Sexuality." In *Augustine and His Critics. Essays in Honour of Gerald Bonner*, edited by R. Dodaro & G. Lawless, 176–97. London: Routledge, 2000.

Lathrop, Gordon. "The Prayer of Jesus and the Great Prayer of the Church." *Lutheran Quarterly* 26 (1974) 158–73.

Leaver, Robin A. "Luther, Martin" In *Grove Music Online*. Oxford Music Online. http://www.oxfordmusiconline.com/subscriber/article/grove/music/17219.

———. *Luther's Liturgical Music: Principles and Implications*. Grand Rapids: Eerdmans, 2007

Lehmann, Karl, and Wolfhart Pannenberg. *The Condemnations of the Reformation Era: Do They Still Divide?* Minneapolis: Fortress, 1980.
Lehmkühler, Karsten. *Inhabitatio: Die Einwohnung Gottes im Menschen.* Göttingen: Vandenhoeck & Ruprecht, 2004.
Lessing, Eckhard. *Abendmahl.* Bensheimer Hefte 72. Ökumenische Studienhefte 1. Göttingen: Vandenhoeck & Ruprecht, 1993.
Lewis, Clive Staples. *The Allegory of Love: A Study in Medieval Tradition.* New York: Galaxy Book, 1963.
Lienhard, Marc. *Luther. Witness to Jesus Christ: Stages and Themes of the Reformers Christology.* Translated by Edvin H. Robertson. Minneapolis: Augsburg, 1982.
Lindbeck, George. *The Nature of Doctrine.* Louisville: Westminster John Knox, 1984.
Lindroth, Hjalmar. *Försöningen: En dogmhistorisk och systematisk undersökning.* Uppsala: Uppsala Universitets Årsskrift, 1935.
Linman, Jonathan. "Martin Luther: Little Christs for the World; Faith and Sacraments as Means to Theosis." In *Partakers of the Divine Nature: The History and Development of Deification in the Christian Traditions*, edited by Michael J. Christensen and Jeffrey A. Wittung, 189-99. Grand Rapids: Baker, 2007.
Loewenich, Walther von. *Luther und der Neuprotestantismus.* Witten: Luther-Verlag, 1963.
―――. *Luthers Theologia crucis.* Witten: Luther-Verlag, 1967.
Lohse, Bernhard. *Luthers Theologie in ihrer historischen Entwicklung und in ihrem systematischen Zusammenhang.* Göttingen: Vandenhoek & Ruprecht, 1995
―――. *Martin Luther's Theology: Its Historical and Systematic Development.* Minneapolis: Fortress, 1999.
Luther, Martin. *Archiv zu Weimarer Ausgabe der Werke Martin Luthers.* Cologne: Bohlau, 1984-.
―――. *D. Martin Luthers Werke: Kritische Gesamtausgabe.* Weimar: Bohlau, 1883-.
―――. *D. Martin Luthers Werke: Weimarer Ausgabe. Briefe.* Weimar: Bohlau, 1883-.
―――. *D. Martin Luthers Werke: Weimarer Ausgabe. Deutsche Bibel.* Weimar: Bohlau, 1883-.
―――. *D. Martin Luthers Werke: Weimarer Ausgabe. Tischrede.* Weimar: Bohlau, 1883-

―――. *Luther's Works.* Edited by Jaroslav Pelikan and Helmut T. Lehman. Philadelphia: Fortress 1955-1986.
―――. *Martin Luther. Studienausgabe.* In collaboration with Helmar Junghans, Reinhold Pietz, Joachim Rogge, and Günther Wartenberg. Edited by Hans-Ulrich Delius. Berlin: Evangelische, 1979-.
MacIntyre, Alasdair. *After Virtue: A Study in Moral Theory.* 2nd ed. Notre Dame: University of Notre Dame Press, 1984.
Maffeis, Angelo. *Teologia della Riforma.* Brescia: Morcelliana, 2004.
Mahlmann, Theodor. "Die Stellung der unio cum Christo in der lutherischen Theologie des 17. Jahrhunderts." In *Unio. Gott und Mensch in der nachreformatorischen Theologie*, edited by Matti Repo and Rainer Vinke, 72-199. Helsinki: Luther-Agricola Gesellschaft, 1996.
Mäkinen, Virpi. *Lutheran Reformation and the Law.* Leiden: Brill, 2006.
Malter, Rudolf. *Das reformatorische Denken und die Philosophie. Luthers Entwurf einer transzendental-praktischen Metaphysik.* Conscientia, Studien zur Bewußtseinsphilosophie, Band 9. Bonn: Bouvier Verlag Herbert Grundmann, 1980.

Mannermaa, Tuomo. *Christ Present in Faith: Luther's View of Justification*. Minneapolis: Fortress, 2005.

———. *Der im Glauben gegenwärtige Christus. Rechtfertigung und Vergottung*. Hannover: Lutherisches Verlagshaus, 1989.

———. "Grundlagenforschung der Theologie Martin Luthers und Ökumene." In *Thesaurus Lutheri. Auf der Suche nach neuen Paradigmen der Luther-Forschung*, edited by Tuomo Mannermaa et al., 17–35. Helsinki: Luther-Agricola Gesellschaft, 1987.

———. "Hat Luther eine trinitarische Ontologie?" In *Luther und die trinitarische Tradition. Ökumenische und philosophische Perspektiven*, edited by Joachim Heubach, 43–60. Erlangen: Martin-Luther, 1994.

———. "Itse ihmisen hyvä tahto on läsnäoleva Kristus. Karl Hollin Luther-tulkinnan filosofinen lähtökohta." In *Teologian näkymiä 1980-luvun alkaessa. Suomalaisen Teologisen Kirjallisuusseuran 90-vuotisjuhlajulkaisu*, edited by Eeva Martikainen & Kalevi Tamminen, 67–74. Helsinki: Suomalainen Teologinen Kirjallisuusseura, 1981.

———. "Justification and Theosis in Lutheran–Orthodox Perspective." In *Union with Christ*, edited by Carl E. Braaten and Robert W. Jenson, 25–41. Grand Rapids: Eerdmans, 1998.

———. *Kontrapunkteja*. Helsinki: Suomalainen Teologinen Kirjallisuusseura, 1980.

———. *Lumen fidei et obiectum fidei adventicium: Uskontiedon spontaanisuus ja reseptiivisyys Karl Rahnerin varhaisessa ajattelussa*. Helsinki: Luther-Agricola Gesellschaft, 1970.

———. *Paralleeleja: Lutherin teologia ja sen soveltaminen*. Helsinki: Suomalainen Teologinen Kirjallisuusseura, 1992.

———. "Theologische Ontologie bei Luther?" In *Nordiskt forum för Studiet av Luther och luthersk teologi*, edited by Tuomo Mannermaa et al., 37–53. Helsinki: Luther-Agricola Gesellschaft, 1993.

———. "Theosis als Thema der finnischen Lutherforschung." In *Luther und Theosis: Vergöttlichung als Thema der abendländischen Theologie*, edited by Simo Peura und Antti Raunio, 11–26. Helsinki: Luther-Agricola Gesellschaft, 1990.

———. *Thesaurus Lutheri: Auf der Suche nach neuen Paradigmen der Luther-Forschung*. Edited by Tuomo Mannermaa et al. Helsinki: Luther-Agricola Gesellschaft, 1987.

———. "Über die Unmöglichkeit, gegen die texte Luthers zu systematisieren: Antwort an Gunther Wenz." In *Luther und Ontologie. Das Sein Christi im Glauben als strukturierendes Prinzip der Theologie Luthers*, edited by Anja Ghiselli et al., 381–91. Helsinki: Luther-Agricola Gesellschaft, 1993.

———. *Von Preussen nach Leuenberg*. Hamburg: Lutherisches Verlagshaus, 1982.

———. "Why Is Luther So Fascinating? Modern Finnish Luther Research." In *Union with Christ: The New Finnish Interpretation of Luther*, edited by Carl E. Braaten and Robert W. Jenson, 1–20. Grand Rapids: Eerdmans, 1998.

Manns, Peter. *Vater im Glauben. Studien zur Theologie Martin Luthers*. Wiesbaden: Steiner, 1988.

Marquart, Kurt E. "Luther and Theosis." *Concordia Theological Quarterly* 64 (2000) 182–205.

Marshall, Bruce. "Justification as Deification and Declaration." *International Journal of Systematic Theology* 4 (2002) 1–17.

Martikainen, Eeva. *Doctrina. Studien zu Luthers Begriff der Lehre*. Helsinki: Luther-Agricola Gesellschaft, 1992.

———. *Doctrina evangelii. Luterilainen oppikäsitys ja sen tulkinta*. Helsinki: Suomalainen Teologinen Kirjallisuusseura, 1985.

Mattes, Mark C. "A Future for Lutheran Theology?" *Lutheran Quarterly* 19 (2005) 439–57.

———. *The Role of Justification in Contemporary Theology*. Grand Rapids: Eerdmans, 2004.

Mattox, Mickey L. "From Faith to the Text and Back Again: Martin Luther on the Trinity in the Old Testament." *Pro Ecclesia* 15 (2006) 281–303.

———. "Luther's Interpretation of Scripture: Biblical Understanding in Trinitarian Shape." In *The Substance of the Faith: Luther's Doctrinal Theology for Today*, edited by Paul R. Hinlicky, 11–57. Minneapolis: Fortress, 2008.

Maxwell, William D. *An Outline of Christian Worship: Its Developments and Forms*. London: Oxford University Press, 1963.

McGrath, Alister E. *Luther's Theology of the Cross: Martin Luthers Theological Breakthrough*. Oxford: Blackwell, 1985.

Meilaender, Gilbert. "Hearts Set to Obey." In *I Am the Lord Your God: Christian Reflections on the Ten Commandments*, edited by Carl Braaten and Christopher Seitz, 253–75. Grand Rapids: Eerdmans, 2005.

Melanchthon, Philipp. *Loci communes 1521. Lateinisch-Deutsch*. Gütersloh: Gütersloher, 1993.

———. *Werke*. Gütersloh: Mohn, 1961.

Messner, Reinhard. *Die Messreform Martin Luthers und die Eucharistie der Alten Kirche: Ein Beitrag zu einer systematischen Liturgiewissenschaft*. Innsbruck: Tyrolia, 1989.

———. "Rechtfertigung und Vergöttlichung—und die Kirche: Zur ökumenischen Bedeutung neuerer Tendenzen in der Lutherforschung." *Zeitschrift für katholische Theologie* (1996) 23–35.

Metzger, Paul Louis. "Mystical Union with Christ: An Alternative to Blood Transfusions and Legal Fictions." *Westminster Theological Journal* 65 (2003) 201–13.

Meyer, Hans Bernhard SJ. *Luther und die Messe: Eine liturgiewissenschaftliche Untersuchung über das Verhältnis Luthers zum Messwesen des späten Mittelalters*. Paderborn: Bonifacius, 1965.

Milbank, John. *Being Reconciled: Ontology and Pardon*. London: Routledge, 2003.

Moltmann, Jürgen. *Der gekreuzigte Gott. Das Kreuz Christi als Grund und Kritik christlichen Theologie*. Munich: Kaiser, 1972.

Mosser, Carl. "The Greatest Possible Blessing: Calvin and Deification." *Scottish Journal of Theology* 55 (2002) 36–57.

Moxter, Michael, and Ingolf U. Dalferth. "Protestant Theology: Germany." In *The Blackwell Encyclopedia of Modern Christian Thought*, edited by Alister McGrath, 489–511. Oxford: Blackwell, 1993.

Neuhaus, Richard John. "On Loving the Law of God." *First Things* 190 (2009) 61–64.

Nichols, Aidan. *The Thought of Benedict XVI: An Introduction to the Theology of Joseph Ratzinger*. New York: Continuum, 2005.

Nilsson, Kjel-Ove. *Simul: Das Miteinandersein von Göttlichem und Menschlichem in Luthers theologie*. Göttingen: Vandenhoeck & Ruprecht, 1966.

Nüssel, Friederike. *Allein aus Glauben: Zur Entwicklung der Rechtfertigungslehre in der konkordistischen und frühen nachkonkordistischen Theologie.* Göttingen: Vandenhoeck & Ruprecht, 2000.

Nygren, Anders. *Agape and Eros.* Chicago: University of Chicago Press, 1982.

Oberman, Heiko A. *The Harvest of Medieval Theology: Gabriel Biel and Late Medieval Nominalism.* Durham, NC: Labyrinth, 1983.

———. *Luther, Mensch zwischen Gott und Teufel.* Berlin: Severin & Siedler, 1982.

Olivier, Daniel. "Der verborgene und gekreuzigte Gott—Das epistemologische Grundgesetz der Theologie nach Luther." In *Lutherische Kirche in der Welt. Jahrbuch des Martin Luther-Bundes* 31 (1984) 55–60.

Olson, O. K. "Contemporary Trends in Liturgy Viewed from the Perspective of Classical Lutheran Theology." *The Lutheran Quarterly* 26 (1974) 110–57.

Olsson, Herbert. *Schöpfung, Vernunft und Gesetz in Luthers Theologie.* Uppsala: Acta Universitatis Upsaliensis, 1971.

Parvio, Martti. "Ehtoollisliturgian ongelmia." *Teologinen Aikakauskirja* 78 (1973) 118–34.

Pelikan, Jaroslav. *From Luther to Kierkegaard.* St. Louis: Concordia, 1950.

Pesch, Otto Hermann. "Twenty Years of Catholic Luther Research." *Lutheran World* 13 (1966) 392–406.

Peters, Albrecht. *Kommentar zu Luthers Katechismen. Band I.* Göttingen: Vandenhoeck & Ruprecht 1990.

———. *Kommentar zu Luthers Katechismen. Band II.* Göttingen: Vandenhoek & Ruprecht, 1991.

———. *Kommentar zu Luthers Katechismen. Band IV.* Göttingen: Vandenhoeck & Ruprecht, 1993.

———. "Luthers Christuszeugnis als Zusammenfassung der Christusbotschaft der Kirche." *Kerygma und Dogma* 13 (1967) 1–26, 73–98.

———. *Mensch: Handbuch Systematischer Theologie Band 8.* Gütersloh: Gerd Mohn, 1979.

———. *Realpräsenz: Luthers Zeugnis von Christi Gegenwart im Abendmahl.* Arbeiten zur Geschichte und Theologie des Luthertums 5. Berlin: Lutherisches, 1960.

Peura, Simo. "Christ as Favor and Gift: The Challenge of Luther's Understanding of Justification." In *Union with Christ: The New Finnish Interpretation of Luther,* edited by Carl E. Braaten and Robert W. Jenson, 42–69. Grand Rapids: Eerdmans, 1998.

———. "The Church as Spiritual Communion in Luther." In *LWF Documentation. The Church as Communion,* edited by Heinrich Holze, 93–131. Geneva: Lutheran World Federation, 1997.

———. "Gott und Mensch in der Unio. Die Unterschiede im Rechtfertigungsvertändnis bei Osiander und Luther." In *Unio: Gott und Mensch in der nachreformatorischen Theologie,* edited by Matti Repo & Rainer Vinke, 33–61. Helsinki: Luther-Agricola-Gesellschaft, 1996.

———. *Mehr als ein Mensch? Die Vergöttlichung als Thema der Theologie Luthers von 1513 bis 1519.* Mainz: von Zabern, 1994.

———. "Die Teilhabe in Christus bei Luther." In *Luther und Theosis,* edited by Simo Peura & Antti Raunio, 121–61. Helsinki: Luther-Agricola-Gesellschaft, 1990.

———. "'Der Vergöttlichungsgedanke' in Luthers Theologie 1518–1519." In *Thesaurus Lutheri, auf der Suche nach neuen Paradigmen der Luther-Forschung,* edited by

Tuomo Mannermaa et al., 171–84. Helsinki: Schriften der Luther-Agricola-Gesellschaft, 1987.

———. "What God Gives, Man Receives: Luther on Salvation." In *Union with Christ: The New Finnish Interpretation of Luther*, edited by Carl E. Braaten and Robert W. Jenson, 76–95. Grand Rapids: Eerdmans, 1998.

Peura, Simo, and Raunio, Antti. *Luther und Theosis: Vergöttlichung als Thema der abendländischen Theologie.* Helsinki: Schriften der Luther-Agricola-Gesellschaft, 1990.

Pfatteicher, Philipp H. *Commentary on the Lutheran Book of Worship: Lutheran Liturgy in its Ecumenical Context.* Minneapolis: Augsburg Fortress, 1990.

Pfatteicher, Philipp H., and Carlos R. Messerli. *Lutheran Book of Worship: Manual of the Liturgy.* Minneapolis: Augsburg Fortress, 1979.

Pieper, Franz. *Christian Dogmatics.* 4 vols. St. Louis: Concordia, 1950–1953.

Pierre d'Ailly. *Quaestiones magistri Petri de Ailliaco cardinalis Cameracensis super libros Sententiarum.* Strassburg, 1490; reprinted, Frankfurt, 1968.

Pluta, Olaf. *Kritiker der Unsterblichkeitsdoktrin in Mittelalter und Renaissance.* Bochumer Studien zur Philosophie 7. Amsterdam: Grüner, 1986.

Ratzinger, Joseph Kardinal. *Theologische Prinzipienlehre: Bausteine zur Fundamentaltheologie.* München: Erich Wewel, 1992.

Raunio, Antti. "Die Gegenwart des Geistes im Christen bei Luther." In *Der Heilige Geist: Ökumenische und Reformatorische Untersuchungen*, edited by Joachim Heubach, 89–104. Erlangen: Luther-Akademie Ratzeburg, 1996.

———. "Luthers politische Ethik." In *Lutherforschung im 20. Jahrhundert*, edited by Rainer Vinke, 151–70. Mainz: Zabern, 2004.

———. "Natural Law and Faith: The Forgotten Foundations of Ethics in Luther's Theology." In *Union with Christ: The New Finnish Interpretation of Luther*, edited by Carl E. Braaten and Robert W. Jenson, 96–124. Grand Rapids: Eerdmans, 1998.

———. *Summe des christlichen Lebens. Die "Goldene Regel" als Gesetz der Liebe in der Theologie Martin Luthers von 1510 bis 1527.* Mainz: Zabern, 2001.

Reed, Luther D. *The Lutheran Liturgy: A Study of the Common Liturgy of the Lutheran Church in America.* Philadelphia: Muhlenberg, 1960.

Ritschl, Albrecht. *Die Christliche Lehre von der Rechtfertigung und Versöhnung.* Vol. 1, *Die Geschichte der Lehre.* Bonn: Marcus, 1889.

———. *Theologie und Metaphysik. Zur Verständigung und Abwehr.* Bonn: Adolph Marcus, 1887.

Ritschl, Otto. *Dogmengeschichte des Protestantismus.* Bd. II, Orthodoxie und Synkretismus in der altprotestantischen Theologie. Erste Hälfte, Die Theologie der deutschen Reformation und die Entwicklung der lutherischen Orthodoxie in den philippistischen Streitigkeiten. Leipzig: Hinrichs, 1912.

Rist, John M. *Augustine.* Cambridge: Cambridge University Press, 1994.

Rosemann, Philipp W. *The Story of a Great Medieval Book: Peter Lombard's Sentences.* Peterborough: Broadview, 2007.

Rowland, Tracey. *Ratzinger's Faith.* Oxford: Oxford University Press, 2009.

Ruokanen, Miikka. *Hermeneutics as an Ecumenical Method in the Theology of Gerhard Ebeling.* Helsinki: Luther-Agricola-Gesellschaft, 1982.

Saarinen, Risto. *Faith and Holiness: Lutheran-Orthodox Dialogue 1959–1994.* Göttingen: Vandenhoeck & Ruprecht, 1997.

———. "Forgiveness, the Gift and Ecclesiology." *Dialog* 45 (2006) 55–62.

———. *God and the Gift. An Ecumenical Theology of Giving.* Collegeville, MN: Liturgical Press, 2005.

———. "Gottes Sein—Gottes Wirken: Die Grunddifferenz von Substanzdenken und Wirkungsdenken in der evangelischen Lutherdeutung." In *Luther und Theosis: Vergöttlichung als Thema der abendländischen Theologie*, edited by Simo Peura und Antti Raunio, 103–19. Helsinki: Luther-Agricola-Gesellschaft, 1990.

———. *Gottes Wirken auf uns: Die transzendentale Deutung des Gegenwart-Christi-Motivs in der Lutherforschung.* Wiesbaden: Steiner, 1989.

———. "Gunst und Gabe. Melanchthon, Luther und die existentielle Anwendung von Senecas Über die Wohltaten." In *Kein Anlass zur Verwerfung: Festschrift für Otto Hermann Pesch*, edited by Johannes Brosseder and Markus Wriedt, 184–97. Frankfurt: Lembeck, 2007.

———. "Klostertheologie auf dem Weg der Ökumene: Wille und Konkupiszenz." In *Luther und das Monastiche Erbe*, edited by Christoph Bultmann et al., 269–90. Tübingen: Mohr/Siebeck, 2007.

———. "The Pauline Luther and the Law: Lutheran Theology Re-Engages the Studu of Paul." In *The Nordic Paul: Finnish Approaches to Pauline Theology*, edited by Lars Aejmelaeus and Antti Mustakallio, 90–113. London: T. & T. Clark, 2008.

———. "Die Teilhabe an Gott bei Luther und in der finnischen Lutherforschung." In *Luther und Ontologie: Das Sein Christi im Glauben als strukturierendes Prinzip der Theologie Luthers*, edited by Anja Ghiselli et al., 167–82. Erlangen: Luther-Akademie Ratzeburg, 1993.

———. "Theosis." *Theologische Realenzyklopädie* 33 (2002) 389–93.

Sasse, Hermann. *This is My Body: Luther's Contention for the Real Presence in the Sacrament of the Altar.* Adelaide: Lutheran, 1977.

Scheible, Heinz. "Luthers Heidelberger Thesen: ein Kompendium seiner Theologie." In *Martin Luther: Die Anfänge der evangelischen Bewegung in Kurpfalz*, 6:121–26. Heidelberg: Heidelberger Bibliotheksschriften, 1983.

———. "Die Universität Heidelberg und Luthers Disputation." *Zeitschrift für die Geschichte des Oberrheins* 131 (1983). Festgabe Gerd Tellenbach zum 80. Geburtstag, herausgegeben von Kommission für geschichtliche Landeskunde in Baden-Württemberg, 309–29.

Schlink, Edmund. "Weisheit und Torheit." *Kerygma und Dogma* 1 (1955) 1–22.

Schmidt-Lauber, Hans-Christoph. *Die Eucharistie als Entfaltung der Verba Testamenti: eine formgeschichtlich-systematische Einführung in die Probleme des lutherischen Gottesdienstes und seiner Liturgie.* Kassel, 1957.

Schulz, Frieder. "Luthers liturgische Reformen. Kontinuität und Innovation." *Archiv für Liturgiewissenschaft* 25 (1983) 247–75.

Seeberg, Erich. *Grundzüge der Theologie Luther.* Stuttgart: Kohlhammer, 1940.

Seeberg, Reinhold. *Lehrbuch der Dogmengeschichte IV/1. Die Entstehung des Protestantischen Lehrbebegriffs.* 1. Aufl. 1898, Unveränderte Nachdruck der 4. Auflage 1933]. Basel: Benno Schwabe, 1960.

Seifried, Mark A. "Paul, Luther, and Justification in Gal 2:15–21." *Westminster Theological Journal* 65 (2003) 215–30.

Seneca, "De beneficiis. On Favours." In Seneca, *Moral and Political Essays*, 181–308. Cambridge: Cambridge University Press, 1995.

Senn, Frack S. *Christian Liturgy: Catholic and Evangelical.* Minneapolis: Fortress, 1997.

———. "Martin Luther's Revision of the Eucharistic Canon in the Formula Missae of 1523." *Concordia Theological Monthly* 44 (1973) 101–18.
———. "The Reform of the Mass: Evangelical, but Still Catholic." In *Catholicity of the Reformation*, edited by Carl E. Braaten and Robert W. Jenson, 35–52. Grand Rapids: Eerdmans, 1996.
Shults, F. LeRon. *Reforming Theological Anthropology*. Grand Rapids: Eerdmans, 2003.
Siggings, J. K. *Martin Luthers Doctrine of Christ*. New Haven: Yale Publications of Religion, 1971.
Simon, Wolfgang. *Luthers Messopfertheologie*. Tübingen: Mohr/Siebeck, 2003.
———. "Worship and the Eucharist in Luther Studies." *Dialog* 47 (2008) 143–56.
Slenczka, Notger. "Die Schrift als 'einege Norm und Richtschnur.'" In *Die Autorität der Heiligen Schrift für Lehre und Verkündikung der Kirche*, edited by K. H. Kandler, 53–80. Neuendettelsau: Freimund, 2000.
Sorabji, Richard. *Emotion and Peace of Mind. From Stoic Agitation to Christian Temptation*. Oxford: Oxford University Press, 2000.
Söhngen, Oskar. *Theologie der Musik*. Kassel: Stauda, 1967.
Spinks, Brayan D. *Luther's Liturgical Criteria and his Reform of the Canon of the Mass*. Grove Liturgical Study 30. Bramcote: Grove, 1982.
Spruit, Leen. *Species Intelligibilis: From Perception to Knowledge*. I. Classical Roots and Medieval Discussions. Leiden: Brill, 1994.
Stählin, Rudolf. "Die Geschichte des christlichen Gottesdienstes." In *Leiturgia I. Handbuch des evangelisches Gottesdienstes*, herausgegeben von K. F. Müller und W. Blankenburg, 9–78. Kassel: Stauda, 1954.
Stolt, Birgit. *Martin Luthers Rhetorik des Herzens*. Tübingen. Mohr/Siebeck, 2000.
Stjerna, Kirsi. "Editor's Introduction." In Tuomo Mannermaa, *Christ Present in Faith: Luther's View of Justification*, xi–xix. Minneapolis: Fortress, 2005.
Suppan, Klaus. *Die Ehelehre Martin Luthers*. Salzburg: Pustet, 1971.
Taylor, Charles. *A Secular Age*. Cambridge, MA: Belknap, 2007.
———. *Sources of the Self: The Making of the Modern Identity*. Cambridge: Cambridge University Press, 1989.
Tiililä, Osmo. *Das Strafleiden Christi: Beitrag zur Diskussion über die Typeeinstellung der Versöhnungsmotive*. Helsinki: Suomalainen tiedeakatemia, 1941.
Tillich, Paul. *The Protestant Era*. Translated by James Luther Adams. Chicago: University of Chicago Press, 1948.
Tjorhom, Ola. *Visible Church–Visible Unity*. Collegeville, MN: Liturgical, 2004.
Trueman, Carl R. "Is the Finnish Line a New Beginning? A Critical Assessment of the Reading of Luther Offered by the Helsinki Circle." *Westminster Theological Journal* 65 (2003) 231–44.
Trelstad, Marit. "The Way of Salvation in Luther's Theology: A Feminist Evaluation." *Dialog* 45 (2006) 236–45.
Tselengides, Demetrios. *He soteriologia tou Lutherou*. Thessaloniki: Filologike kai theologike Bibliotheke, 1991.
Työrinoja, Reijo. "Nova vocabula et nova lingua: Luther's Conception of Doctrinal Formulas." In *Thesaurus Lutheri. Auf der Suche nach neuen Paradigmen der Luther-Forschung*, edited by Tuomo Mannermaa et al., 221–36. Helsinki: Schriften der Luther-Agricola-Gesellschaft, 1987.
———. "Opus theologicum. Luther and medieval theories of action." *Neue Zeitschrift für Systematische Theologie und Religionsphilosophie* 44 (2002) 119–53.

———. "Proprietas Verbi, Luther's Conception of Philosophical and Theological Language in the Disputation: Verbum caro factum est (Joh 1:14), 1539." In *Faith, Will and Grammar: Some Themes of Intensional Logic and Semantics in Medieval and Reformation Thought*, edited by Heikki Kirjavainen, 141–78. Helsinki: Publications of Luther-Agricola-Society, 1986.

Vercruysse, Jos. E. "Gesetz und Liebe: Die Struktur der 'Heidelberger Disputation' Luthers (1518)." *Lutherjahrbuch* (1981) 7–43.

———. "Luther's Theology of the Cross: Its Relevance for Ecumenism." *Centro pro Unione* 35 (1989) 2–11, 19.

———. "A Theology of the Cross and the Church as Sacrament." *Unum omnes in Christo: In unitatis servitio*. Miscellanea Gerardo J. Békés OSB octogenario dedicata. Vol. I. Directione András Szennay OSB curavit Ádám Somorjai OSB, 453–70. Pannonhalma: Bences Foapatsag 1995.

———. "Theology of the Cross at the Time of the Heidelberg Disputation." *Gregorianum* 57 (1976) 523–48.

Urbano, Pedro. "Christus in fide adest. Cristo presente en el creyente o la teologia de la deification in Lutero." *Scripta theologica* 32 (2000) 757–800.

Vainio, Olli-Pekka. "Christ for us and Christ in us—Mutually Exclusive? Different Aspects of Justification in the Early Lutheranism from the Viewpoint of Certainty of Salvation." In *Luther between Present and Past*, edited by Ulrik Nissen et al., 89–106. Helsinki: Luther-Agricola Gesellschaft, 2004.

———. *Justification and Participation in Christ: The Development of the Lutheran Doctrine of Justification from Luther to the Formula of Concord*. Leiden: Brill, 2008.

Vajta, Vilmos. *Die Theologie des Gottesdienstes bei Luther*. Stockholm: Svenska kyrkans diakonistyrelse, 1950.

Wegman, H. A. J. "Genealogie des eucharistischen Hochgebetes." In *Archiv für Liturgiewissenschaft* 33 (1991) 193–216.

Wendebourg, Dorothea. "Den falschen Weg Rom zu Ende gegangen? Zur gegenwärtigen Diskussion über Martin Luthers Gottesdienstreform und ihr Verhältnis zu den Traditionen der Alten Kirche." *Zeitschrift für Theologie und Kirche* 94 (1997) 437–67.

———. "Noch einmal 'Den falschen Weg Roms zu Ende gegangen?' Auseinandersetzung mit meinen Kritikern." *Zeitschrift für Theologie und Kirche* 99 (2002) 400–440.

Wengert, Timothy J. "Luther's Cathechisms and the Lord's Supper." *Word & World* 17 (1997) 54–60.

Wenz, Gunther. "Unio. Zur Differenzierung einer Leitkategorie finnischer Lutherforschung im Anschluss an CA I-VI." In *Unio: Gott und Mensch in der nachreformatorischen Theologie*, edited by Matti Repo and Rainer Vinke, 333–80. Helsinki: Luther-Agricola Gesellschaft, 1996.

Wetzel, Christoph. "Träger des Liturgischen Amtes im evangelischen Gottesdienst bei dem Apostel Paulus und bei Martin Luther." In *Leiturgia: Handbuch des evangelischen Gottesdienstes*, edited by K. F. Müller and Walter Blankenburg, 270–340. Kassel: Johannes Stauda, 1961.

White, Graham. *Luther as Nominalist*. Helsinki: Luther-Agricola-Society, 1994.

Wicks, Jared. *Cajetan und die Anfänge der Reformation: Katholisches Leben und Kirchenreform im Zeitalter der Glaubensspaltung*. Vereinschriften der Gesellschaft zur Herausgabe des Corpus Catholicorum 43, edited by Erwin Iserloh. Münster: Aschendorf, 1983.

———. "Roman Reactions to Luther: First Year (1518)." *Catholic Historical Review* 69 (1983) 521-62.
Wieneke, Josef. *Luther und Petrus Lombardus*. St. Ottilien: EOS, 1994.
Wislöff, Carl, Fr. *Abendmahl und Messe: Die Kritik Luthers am Messopfer*. Arbeiten zur Geschichte und Theologie des Lutherthums. Band 12. Berlin: Lutherisches, 1969.
Yeago, David. "Ecclesia Sancta, Ecclesia Peccatrix: The Holiness of the Church in Martin Luther's Theology." *Pro Ecclesia* 9 (2000) 331-54.
———. "Martin Luther on Grace, Law and Moral Life." *The Thomist* 62 (1998) 163-91.
Zumkeller, Adolar. *Erbsünde, Gnade, Rechtfertigung und Verdienst nach der Lehre der Erfurter Augustinertheologen des Spätmittelalters*. Würzburg: Augustinus, 1984.
Zur Mühlen, Karl-Heinz. "Die Heidelberger Disputation Martin Luthers vom 26. April 1518. Programm und Wirkung." In *Semper apertus*. Sechshundert Jahre Ruprecht-Karls-Universität Heidelberg 1386-1986. Festschrift in sechs Bänden. Bd. I. Mittelalter und frühe Neuzeit 1386-1803, edited by Wilhelm Doerr, 188-213. Berlin: Springer, 1985.
———. "Kreuz V-VII, Reformationszeit-19. Jahrhundert." *Theologische Realenzyklopädie* 19 (1990) 762-68.
———. "Luthers Kritik am scholastischen Aristotelismus in 25. These der 'Heidelberger Disputation' von 1518." *Lutherjahrbuch* (1981) 54-79.
———. *Reformatorisches Profil: Studien zum Weg Martin Luthers und der Reformation*. Göttingen: Vandenhoeck & Ruprecht, 1995.

Subject Index

aesthetics, 211, 217–19, 222
annihilation, 47, 49, 54, 56, 139, 155, 170
anthropology, 20, 27–58, 189–91, 201
antinomianism, 93, 148
apprehension, 37, 70, 139–43, 149, 172
Aristotelianism, ix, 28–29, 53, 120, 141, 157, 159, 161–63, 169, 170–72
atonement, 19, 227, 229
Augustinianism, 1–2, 4, 9, 12, 14, 22, 35, 60, 81, 83, 86, 138, 152, 157, 202

baptism, 20, 27, 51, 79, 87, 91, 95–108, 133, 115, 131, 134, 154, 199, 215, 221, 224
beauty, 39, 75, 217–22

catechism, 81, 89–90, 95, 101, 107, 109–10, 112, 114, 126, 128, 220–21, 224, 229–31
communicatio idiomatum, 7, 62–63, 66, 68, 114, 134, 139, 182
communitarianism, 1–2
concupiscentia, 45, 65, 75–76, 80, 168, 201, 204
condescendence, 70–71, 74–76, 79
contraception, 204
conscience, 22, 42, 56–57, 67, 123, 132, 148, 153, 178, 188, 194–96, 215, 226
Creed, 81, 84, 89–91, 94, 111–12, 122–23, 221, 224, 229–30
creation, 32, 60, 64, 77, 83, 90–91, 95–98, 112, 134, 137, 137, 139, 144, 150, 166, 171, 179, 188–89, 194, 199–201, 204, 207, 211, 213, 220, 222, 229

devil, 32, 35, 63, 67, 69, 102, 150, 194, 207, 213, 221, 222
disputation, 33, 46, 81, 86, 92, 93, 156–71, 220

Eastern Orthodoxy, 5, 20, 28, 60, 123, 127, 218
ecclesiology, 4, 7, 16, 18, 126, 130, 154, 191, 193, 215
ecumenism, viii, xiv, 46, 11–12, 27, 120, 155, 159
Eucharist, 22–23, 66, 72, 77, 79, 108–37, 154, 199, 215, 224
evangelical Catholicity, 4, 12, 16

faith
  aesthetics and, 217–21
  apprehending, 40–42, 61, 70, 138–50, 226
  baptism and, 99–103
  Christ present in, 4, 7–10, 21, 47, 148, 167, 229–31
  as substance, 1, 14–16
  Eucharist and, 109–10, 113–14, 123, 128, 136
  fides Christi, 227
  fides Christo formata, 48, 54–58, 144–45
  fides charitate formata, 144, 203
  fides infantium, 96, 103–7
  liberal Protestantism and, 1, 108, 162
  love and, 16, 55, 135, 143–53, 181, 207–9, 216
  St. Mary's, 177–81
  three powers of, 24
  personal, 61, 90

faith (cont.),
  philosophy and, 30, 43, 52–53, 121
  word and, 45–46
favor, 17–20, 23–25, 71–72, 81, 85, 103, 111, 187, 215, 227, 228–229
filioque, 59, 85–86
forgiveness, 7, 17–18, 56–57, 70, 96, 102, 109–11, 114, 123, 128–29, 140, 147, 149, 151, 193–94, 200, 202, 227–28

gift, 11, 17–26, 37, 41–42, 58, 72, 91, 93, 96, 98–114, 117–99, 122, 126, 133–37, 140, 151, 166, 168, 182, 190, 195, 195, 196, 198, 210–14, 217, 219–23, 226–30
Golden Rule, 10, 17, 52, 190–92
guilt, 65, 67, 69, 129, 138, 177–78

hope, 14–15, 34–35, 39, 41, 153, 179, 228
humility, 56, 160, 165, 174–78, 181

imago Dei, 27, 34–49
imputation, 21, 140, 143, 149, 151–52, 228
incarnation, 30, 45, 61–62, 65, 71–79, 91, 99, 109, 139, 182
intellect, 2, 35, 39, 41–42, 87–88, 141–44, 166, 202–3, 221, 223

justification, 5–25, 28, 45, 47–48, 54, 57, 65, 67, 70–71, 100–111, 120, 126–27, 138–40, 145–55, 163, 167, 211, 216, 218, 227–29
Joint Declaration on the Doctrine of Justification, 6

kenosis, 64–68, 74–76, 79

law, 16–17, 22, 32–33, 45, 48–49, 52–53, 55–57, 64, 67, 69, 91, 93, 124, 140, 144–50, 153–54, 157, 166–67, 173, 188, 190–92, 199, 206–7, 211, 219, 222, 226, 229
Leuenberg Agreement, 6
liberation theology, 151, 155
libertinism, 146, 148
libido, 200–202
love, 16, 30, 37–38, 43, 52, 55–57, 88, 90–91, 156–57, 167–70, 181–82, 201–10, 214, 216, 219, 223
  agape, 8, 112, 191, 203, 206–7
  courtly love, 187
  faith and love, 16, 55, 135, 143–53, 181, 207–9, 216
  God's love, 74, 78, 84–85, 112–16, 119, 172–74, 178, 193, 220, 227
  Mannermaa on Nygren, 8–10
  love between man and woman, 186–92, 205–9
  love of neighbours, 114–15, 124, 133, 151, 175, 188, 229
  self-love, 64–65, 71, 75–76, 166, 171, 201
  True Love Waits, 195

mariology, 173–74, 181–85
marriage, 22, 25, 186–217
metaphysics, 9, 39, 92, 108, 120, 158–63, 171
music, 210–22
mysticism, 8, 12–13, 21–22, 135, 143, 149, 181, 206, 211
natural Theology, 210, 220
nominalism, 1, 12, 118

ontology, 5, 11, 21, 27–31, 97, 159, 161–63, 171
ordo caritatis, 9, 144, 202–4
ordo salutis, 143

participation, 8, 10–12, 15, 17, 22–23, 25, 27–28, 30–31, 36–40, 45, 56, 58, 96, 103–6, 123, 140–43, 147–51, 163, 171, 223, 227–29
pelagianism, 148–49, 154, 172
perception, 14, 32, 44, 142, 159, 169, 217, 220
philosophy and theology, 31–34, 42–47, 58, 120–21, 155–72
Platonism, 28, 170–71, 211
Porvoo Agreement, 6
postliberalism, 5–6

Radical Orthodoxy, 1–2, 146
reason, 30–35, 37, 38, 42–46, 49–57, 175–76, 179–82, 186, 188–91, 201
relationality, ix, 18–19, 22–23, 28–30, 34, 51, 58, 161
righteousness
    becoming righteous, 15, 25, 47–49, 51, 54–58, 90, 105, 113, 143–53, 167–68, 192, 194
    Christ's righteousness, 28, 40–42, 45, 68–72, 115, 139–140, 183, 225–28
    iustitia activa et passiva, 226
    original righteousness, 37

sacrifice, 18–19, 21–23, 117–26, 132–37
sadness, 213, 221
sanctification, 7, 25, 46, 60, 147, 150–52, 154, 228–29
satisfaction, 67–70, 139
sexuality, 75, 186–209, 217
simul iustus et peccator, 47, 152–53, 217–18
sin, 53–59, 71, 115–20, 140, 170, 196–97
    defined, 67
    original sin, 39, 88, 189
    Christ and sin, 39–40, 65, 68–70, 74–76
    Christians as sinners, 47–51, 148–54
    St. Mary and sin, 183–84
    Sex and sin, 199–202, 217
soul, 25–26, 29, 32, 35–52, 72, 82, 85–88, 106, 118, 143–44, 170, 177, 212, 215–16, 219
species intelligibilis, 142
Spe Salvi, 14–16

Theotokos, 182, 185
theosis (deification), 5, 10–13, 27–28, 65, 152, 155, 160, 163
transformation, 10, 13, 28, 149
Trinity, 17, 29, 30, 59–61, 69, 80–97, 112, 152, 224
    psychological analogy of Trinity, 82, 86–89
    appropriations, 60, 84, 97, 90
unio
    Union with Christ (*Unio cum Christo*), 7–12, 22, 25–28, 48, 51, 55, 58, 70–71, 76, 79, 96–97, 100, 106, 139–47
    Union of Christ's natures, 39, 62–64, 140
    Union of Word and faith, 46
    Union between the receivers of Eucharist, 113–15

via moderna, 32, 81, 86, 92
vow of celibacy, 186, 193–96

will, 20, 35, 38, 41–42, 49–50, 53–57, 60, 87–91, 141–41, 144, 149, 151–52, 157, 166, 178, 172, 189, 216, 221

Name Index

Aquinas, Thomas, 38, 117, 141, 146, 202, 217
Althaus, Paul, 69, 95, 101, 115
Augustine, 19–20, 38, 80–86, 89, 117, 127, 146, 152, 157, 201–4, 211, 224–25
Aulen, Gustav, 67
Aristotle, 46, 141–42, 159, 168–71

Balthasar, Hans Urs von, 217–18
Barth, Karl, 5, 9, 13, 88, 157
Bauer, Karl, 170
Bayer, Oswald, 34, 36, 221
Begbie, Jeremy, 216
Bell, Daniel M. Jr., 151
Benedict XVI, 1, 14–16, 24, 145–50
Besserer, Adam, 129–30
Beutel, Albrecht, 29
Biel, Gabriel, 81–86, 168
Bielfeldt, Dennis, 86
Billings, J. Todd, 12
Blankenburg, Walter, 211
Blaumeiser, Hubertus, 162
Block, Johannes, 104, 165, 211
Boehme, Armand J., 125
Bonhoeffer, Dietrich, 11
Bornkamm, Heinrich, 2, 162
Braaten Carl E., viii, 5, 9, 12, 127, 132, 162
Brand, Eugene L., 125
Brecht, Martin, 56, 92, 157
Brightman, F. E., 123
Brilioth, Yngve, 125
Bring, Ragnar, 67
Briskina, Anna, 13

Cabié, Robert, 122
Christensen, Michael J., 13
Cleve, Fredric, 111

Dales, Richard, C. 170
Dalferth, Ingolf U., 158
Delius, Walter, 157
Denifle, H., 151, 200
Devasahayam, V., 155
Dieter, Theodor, 29, 31, 47, 162
Dilthey, Wilhelm, 108

Ebeling, Gerhard, 14–15, 29–31, 108–9, 158–61
Ellwein, Eduard, 161
Erasmus, 20, 215–16

Fiennes, Joseph, 138
Finlan, Stephen, 13
Flogaus, Reinhard, 11, 13
Forde, Gerhard O., 118, 120, 155, 162
Forsberg, Juhani, 16, 132

Gollum, 138
Gregory, Eric, 152
Gregory the Great, 219, 224
Gritsch, Eric W., 173
Guicharrousse, Hubert, 211

Hacker, Paul, 15
Hallonsten, Gösta, 13
Hardt, Tom. G. A., 111
Harnack, Adolf von, 108
Hart, David Bentley, 218
Hays, Richard, 143
Heinimäki, Jaakko, 192
Helmer, Christine, 2, 80–81, 92–94
Herms, Eilert, 89
Hilary of Poitiers, 81
Hilgenfeld, Hartmut, 111
Holm, Bo, 11
Huovinen, Eero, 6, 16, 27, 34, 36–37, 101, 103, 141

Hütter, Reinhard, 13, 148, 154, 191
Hägglund, Bengt, 31, 36, 228
Hänggi, Anton, 123

Iserloh, Erwin, 4, 14–15, 117

Jansen, Rainer, 80, 87–91, 96
Jasper, R. C. D., 123
Järveläinen, Petri, 192
Jenson, Robert W., viii, 5, 9, 12, 125, 127, 132, 162
John Duns Scotus, 1, 82, 84, 86, 92
Jorgenson, Allen G., 12
Junghans, Helmar, 170
Jungmann, Josef A., 124
Juntunen, Sammeli, 10, 16, 31, 47, 139, 149, 159, 161, 217

Karlstadt, Andreas, 109
Kass, Amy A., 20
Kärkkäinen, Pekka, 10, 16–17, 32
Kärkkäinen, Veli-Matti, 12, 155
Kazoh, Kitamori, 155
Kharimov, Vladimir, 13
Kirjavainen, Heikki, 79, 163
Kitanov, Severin, 86
Kittilä, Seppo, 19
Knuuttila, Simo, 86, 92
Kolb, Robert, 28
Kotila, Heikki, 125
Kretschmar, Georg, 188–89, 195, 206–7
Krodel, Gottfried G., 125
Krummacher, Christoph, 211

Lamberigts, M., 201
Lathrop, Gordon, 125
Lähteenmäki, Olavi, 186, 188, 190, 198, 200, 204

Leaver, Robin A., 210–11, 213
Lehmann, Karl, 4, 6
Lehmkühler, Karsten, 11
Lessing, Eckhard, 111

Lewis, Clive Staples, 187
Lienhardt, Marc, 60–64
Lindbeck, George, 5, 61
Lindroth, Hjalmar, 67
Linman, Jonathan, 13
Loewenich, Walther von, 155, 158–61
Lohse, Bernhard, 36, 81

MacIntyre, Alasdair, 1
Maffeis, Angelo, 11–12
Mahlmann, Theodor, 11, 17
Malter, Rudolf, 161
Mannermaa, Tuomo, 4–14, 17–18, 22, 25, 28–31, 65, 95, 142, 145, 149, 159, 162–63
Manns, Peter, 4, 6
Marquart, Kurt E., 12
Marshall, Bruce, 12–13, 152
Martikainen, Eeva, 154, 160, 162
Mattes, Mark C., 12, 21–22
Mattox, Mickey L., 80, 93
Maxwell, William D., 125
Mäkinen, Virpi, 17
McGrath, Alister E., 155, 162
Meilaender, Gilbert, 154
Melanchthon, Philipp, 17, 23–24, 194, 207
Messerli, Carlos R., 125
Messner, Reinhard, 11–12, 111, 133
Metzger, Paul Louis, 12
Meyer, Hans Bernhard, SJ, 111
Milbank, John, 1, 12–13, 17
Moltmann, Jürgen, 155
Mosser, Carl, 12
Moxter, Michael, 158
zur Mühlen, Karl-Heinz, 29, 159, 161–62, 170
Müller, Alfred Dedo, 210

Neuhaus, Richard John, 147–48
Nichols, Aidan, 15
Nilsson, Kjel-Ove, 61–67
Nüssel, Friederike, 65, 149

Name Index

Nygren, Anders, 8–9

Oberman, Heiko, 1, 168, 190, 195, 200, 208
Oecolampadius, Johannes, 109
Olivier, Daniel, 161
Olson, O. K., 125
Olsson, Herbert, 67
Osiander, Andreas, 28, 139

Pahl, Irmgard, 123
Pannenberg, Wolfhart, 4
Parvio, Martti, 125
Pelikan, Jaroslav, 2
Pesch, Otto Hermann, 4
Peter Lombard, 80–88, 189
Peters, Albrecht 29, 36, 61, 67, 89, 96, 108, 110–11, 129
Peura, Simo, 6, 10, 15–17, 23, 27–28, 114, 143, 154, 160, 162
Pfatteicher, Philipp H., 125
Pieper, Franz, 114
Pierre d'Ailly, 81, 83–85, 92
Plato, 170
Pluta, Olaf, 170
Pythagoras, 171

Ratzinger, Joseph Kardinal, 114, 146
Raunio, Antti, 9–10, 16, 144, 160, 203
Reed, Luther D., 125
Rist, J., 201
Ritschl, Albrecht, 11, 158–159
Ritschl, Otto, 160
Rosemann, Philip W., 80
Rowland, Tracey, 146
Ruokanen, Miikka, 159

Saarinen, Risto, 5, 11, 13, 18, 24, 29, 60, 86, 109, 140, 152, 158–59, 162
Sasse, Hermann, 111
Scheible, Heinz, 157
Schleiermacher, Friedrich, 11, 108

Schlink, Edmund, 161
Schmidt-Lauber, Hans-Christoph, 125
Seeberg, Erich, 67, 160
Seeberg, Reinholdf, 160
Seifried, Mark A., 12
Senn, Frack S., 117, 122, 125
Seneca, 19, 23
Senfl, Ludwig, 212
Servetus, Michael, 93–94
Shults, F. LeRon, 29
Simon, Wolfgang, 23, 111, 117, 131, 133, 136
Slenczka, Notger, 225
Söhngen, Oskar, 211
Spinks, Brayan D., 125
Spruit, Leen, 142
Sorabji, Richard, 20
Stählin, Rudolf, 123
Stolt, Birgit, 215
Stjerna, Kirsi, 9
Suppan, Klaus, 186, 188, 190, 193, 199

Taylor, Charles, 2
Tiililä, Osmo, 67
Tillich, Paul, 211–22
Tinctoris, Johannes, 212
Tjorhom, Ola, 4
Trueman, Carl R., 12
Trelstad, Marit, 155
Tselengides, Demetrios, 13
Työrinoja, Reijo, 51, 79, 163

Urbano, Pedro, 11–12

Vainio, Olli-Pekka, 10, 16–17, 67, 149
Vajta, Vilmos, 111

Wegman, H. A. J., 123
Wendebourg, Dorothea, 126
Wengert, Timothy J., 110
Wenz, Gunther, 11

Wetzel, Christoph, 210–11
White, Graham, 30, 32, 79, 85, 92–93, 159, 163
Wicks, Jared, 157
Wieneke, Josef, 80–88
William Ockham, 1, 4, 81
Wislöff, Carl, Fr., 132
Wittung, Jeffrey A., 13
Wolferinus, Simon, 130–32

Yeago, David, 13

Zumkeller, Adolar, 81
Zwingli, Ulrich, 63, 66, 77, 109, 121, 130–31, 207

www.ingramcontent.com/pod-product-compliance
Lightning Source LLC
Chambersburg PA
CBHW030822230426
43667CB00008B/1336